TITANIC

The
Great Lakes
Connections

CRIS KOHL

TITANIC

The
Great Lakes
Connections

CRIS KOHL

SEAWOLF
Communications

West Chicago

TITANIC, THE GREAT LAKES CONNECTIONS
BY CRIS KOHL

COPYRIGHT © 2000 BY SEAWOLF COMMUNICATIONS, INC.

ALL RIGHTS RESERVED

SOFTCOVER ISBN 0-9679976-0-7
SPECIAL LIMITED EDITION HARDCOVER ISBN 0-9679976-1-5

LIBRARY OF CONGRESS CARD NUMBER: 00-191702

SEAWOLF COMMUNICATIONS, INC.
P.O. BOX 66
WEST CHICAGO, IL 60186
USA
Tel: (630) 293-8996   Fax: (630) 293-8837   Email: SeawolfRex@aol.com
Visit our website at www.SeawolfCommunications.com

NOTE: Photo credits are shown in terms of the author's source for the photograph rather than a specific photographer who might have taken it, except where the photographer is known and specifically named.

Printed and bound in the United States of America

FIRST EDITION: DECEMBER, 2000

05 04 03 02 01 00   9 8 7 6 5 4 3 2 1

Cover photo: *The dramatic bow was one of the few portions of the TITANIC shipwreck to remain relatively intact after the ship's two-and-a-half-mile plunge to the North Atlantic Ocean floor in 1912. Located in 1985, 73 years after the tragic sinking which claimed over 1,500 lives, TITANIC has maintained her reputation as the world's most famous shipwreck.* (PHOTO BY RALPH WHITE, USED WITH PERMISSION.)

To my father,

Lorenz Kohl
(1917-1982)

and to my mother,

Erika Kohl

for their courage
and determination,
for losing sight of shore in order
to find new lands and new lives,
for taking me across the
North Atlantic Ocean
by ship five times,
and, finally,
for settling in the heart of
the Great Lakes.

Acknowledgements

Many individuals and numerous organizations, including their very helpful staff members, provided assistance in the production of this book. The author sincerely thanks the following, and anyone he may have inadvertently overlooked, for all of their help:

Joan Forsberg, High Lake, Illinois; Walter Lord, the Dean of *Titanic* researchers; Robert McGreevy, marine artist, Grosse Pointe Woods, Michigan; Jim Clary, marine artist, St. Clair, Michigan; Alice Solomonian, St. Catharines, Ontario; Joan Stickley, Jamestown, Rhode Island.; Ethel Rudolph, San Diego, California; Alan Hustak, Montreal; Edward Goyette, Director, *Willis Boyer* Museum, Toledo, Ohio; William Fox, Williamsburg, Virginia; Edward Kamuda of the *Titanic* Historical Society, Indian Orchard, Massachusetts; the Archives of Ontario (Toronto, Ontario); the Library of Michigan (Lansing, Michigan) and especially Carey Draeger; the Illinois State Historical Library (Springfield, Illinois); the Wisconsin State Historical Society Library (Madison, Wisconsin); the Ohio Historical Society Library (Columbus, Ohio); the Indiana State Historical Library (Indianapolis, Indiana); the Minnesota Historical Society Library (St. Paul, Minnesota); the State Library of Pennsylvania (Harrisburg, Pennsylvania); the New York State Historical Library (Albany, New York); the National Archives of the United States, Washington, DC; the National Archives of the United States, Great Lakes Region (Chicago, Illinois); the Great Lakes Collection of the Milwaukee Public Library/Wisconsin Marine Historical Society, and Paul Woehrmann, Suzette Lopez, and Virginia Schwartz in particular; the Historical Collections of the Great Lakes, Center for Archival Collections, Bowling Green (Ohio) State University, and Robert Graham in particular; the Great Lakes Historical Society, Vermilion, Ohio; the Dossin Marine Museum, Detroit, Michigan, and John Polascek, Curator, in particular; the Oswego (New York) County Historical Society, and Terry M. Prior, Curator, in particular; the Public Archives of Nova Scotia, Halifax, and Garry Shutlak in particular; the Mariners' Museum, Newport News, Virginia, and especially Claudia Jew; Harland and Wolff, Belfast, Northern Ireland; the Ulster Folk & Transport Museum, Holywood, Northern Ireland; the Steamboat Historical Society of America, Providence, Rhode Island; the Chicago Historical Society; the University of Toronto Archives; the Chatham (Ontario) Public Library; the Windsor (Ontario) Public Library; the Sarnia (Ontario) Public Library; the St. Marys (Ontario) Museum; the Swan Library, Albion, New York; the Dowagiac (Michigan) Public Library; the Grand Rapids (Michigan) Public Library; the Pontiac (Michigan) Public Library; the Manatee County Public Library, Central Location (Bradenton, Florida); the Benton Harbor (Michigan) Public Library; the Mead (Sheboygan, Wisconsin) Public Library; the Green Bay (Wisconsin) Public Library, and Mary Jane Herber in particular; the Manitowoc (Wisconsin) Public Library; the Chicago (Illinois) Public Library, Harold Washington Library Center; the Sulzer Regional Library (Chicago, Illinois); the West Chicago (Illinois) Public Library; the St. Charles (Illinois) Public Library; the Gail Borden (Elgin, Illinois) Public Library; and the Reddick Library, Ottawa, Illinois.

Special thanks to Ralph White of Los Angeles for the use of his excellent photograph on the cover.

Contents

Maps

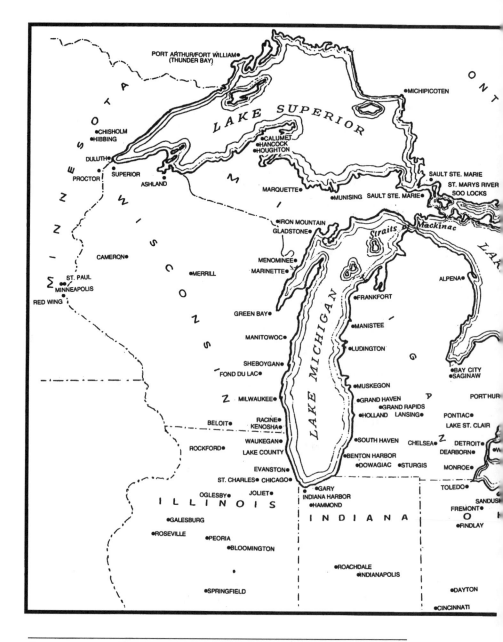

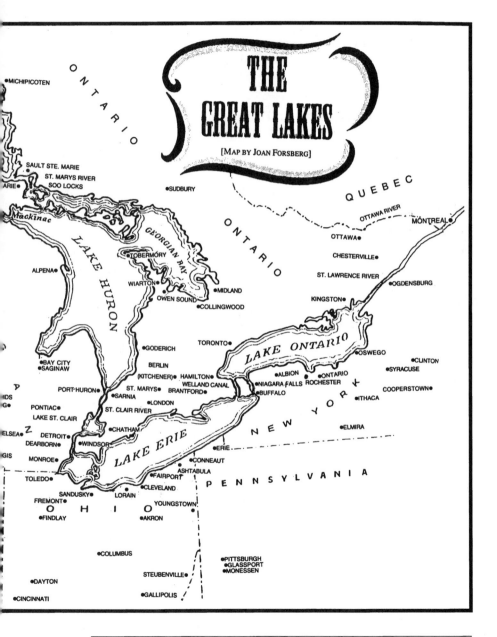

THE
GREAT LAKES
[MAP BY JOAN FORSBERG]

●MICHIPICOTEN

ONTARIO

QUEBEC

SAULT STE. MARIE
ST. MARYS RIVER
SOO LOCKS
ARIE●
●SUDBURY

OTTAWA RIVER
MONTREAL●

OTTAWA●

ONTARIO

CHESTERVILLE●

ST. LAWRENCE RIVER
●OGDENSBURG

Mackinac

GEORGIAN BAY

●TOBERMORY

LAKE HURON

ALPENA●

WIARTON●
●MIDLAND
OWEN SOUND
●COLLINGWOOD

KINGSTON●

●GODERICH

TORONTO●

LAKE ONTARIO

●OSWEGO
●CLINTON

BAY CITY●
●SAGINAW

BERLIN
(KITCHENER)● HAMILTON●
WELLAND CANAL

●ALBION
NIAGARA FALLS ROCHESTER
●ONTARIO
●SYRACUSE

COOPERSTOWN●

PORT·HURON●
ST. MARYS● BRANTFORD●
●BUFFALO
●ITHACA

IDS●
G●
SARNIA
●LONDON

NEW YORK

PONTIAC●
LAKE ST. CLAIR
ST. CLAIR RIVER

ELSEA● Z DETROIT●
●CHATHAM
●ELMIRA

DEARBORN● ●WINDSOR

LAKE ERIE

GIS MONROE●
●ERIE

●CONNEAUT

TOLEDO●
ASHTABULA
●FAIRPORT

PENNSYLVANIA

SANDUSKY● LORAIN
●CLEVELAND

FREMONT●
YOUNGSTOWN●

OHIO

●FINDLAY
●AKRON

●COLUMBUS

●PITTSBURGH
●GLASSPORT
●MONESSEN

STEUBENVILLE●

●DAYTON

●CINCINNATI
●GALLIPOLIS

Some Statistics Regarding
Great-Lakes-Bound
Passengers on *Titanic*

Illinois: A total of 86 passengers on *Titanic* were bound for this state. From these, there were 23 survivors and 63 deaths. For the city of Chicago alone, which 61 passengers made their goal, only nine survived while 52 perished.

Indiana: Only seven passengers on *Titanic* were heading for Indiana destinations; three survived while four died.

Michigan: Of the 64 passengers heading for points in this state, 27 survived *Titanic's* sinking; 37 perished. From the 24 who made the city of Detroit their goal, 13 survived and 11 died.

Minnesota: In all, 29 people were bound for Minnesota, with the survival rate being almost evenly split: 14 lived and 15 died.

New York (western part): A total of 35 people were heading to locations in upstate New York relatively close to the Great Lakes. Of these, 14 survived, while 21 perished.

Ohio: From a total of 46 passengers bound for Ohio destinations, a balanced 23 survived and 23 died.

Ontario: Of the 41 people who made various places in Ontario, the only Canadian Great Lakes political entity, their destinations, only eight survived, while 33 perished.

Pennsylvania (western part): From the 18 people heading here, six survived while 12 died.

Wisconsin: An even 20 passengers were bound for the state of Wisconsin, and an even ten survived and ten perished in *Titanic's* sinking.

TOTAL: 345 *Titanic* passengers were heading to Great Lakes destinations, of whom 128 survived and 217 perished.

Introduction

TITANIC! It's an infamously fascinating word. The name of this ship is one of the most widely recognized and most strongly emotive words in any language on this entire planet. The very sound of it causes instant universal recognition in people from Chicago to Shanghai and Rangoon to Roanoke, similar to the words COCA COLA and PASSPORT, but with substantially different effect. The very sound of TITANIC reverberates with heroic and tragic drama akin to the word EVEREST (indeed, *Titanic* is the Mount Everest of shipwrecks, it is the water world's grimacing Chomolungma, it is the mother of all maritime disasters). Virtually everyone on our planet has heard at least something of TITANIC, the ship which sank on April 15, 1912, with enormous loss of life after colliding with an iceberg on her maiden voyage.

In a attempt to explain the universality of emotional response to the *Titanic* disaster, the Toronto *Mail and Empire* newspaper in 1912 stretched a fact, but still made a relevant point: "Veteran newspapermen in New York who can speak from an experience of fifty years, say that writing the story of the wreck of the *Titanic* was the biggest task they had to accomplish in all that time. The *Slocum* disaster, the burning of the Brooklyn theater, the Johnstown flood, the Martinique earthquake and the earthquake and fire at San Francisco are among the big stories of late years, but in nearly all of these the interest was somewhat localized. In the *Titanic* there were victims from nearly every city in the world...."

This book will attempt to fill some of the gaps in the *Titanic* story. Many of the people on board the ill-fated luxury liner had lived most of their lives in Great Lakes towns and cities in Michigan or Ohio or Wisconsin, and were in the process of heading home from business or vacation or, in a couple of instances, a honeymoon. Many others hoped to reach destinations which they had never before seen, hoping to create new lives and homes in a New Land. In 1912, the immigration movement to the Great Lakes region and to the West was at a peak. This book will tell many hitherto untold stories of those people.

This book will also relate how Great Lakes area newspapers told the jarring tale of *Titanic's* loss and the resulting events, complete with certain glaring inaccuracies and all-too-human prejudices.

One chapter will relate the parallel story of a Great Lakes ship being constructed at the same time as *Titanic* and described in superlatives as lofty as those used for the larger leviathan. The resulting story of the *City of Detroit III* shows similarities to *Titanic* (such as an accident with another ship prior to the maiden voyage), but with different endings.

The loss of *Titanic* prompted changes in maritime legislation that had far-reaching effects upon shipping in the Great Lakes. Proposed changes were basically beneficial in nature, and affected principally the number of lifeboats and trained crew on board each ship, and the operation of wireless (radio) transmissions. These proposals met, surprisingly, with loud and powerful opposition, and not all of these proposals ended with positive results, as the catastrophic loss of life in the *Eastland* accident showed.

Artists having *Titanic*/Great Lakes connections are featured in one chapter, and finally, there is the story of a turn-of-the-century writer who, in 1898, wrote a prophetic tale about the world's largest ocean liner sinking on its maiden voyage after striking an iceberg in the North Atlantic, with enormous loss of life because of insufficient lifeboats. His ship was named *Titan*. Fourteen years later, a shocking amount of what Morgan Robertson had described in his novella actually happened to *Titanic*. This author, born and raised along the shores of Lake Ontario, was the son of a Great Lakes captain.

Many factors joined forces to propel the writing of this book.

Somewhere in my youth I read the book, *A Night to Remember*, Walter Lord's fascinating and lively 1955 account of the loss of *Titanic*. I know why I was immediately hooked on the story's details: they were episodes which I, with the singularly few experiences of my short life at that time, could clearly imagine. I had watched icebergs in the North Atlantic quite close to us slide forebodingly past the steel hull of our passenger ship. Nearly forgotten vignettes of lifeboat drills sprang from hidden recesses of my child's mind; I recalled the calming words spoken softly to me by my parents when all passengers were ordered to don lifejackets and report to their designated area of the ship to await further orders during something called a lifeboat drill. I remembered how my mother, composed and undisturbed, reassured me as she tied the strings of my tiny lifejacket that this was merely a practice in the event that something should go amiss during our Atlantic Ocean crossing.

"But of course, nothing will go wrong because ships today are much safer than they used to be," she uttered to me with certainty.

I clutched tightly at my brown teddy bear. I never lost sight of my furry companion as we crossed the Atlantic Ocean when I was five years old. Gazing at the vast, black waters of the sea, staring at the occasional white iceberg slipping past, and viewing the lifeboats (why were these many small boats sitting on our big boat?) combined to make me and my teddy bear suspect that there was more to this setting than we could understand.

Years later, after reading *A Night to Remember* and other shipwreck stories to which I had become addicted, and having watched the survivors of the *Andrea Dorea* sinking on black-and-white television land safely at their New York dock (did my mother really tell me that nothing could go wrong with ships today because they were much safer than they used to be?), I was aware of that element of drama and adventure presented by the situation where human beings place themselves on board an enormous object made of steel (how steel could float was still beyond me), move straight out towards the unbroken horizon of endless water on this object, lose sight of shore, and, after several days of nonstop motion void of anything man-made save the occasional outline of a ship passing in the distance, successfully make a landfall and return to civilization, with its television, traffic jams and daily routines. It was already a fast, modern world on land back then.

The very young future writer and his mother and father traveled in steerage on board the immigrant ship, *Beaverbrae. Titanic* had sunk in these waters less than 40 years earlier. (PHOTO BY LORENZ KOHL)

When I crossed that ocean by ship again at age eleven, my brown teddy bear stayed in storage while I interested myself in reading adventure books and learning how to play chess from the older boys on board. I was fourteen years of age when I last crossed the North Atlantic by ship, and that time I photographed those icebergs and lifeboats. My teddy bear, again in storage, had become relegated to my past.

At about that time, the per person cost of flying across the Atlantic Ocean had come down so much that it actually put the old steamers that were still eking out a living on trans-Atlantic runs out of business. My family had crossed the ocean several times by ship only because it was the cheapest way to cross. On our first transit, we were steerage passengers immigrating to a new land; subsequent crossings were made in Second Class accommodations. Some time in the 1960's, it became less dear financially to take an airplane (or was it still spelled "aeroplane" then?) across the ocean in about 12 hours time than it cost to sail on a beautiful ship for a week. Some time in the 1960's, people started running out of time and developed a thing called haste, and the prospect of spending seven days at sea to reach a destination attained in only half a day in an aircraft seemed absurd in this new "jet age." The unique social experience of leisurely sailing across an ocean in resort-like comfort was replaced by a speedy flight while crammed into tight chairs and breathing bad air. To say that the demise of the trans-Atlantic passenger ship trade by the 1960's was a lamentable loss of custom, experience, etiquette and way of life is a strong understatement.

When the author, at the age of 14, crossed the North Atlantic by ship for the final time, he photographed lifeboats, davits and other parts of the passenger vessel *Arkadia*.

My family finally settled in Windsor, Ontario, in the hub of the Great Lakes region, but the experience of travel was by then too deeply ingrained for me to stay in any one place too long. I began reading accounts of small vessels sailing to exotic places like Tahiti, and when I was 15 years old, I painstakingly drew up detailed plans for a seven-year voyage around the world (that trip is still pending). Since then, I have travelled liberally, taken courses and taught courses on seamanship, piloting and navigation, owned several vessels of both the sail and power types and operated them on all of the five Great Lakes, and run chartered sailboats in the Florida Keys and the Bahamas. My love of ships and the water deepened.

One of the numerous North Atlantic icebergs photographed by the author from the deck of *Arkadia*.

With college beard abandoned for career, I honestly tried to settle down and grow roots in one location. I was now teaching *A Night to Remember* to high school classes, but my true ambition was to write stories like that myself. My first book on Great Lakes shipwrecks was published in 1985. While I was finishing the research on that book, Robert Ballard and the joint American-French expedition located, photographed and positively identified the submerged remains of the colossal liner *Titanic* under two and a half miles of Atlantic Ocean water.

On a whim probably spurred on by all of the publicity about the newly-located shipwreck, I decided to see what the local newspaper where I was living in Ontario had written about the loss of *Titanic* in 1912. Much to my surprise, a series of short newspaper articles dramatically outlined the frenzy and distress of a local man who was awaiting the arrival of his wife and two children. Unfortunately, they were steerage passengers who were lost when *Titanic* sank.

With this discovery, the *Titanic* story suddenly developed more immediacy for me. Over the next several years, whenever I researched a Great Lakes shipwreck for another book or a magazine article, or when I did research work for my Masters degree in History, I investigated what local newspapers reported about the loss of *Titanic* in 1912. The results were always fascinating, and the pile of research notes and photocopied articles on *Titanic* grew in proportion to the writing I did on Great Lakes maritime history.

I read all of the new *Titanic* books as soon as they came off the presses, being forced to increase my reading speed after the 1997 release of the magnificent James Cameron film version of the sinking. Even with the abundance of published *Titanic* material at that time, I knew that many of her stories had yet to be told. I also realized that I wanted to write those stories and teach people in the Great Lakes area that, whether we liked it or not, we were connected to *Titanic's* loss in several ways. Although the ship sank in the Atlantic Ocean in 1912, time and distance cannot keep *Titanic* at arm's length from those of us who live today in the area of the Great Lakes. The legacies and reminders are far too numerous to shrug off.

     *   *   *   *   *   *   *   *

I am aware of two suitably related circumstances about my setting: this Chicago-area heritage house where I wrote these words and the rest of this book was constructed in 1912, the year *Titanic* sank, and *Titanic* sank exactly 88 years ago today. The house is holding up excellently because it has received regular maintenance, but the remains of *Titanic* on the ocean floor are disintegrating from saltwater bacteria eating the steel. Soon only the artifacts which have been recovered and conserved will remain as material evidence of the world's most famous shipwreck and its many stories.

Sadly, only five of the 705 *Titanic* survivors remain alive in the world today, 88 years after that magnificent ship sank: two in England, one in France, and two in North America. One of the latter is a Great Lakes area survivor, living the end of her life quietly in a Michigan nursing home. She is 96 years old. The story of her survival when she was eight is in this book.

A brown teddy bear, now a bit threadbare with age, sits upright in this safe, motionless room, and has happily retired from those bobbing ocean crossings, his purpose as a child's companion successfully accomplished long ago. Today, ever the ally, he seems to give his endorsement to the words I write.

One day, all that will remain are the stories.

C. K.
High Lake, Illinois
April 15, 2000

Prologue

The giant ship surged down the launchramp like a greased skyscraper on its side, a slow but steady and unstoppable missile. The 14,000 tons of streamlined steel plunged into the Detroit River, forcing an enormous geyser of fresh water into the air. A massive crowd of onlookers cheered wildly as the unwieldy hull bobbed from side to side, gradually becalming itself once afloat, then sitting tall with erect majesty in the center of the Great Lakes.

The date was Saturday, July 1, 1911. This newly-launched ship, with a length of 617 feet and a beam of 67 feet, was longer than the new U.S. government dreadnaught war vessels and was exceeded in size by only a handful of the world's great ocean liners. The Shenango Steamship and Transportation Company of Pittsburgh, which had commissioned her construction, proudly named the massive colossus *Col. James M. Schoonmaker,* after the Civil War hero who was also the company's general manager and the owner's son-in-law.

But the proudest of them all that day was the ship's builder.

The Ecorse Shipyards of the Great Lakes Engineering Company at Detroit had just launched the largest steel bulk freighter in the world.

◆   ◆   ◆   ◆   ◆   ◆   ◆   ◆

Exactly 32 days earlier, on May 31, 1911, on the other side of the Atlantic Ocean, another ship had been launched. So proud was the city of this new ship that hundreds of trolley cars brimming with excited onlookers ran special trips to the yard. Thousands of spectators filled every vantage point in and around the shipyard vying for a chance to view this magnificent event. Men waved their caps, women and children fluttered handkerchiefs, and they all cheered loudly while tugboats blew their steam whistles incessantly. J. P. Morgan, Bruce Ismay, Lord Pirrie, the Lord Mayor of Belfast and other company officials and dignitaries, viewing this unique spectacle from their privileged lookout in the grandstand, preened and beamed as the immense hull slid down the launchramp.

But the proudest of them all that day was the ship's builder.

The Harland and Wolff shipyard of Belfast, Ireland, had just launched *Titanic,* the largest and most luxurious passenger steamer in the world.

◆   ◆   ◆   ◆   ◆   ◆   ◆   ◆

The new *Col. James M. Schoonmaker,* after a three-month-long outfitting, embarked on her maiden voyage in early October, 1911, loaded at Toledo, Ohio, with a record-breaking 13,000-ton cargo of coal for upbound delivery to Duluth on the far western shores of Lake Superior. On October 13th, the biggest freight carrier afloat cleared Duluth for her first downbound trip with almost 11,000 tons of iron ore, a remarkably large load. The ship's owners beamed with pride.

At the end of the 1911 Great Lakes shipping season, before ice formed to block the waterways of the inland seas, the *Schoonmaker* went into winter mooring at Ashtabula, Ohio, on Lake Erie.

◆   ◆   ◆   ◆   ◆   ◆   ◆   ◆

An unusually severe winter delayed the opening of navigation on the Great Lakes in early 1912. By April, normally a time when grain or ore-filled freighters were departing Duluth for transit to southern ports, the Great Lakes fleets remained in safe harbors, not attempting to break through the extensive fields of ice that covered and blocked the lakes and rivers. Duluth, in fact, reported harbor ice 36 inches thick. Shipping companies received word on good authority that Lake Superior had frozen over entirely that winter for the first time in recorded history. "There never was such a winter," decried the old-timers, declaring the lakes un-navigable. The ships would just have to wait it out.

◆   ◆   ◆   ◆   ◆   ◆   ◆   ◆

During that wait, on a fateful weekend in mid-April, 1912, strange events occurred on the Great Lakes.

Various Lake Erie ports reported an immense tidal wave that swept the south shore. This was indeed odd, as there are no tides on the inland seas. At Painesville, Ohio, lake ice was washed 600 feet back up the river, and huge icebergs, the likes of which had never before been seen on the Great Lakes, were observed out in Lake Erie.

At Ashtabula, the tidal wave swept the large steel steamer, *Sahara,* from her moorings, throwing her against the even larger *Col. James M. Schoonmaker.* The *Schoonmaker's* light upper works at the bow were entirely smashed. By some miracle, no lives were lost during this aberration of Nature. The ship could be repaired.

The date of this report outlining the damage to the *Col. James M. Schoonmaker,* the largest freighter in the world, was Sunday, April 14, 1912.

On that day, about a thousand miles away in the North Atlantic Ocean, a fateful event of greater magnitude and more serious consequence was about to take place. The palatial *Titanic,* the largest passenger steamer in the world, having finally completed her ten-month-long outfitting, was making speedy headway towards New York City on her maiden voyage across the ocean with over 2,200 people on board, and she was about to strike an iceberg.

Titanic would be far less fortunate than the *Schoonmaker.*

◆   ◆   ◆   ◆   ◆   ◆   ◆   ◆

These are the stories of *Titanic's* Great Lakes connections.

1 The Collision

Everything about *Titanic,* the White Star Line's newly-launched passenger ship, excited the world of transportation. She was not only the largest manmade movable object that the world had ever seen, but also, as implied by newspaper advertisements, the most luxuriant: "French à la Carte Restaurant... Turkish and Electric Baths... Swimming Pool... Four Elevators... Gymnasium... Veranda Café... Palm Court... Squash Racquet Court...."

Marine experts studied the plans, examined the hull, and proclaimed *Titanic* to be "practically unsinkable." As word of mouth fired news of this colossal new ship throughout the world's ports and to the ears of seasoned and green travellers alike, the cautious disclaimer, "practically," disappeared from the descriptions. In the public's eyes, there was absolutely no need for concern about safety at sea with this ship. *Titanic* simply could not sink.

Titanic, from *Beeson's Marine Directory,* 1912

Besides being a gigantic gem amazing to one's sight and indulgent towards one's comfort, *Titanic,* on her maiden voyage, also felt the need to prove another strength: speed. The White Star Line had just recently begun promoting its ships, *Titanic* and *Olympic,* as

"The Largest Steamers in the World." The company was well aware of the advertised claim to fame of its chief rival, the Cunard Line, for its fleet, which included *Mauretania, Lusitania, Saxonia* and *Carpathia*: "The Fastest Steamers in the World."

A record-breaking ocean crossing on *Titanic's* debut voyage would be the perfect surprise bombshell to drop upon the Cunard Line. With arrival at New York City harbor scheduled for Wednesday morning, April 17, 1912, it would be an incredible accomplishment for the ship to reach port on Tuesday evening, well ahead of schedule. How the First Class passengers would lavish acclaim upon the vessel, her captain, her builder and her owners. How the press would applaud, and in what glowing terms they would relay their reverence to their legions of readers. How the rivals would cringe with envy. What an introduction to society for the exquisite maiden named *Titanic*!

But at that very moment, icebergs were drifting down from the bleak Arctic like starving wolf packs desperately ranging into unfamiliar territory in quest of food. It had been a milder than usual Arctic winter, so the warmth prompted larger ice fragments to break off Greenland's glaciers in greater numbers. Increased size produced greater longevity, allowing the northern current to carry the icebergs beyond previously established southern limits. The trans-Atlantic shipping lanes for the month of April were already set further south than they were during the summer months. But they were not set far enough for the unusual spring of 1912. The unexpected presence of a vast army of ice titans menaced the vessels utilizing the prescribed shipping lanes.

Titanic, power-drugged with seeming invincibility, sped through the iceberg field, ignoring numerous ice warnings that had been sent by wireless from other ships that had slowed down or stopped completely. They would not risk damage or destruction while blindly traversing this obstacle course by night. *Titanic,* however, with deck lights defiantly ablaze, plowed headstrong into the dark danger zone.

The night lookouts spotted the huge iceberg when their ship was an estimated 1,500 feet from it. They rang the crowsnest bell and speedily communicated the problem to the bridge. There, First Officer Murdoch ordered the rudder hard left and the ship's engines reversed. In his split-second need to make a crucial decision, and likely because this was the ship's maiden voyage and her handling characteristics were not yet known or familiar, he forgot that only the two outer propellers could be put into reverse; the main center propeller, which controlled the rudder (and hence the direction the ship took), simply stopped altogether. *Titanic* turned towards the left extremely slowly with the two outer props in reverse and the main propeller providing no current to activate the rudder. Had the order been given for the left outer propeller to be reversed, with the right and center propellers maintaining their forward thrust, *Titanic* would have swung left further and faster, and missed the iceberg completely.

At 11:40 P.M., Sunday night, April 14, 1912, *Titanic* struck the immense iceberg a long, glancing blow along the ship's starboard bow side. An intermittent slender line of fractured steel plates and popped rivets 300 feet long left thin openings in the side of the ship, admitting powerful jets of ice-cold saltwater into several of the forward compartments. The ship slowly began to fill with water. The unthinkable and the unspeakable had commenced. The unsinkable ship of dreams was heading to the bottom of the North Atlantic Ocean.

During the 10 seconds of impact when intermittent stretches of *Titanic's* hull scraped along the barely submerged extension of the vast iceberg, most passengers had already retired for the night, the fifth of their seven night trans-Atlantic voyage.

Titanic at the moment of impact with the iceberg. This depiction exaggerates the width (a gash that size would have sunk Titanic within minutes), but does not show the entire length of the intermittent thin gashes.   *SCIENTIFIC AMERICAN*, APRIL 27, 1912.

Survivors' vivid accounts indicate that virtually all of them were able to recall the sensation of *Titanic's* impact with the iceberg. To those travelling First Class, with their staterooms in the middle upper portion of the ship, very little was heard or felt compared to the noisy, jarring scrape which physically jolted and alarmed many of the Third

Class men who were bunked in almost the lowest portion of the bow, closest to the ship's actual contact point with the ice.

This iceberg, photographed by the Chief Steward on the German ship, *Prinz Adelbert,* on April 15, 1912, near the scene of *Titanic's* sinking, is the most likely candidate for authenticity (from several that were photographed by a few people on different ships claiming to have captured an image of *"the* iceberg that sank the *Titanic"*). The Chief Steward took this picture because of the scar of red paint he noticed running along the iceberg's base, implying a recent collision; in fact, he had not yet heard about *Titanic's* accident when he snapped the shutter!   COURTESY OF WALTER LORD.

Over a quarter of the total *Titanic* passengers, proportionately represented in all classes, were bound for Great Lakes destinations. Of the 1,343 passengers aboard, 346 of them were heading for communities along or within about 100 miles of, the inland seas; only 128 of them would survive the sinking.

First Class passengers and wealthy, young newlyweds Dickinson (25) and Helen (19) Bishop, returning to Dowagiac, Michigan, from a three-month-long honeymoon in Egypt and the Mediterranean, felt and heard nothing when *Titanic* grazed the iceberg, Helen had retired for the night and Dickinson was seated in a stateroom chair reading a book when the ship struck. Several minutes passed before someone pounded on their door and told them to report to the deck. They dressed hastily.

On deck, officers assured the Bishops that there was no danger and they could return to their cabins. Back in B-49, the couple again prepared for bed, but were soon disturbed by repeated knocking. Their friend, Albert Stewart, warned them that the ship was listing.

Mechanically, the Bishops dressed and returned once more to deck level. They were getting good at this drill.

First Class passengers Dickinson and Helen Bishop, from Dowagiac, Michigan, were among several honeymoon couples on board *Titanic*. AUTHOR'S COLLECTION.

The chill of the April night on the ocean prompted Helen to ask Dickinson to return to their cabin for her muff. The young husband obliged quickly and unquestioningly. No sooner had he reached his goal than his wife appeared hot on his heels in continuation of this apparent screwball comedy of movement. But the situation was losing its humor: Helen reported that all passengers had been ordered to don lifejackets. A soft-hearted steward had allowed Helen to keep her new pet, a little dog she named Frou Frou, in their cabin. She left the dog behind, knowing there would be neither room nor sympathy for an animal in a lifeboat compared to the lives of women and children.

Newlyweds John and Nelle Snyder from Minneapolis retired at 10:30. John was sound asleep when Nelle nudged him awake and told him that something was wrong. He arose, threw on a bathrobe, and flagged down an assistant steward in the companionway.

"The ship has struck sideways against an iceberg, but she's pursuing her regular course," he responded cheerily.

John returned to Nelle. Only later when they heard the Bishops, another honeymooning couple quartered in the stateroom across the hall from theirs, leaving their quarters did the Snyders do the same.

Walter and Mahala Douglas of Minneapolis, Minnesota, in their First Class stateroom, described the impact as being "not great to us." They felt the engines stop, "then they went on for a few moments, then stopped again." After a very long time of no activity whatsoever on the ship --- no officers, no stewards, no orders, no answers --- they started seeing passengers wearing lifejackets. So the Douglas couple dressed warmly (she in her fur coat) and left their cabin with three lifejackets, the extra one for their maid, Bertha LeRoy.

John and Nelle Snyder and Walter and Mahala Douglas hailed from Minneapolis, Minnesota. The Snyders were another couple returning on *Titanic* from their honeymoon.   AUTHOR'S COLLECTION.

First Class passenger Martha Stone, from Cincinnati, Ohio, slipped a kimono over her night dress, put on her slippers, and walked into the corridor, where, from overhead, she heard the steady loud blast of valves releasing steam. An officer assured her that they had simply stopped to assess damages, and that there was no danger. Not long afterwards, both Martha and her maid, Amelia Icard, donned lifejackets and walked up to the lifeboat deck.

Ann Isham of Chicago.
AUTHOR'S COLLECTION.

Chicago socialite Ann Isham, who had spent the last decade of her 50 years living in Europe, boarded *Titanic* at Cherbourg, France, anticipating spending the summer of 1912 with her brother, Edward, in New York City. She kept largely to herself in her First Class cabin, C-49, and when *Titanic* struck the iceberg, she noticed nothing.

Miss Constance Willard, enjoying the quiet of the First Class cabin she had all to herself, had just put down a book she was reading in bed. A "tremendous crash" prompted her to sit up suddenly. She felt a peculiar sensation that something had happened which she had been expecting. Then she remembered a prophecy, made to her years ago by a sinister fortune teller in her home town of Duluth, Minnesota, warning that she would die when she was approaching 21 years of age. She was, in fact, 21, but she worried that the prediction might be a late bloomer. She repeatedly rang the bell for a steward, and when one finally appeared, his face wore a frightened expression. He told her to dress and get out on deck. So she dressed, aimlessly, and prepared to leave her room, but before doing so, she peered at the image in the mirror for a long time, trying to understand why she was not alarmed, only interested, at the prospect of never reaching America.

Constance Willard from Duluth.
AUTHOR'S COLLECTION.

Also from Duluth and also in First Class, William and Alice Silvey had retired, but were not yet asleep when the collision occurred. They had spoken earlier in the evening about the increased vibration of the ship, with William explaining to his wife that *Titanic's* speed had been increased. They listened now, could still hear the engines (Alice later claimed that the engines were not shut down until about 30 minutes after the impact), heard a commotion outside, and got up and dressed.

Chicagoan Ida Hippach did feel the shock of the collision, although she admitted that it was "a mild one." Jean, her 16-year-old daughter, slept through it and did not awaken until "the roar of escaping steam from some quarter of the mangled boat" reached them. They put on some wraps and left their cabin. Outside, people talked about the ship having struck an iceberg, but that there was no danger. Ida's curiosity was piqued. "When I heard there was an iceberg in sight, I immediately made up my mind that I would go out on deck and see it, for I had never seen an iceberg before in my life." An officer passed them. "Ladies, go back to bed. You'll catch cold."

They returned to their stateroom, not to return to bed, but to dress warmer for their planned iceberg viewing. When they emerged again on deck, another officer told them to put on their lifejackets. Things had taken a serious turn. The Hippachs did as they were told.

Ida Hippach and her daughter, Jean, from Chicago.
AUTHOR'S COLLECTION.

Major Arthur Peuchen recalled, "On Sunday evening, I dined with Mr. Markland Molson, Mr. and Mrs. Allison, and their little girl. Everything was exceptionally bright. Then I went to the smoking room and met Mr. Beatty, a partner of Mr. Hugo Ross of Winnipeg, formerly of Toronto. I also met Mr. McCarthy of the Union Bank of Vancouver, and a financial man from Toronto. Talk was unusually bright. This was at about 11 o'clock. Then I said, 'Good-night. I am going to turn in.' I had just reached my berth when I heard a dull thud. It was not like a collision, and I didn't think it serious. That's extraordinary, I thought, and went up to see. I ran upstairs and, on the way, met a friend, who laughingly said that we had struck an iceberg, and we went up on deck."

Self-made millionaire Hudson Allison, who divided his time between his workplace in Montreal and the family farm where he was born on December 9, 1881, at Chesterville, Ontario, had been in Europe on business since November, 1911. The object of his working vacation was to interest British capitalists in the British and Canadian Lumber Corporation, a $20,000,000 concern with vast lumber tracts in British Columbia backed with New York money. Accompanying him were his wife Bess (which one Toronto newspaper coldly described as "a Milwaukee woman"; Hudson had met and married her in Milwaukee on December 9, 1907), their children, Helen Loraine, who was three, one-year-old Trevor, and four recruits from England: two nannies, Sarah Daniels and Alice Cleaver, a cook, Mildrid Brown, and a chauffeur, George Swane. The Allisons paid a small fortune to be among the prominent people on *Titanic's* maiden voyage: £151 ($760 U.S.), for luxury First Class staterooms C-22 and C-26.

Caroline Bonnell shared a First Class stateroom with her cousin, Natalie Wick. Elizabeth Bonnell, Caroline's aunt, was in a stateroom nearby, and Natalie's father and stepmother, Colonel George and Mary Wick, were quartered in one not far away. The members of the Wick-Bonnell entourage looked up to the colonel, "the leading businessman of Youngstown, [Ohio]", as their group leader.

Col. George D. Wick and his wife, Mary, from Youngstown, Ohio.
AUTHOR'S COLLECTION.

Miss Caroline Bonnell
(left) shared a cabin with
her cousin, Natalie Wick
(center); Caroline's aunt,
Elizabeth Bonnell (right)
had one nearby. All were
bound for Youngstown.
AUTHOR'S COLLECTION.

Everyone had retired for the night. Caroline and Natalie closed
their port because, unlike previous evenings on board, it was uncomfortably cold this night. Suddenly they heard a discomforting grating
sound. Natalie peered through their porthole and saw what looked like
a mountain of ice behind them. Meanwhile, men on deck were picking up huge chips that had been shaved off the iceberg when *Titanic*
passed, and with great merriment were throwing them at each other.

"Well, thank goodness, now we'll see our first ice mountain at
last!" one of the young women crowed. Dress skirts thrown hastily
over night clothing, with fur coats atop everything, the excited ladies
left their cabin. Then the ship's engines stopped.

On the Second Class decks, passengers were also mobilized by the
impact. Nellie Becker and her three children were returning to Benton
Harbor, Michigan, while her husband stayed behind in India to
complete some missionary work. Their youngest, Richard, had contracted a serious disease there, and the Beckers, who had already lost
one son to illness in India, were determined to save this one's life with
treatment in America. All four of the family members were asleep in
their stateroom when the ship struck the iceberg. Nellie claimed that
they felt "only a slight jar," but then suddenly the engines stopped,
which "is a bad sign on shipboard when the ship is in the middle of
the ocean." Nellie, slipping quickly into a robe and slippers, stepped
into the hallway and confronted a steward. "Nothing is the matter,

Madam. We've just had a little accident. They're going to fix it and then we'll be on our way. Please go back to bed."

Nellie did as ordered, but was unable to sleep. The pounding above her head and people whistling and singing as though nothing was wrong troubled her. She again ventured into the hallway.

MRS. A. O. BECKER and TWO CHILDREN, RUTH and MARIAN

This time, a steward started fastening the life preserver in his hands onto her, and gave the order to hurry to the deck. Nellie instead rushed back to her stateroom to collect her family.

"Ruth, help me put shoes and socks on the younger children," she told her twelve-year-old. "We have to go up on deck, and we don't want them to get cold."

Without tying the children's laces, Nellie and Ruth Becker rushed out of their stateroom towards the upper deck with four-year-old Marion and the baby Richard in tow.

Norman and Bertha Chambers of Ithaca, New York, in bed at the time of the collision, "noticed no great shock, the loudest noise by far being that of jangling chains whipping along the side of the ship." When the order to don lifejackets and go to the boat deck was given, they dressed warmly and, after sending his wife ahead, Norman opened his bag, removed his automatic pistol and slipped it into the pocket of his heavy overcoat. He prepared for anticipated trouble.

Daisy Minahan of Green Bay, Wisconsin, was awakened by the crying of a woman (whom she later identified as Mrs. John Jacob Astor) in the passageway. She awakened her brother, Dr. William

Minahan and his wife, Lillian. The doctor dressed, the women threw kimonos and blankets over their night garments, and all went on deck.

Two Wisconsin passengers: Daisy Minahan of Green Bay and her brother, Dr. William Minahan, from Fond du Lac. AUTHOR'S COLLECTION.

Ellen Toomey from Indianapolis. AUTHOR'S COLLECTION.

Ellen Toomey felt a "slight shock, but nothing serious." A short time later, a steward ran past her Second Class cabin and ordered the women within to take down the lifebelts and put them on. In her haste, the 50-year-old Miss Toomey, returning home to Indianapolis, left behind her satchel containing her tickets and money.

Jessie Trout, returning to Columbus, Ohio, from a visit with relatives in Scotland after the accidental death of her railroad switch-man husband the previous September, was immediately awakened by the sound when the ship struck. She looked out the porthole and saw the iceberg passing, reminiscent of "the roots of a double tooth that has been pulled." She remained in her cabin until about 12:30, when the Second Class purser told her to don a lifejacket and proceed to the boat deck. Jessie threw a top coat over her night clothes and headed up. Somewhat unglued by the commotion about her, she remembered something important and returned to her cabin to get her back comb, which was her husband's last gift to her before he died.

Jessie Trout from Columbus, Ohio.
AUTHOR'S COLLECTION.

Emily Richards was shaken awake in her Second Class cabin by her mother, Elizabeth Hocking, shortly after the collision.

"There is surely some danger. Something has gone wrong," the older woman warned.

Emily had heard nothing as she slept, but she donned slippers and a coat, and, after dressing her children, three-year-old William and baby George, they all went on deck.

"Everybody put on your life preservers before coming on deck," a steward shouted down in a calm voice to the emerging passengers.

Akron-bound, Emily Richards and children, and her mother, Elizabeth Hocking.
AUTHOR'S COLLECTION.

Minutes later, lifebelt-garbed Elizabeth Hocking, matriarch of a major family move from England to Akron, Ohio, where her sons lived, scampered away to find her other daughter, Nellie Hocking, 20, her son, Richard Hocking, 23, who was guiding the family to their new home in America, and her younger sister, 45-year-old Ellen Wilkes.

"Get up Dagmar! The ship has hit something!" Dagmar Bryhl, a 20-year-old from Skara, Sweden, was already awake from the jar of their ship hitting the iceberg. The man knocking on her Second Class cabin door was her fiancée, Ingvar Enander, a year older than she. The pair was enroute to Rockford, Illinois, for a summer visit to her uncle Oscar Lustig and three aunts, Mrs. Charles Ellison, Mrs. Charles Landstedt and Mrs. Ida Gustafson. Dagmar's brother, Kurt Bryhl, shared a cabin with Ingvar, but unlike the other two, he was emigrating to America. Dagmar dressed and joined the two men on deck.

The Reverend John Harper, on his way from London to preach at a series of revival meetings in Chicago, was travelling in Second Class with his six-year-old daughter, Nina, and her aunt, Miss Jessie Leitch, who had helped enormously in looking after the child since the death of her mother two years earlier. They had appreciated a truly fine sunset from *Titanic's* deck that Sunday evening, and, noting the excellent weather, Reverend Harper commented, "It will be beautiful in the morning."

"When we were awakened by the sound of the collision, we were told to go to deck A," stated Miss Leitch later. "Reverend Harper packed up little Nina in a blanket and kissed her."

The Chicago-bound
Rev. John Harper.
AUTHOR'S COLLECTION.

Lyyli Silven, 18, hastily slipped on a thick skirt over her night dress and investigated the collision. She shared a Second Class cabin with another young woman from Finland, but she sought her cousin, Anna Lahtinnen, and her minister husband, William, with whom Lyyli was heading to Minneapolis. When she finally found them, Anna nervously told Lyyli to leave them, as they wished to be left alone in each other's company. A resigned William casually puffed on a cigar. Lyyli's sense of survival was stronger than theirs. She moved on.

Jane Quick and her two daughters, eight-year-old Winifred and four-year-old Phyllis, were returning home to Detroit after a visit to Jane's relatives in England. They had retired to their cabin by 9:00 o'clock that Sunday evening, and were asleep when a lady passenger tapped on their door.

"Hurry onto the deck. There has been an accident," she called.

Jane hurriedly put what clothing she could onto Winifred and herself, when the steward appeared with the command to put on life-belts. Jane wrapped a shawl around Phyllis, who was sound asleep on the berth, took her children and hastened on deck. A man expertly placed lifebelts on the two girls, as well as onto Jane, and guided them up an iron ladder to the waiting lifeboats. They never saw him again.

Jane Quick and her two daughters, Winifred and Phyllis, made Detroit their destination.
AUTHOR'S COLLECTION.

Anna Hamalainen (or Hamlin, the anglicized version which she and her husband preferred to use in Detroit where they lived) was returning from Finland with her year-old son, Viljo, and a home town friend who was excited about moving to America, 18-year-old Marta Hiltunen, six years Anna's junior. They shared a Second Class cabin, to which they retired after ten o'clock on that Sunday night. Marta slept in her berth, but Anna fell asleep on the couch with her baby, who had been restless. The jar of the ship as she struck the iceberg awakened both Anna and Marta.

"It was not a hard collision," claimed Anna. "Just a little bump and then a grinding that lasted for a minute or two. So slight was the shock that I didn't consider it of enough importance to investigate, even when I felt the engines stop." Both young women dropped asleep again, but hard pounding on their door soon awoke them.

"Get up! Get dressed! The ship has collided with an iceberg!" shouted a man's voice.

Third Class passengers Helmina Nilsson and Elin Braf, two adventurous, single women, shared a steerage cabin near *Titanic's* stern with fellow Swede Alice Johnson, who was returning to St. Charles, Illinois, with her two young children, Harold and Eleanor. Elin, who was only 20 but the better-travelled of the unmarried women, talked excitedly of returning to Chicago to her sister's house on Roscoe Street, while Helmina, six years older, was heading for nearby Joliet, where three of her brothers and a sister lived and worked. Both young women came from Ramkvilla, Småland, Sweden, and both, in spite of Elin's familiarity with the United States and Helmina's inability to speak English, eagerly looked forward to new lives in the new land. The ladies had also met fellow Swedes Ernest Aronsson and Gustaf Edvardsson; Helmina seemed especially pleased, as both of these young men also made Joliet, Illinois, their destination.

Swede Helmina Nilsson
was bound for Joliet, Illinois.
AUTHOR'S COLLECTION.

Helmina was the only one still awake when the ship hit the iceberg, the shock tossing her against the wall and knocking things from the table. Elin Braf and Alice Johnson woke with a start and soon heard the din of people walking around the ship.

"What is all the commotion about?" Alice asked an immigrant girl across the passage.

"We have reached New York. We must hurry and get ready to land!" came the response as the eager young woman busily started packing a big lunch in anticipation of the three-day train ride she said lay ahead of her.

But Alice was skeptical about the impact arising from *Titanic* docking in America. She put on some clothes and ran on deck, where she was told that the ship was sinking and that passengers were going to be removed in lifeboats. She speedily returned to her cabin to inform her cabin mates and to dress her two small children.

The women dressed hastily, but then Elin lingered to pack her few personal possessions, in particular a doll which she kept with her in the cabin as an intended gift for her niece.

"We have to go quickly! Leave those things now!" exclaimed an anxious Helmina in Swedish. But Elin, who had already crossed the ocean twice and felt much more secure in this "unsinkable" ship than she had in any of the others, showed no excitement and expressed no fear. She remained casual, carefully packing things into her bag. Daring to wait no longer, Helmina tossed a shawl around her neck and rushed to the deck above her as quickly as possible.

The Johnson family, visiting in Europe, was now returning to St. Charles, Illinois. From left to right, Harold, his mother, Alice, and his sister, Eleanor. AUTHOR'S COLLECTION.

Henry Davison and his wife Mary, from Bedford, Ohio, were in bed when they heard the crash. He went to investigate. "Come on deck. We've hit an iceberg!" he shouted to his wife upon his return. Mary heard a woman scream and she suddenly felt very frightened.

A young Englishman named Edward Dorking, enroute to making his fortune in America via his uncle Frederick Cooke's home in Oglesby, Illinois, was busily play-

Mary Davison was returning to Bedford, Ohio. AUTHOR'S COLLECTION.

ing cards with colleagues in the Third Class music room on the Shelter Deck (D Deck) near the top of *Titanic's* stern. The collision threw him from his bench, and the "grinding noise" made them all aware that something was seriously amiss.

Philip Zenni was heading for Dayton, Ohio. AUTHOR'S COLLECTION.

Philip Zenni, a young Syrian "of quick mind and Americanized manners" (he had lived in Youngstown, Ohio, for several years, altered his original name, Fahim Leeni, to a less foreign-sounding one, and was enroute to Dayton), was shaken awake by a companion who heard the crash of *Titanic* against the iceberg. The engines, he noticed, ran with a "strange noise," and among his fellow steerage passengers, there was "considerable confusion." Zenni pulled on a pair of trousers and headed up towards the boat deck.

Victor Sunderland shared a Third Class cabin with other men deep in *Titanic's* bow, and to him, the collision was only a slight jar similar to the effect of a basket of coal dropped onto an iron plate. A steward told them that they should go back to bed. Only when water began pouring in under their cabin door did they think anything was wrong, and Victor wondered if he would ever see his uncle in Cleveland.

Nearby, Milwaukee-bound Anton Kink and his brother, Vincenz, shared a steerage cabin with four other European men. There was a "crash like an earthquake, and the boat continued to quiver for a time," Anton recounted later, "but we were not thrown from our berths." The men headed to the stern to warn their family members.

Cleveland was Victor Sunderland's destination. AUTHOR'S COLLECTION.

Neshan Krekorian, a young Armenian, was encouraged by his father to emigrate to Canada as a means of escaping the religious pogroms in his own country. Once established there, he was determined to earn enough money to send for his younger brothers. Neshan was not travelling alone, as four others from his village of Keghi were with him. Yet he felt oddly alone when he gazed through the open porthole in his steerage cabin on board *Titanic* and sighted a distant iceberg for the very first time in his life. The air felt so cold that he slept in his bunk fully dressed, having removed only his boots. When the ship collided with one of those icebergs, Neshan felt the ship tilt to one side. He jumped out of bed, put on his boots, and headed towards the deck. From that point on, it became every man for himself.

Austro-Hungarian Franz Karun, returning to Galesburg, Illinois with his four-year-old daughter, Manca, was fast asleep when *Titanic* hit the iceberg. They dressed, donned lifejackets, and headed up.

Twelve-year-old Banoura Ayoub awoke from the shock of the collision, as did her cousin, John Thomas of Columbus, Ohio, and his 15-year-old son, John Thomas, Jr. Mr. Thomas left to find out what had happened. He returned shortly and went back to bed. "The officers said there was no danger," he said confidently to the two.

Banoura Ayoub and her cousin, John Thomas, of Columbus, Ohio. AUTHOR'S COLLECTION.

Over an hour later, Banoura awoke and, seeing water on the cabin floor, bestirred her cousin. He, in turn, found that his son was gone. John told the girl to run up to the deck while he hunted for John Jr.

Arriving on deck, Banoura saw John Jr., who disappeared again below deck immediately after she told him about his father's search. Simultaneously, the elder John came up a different set of stairs. Normally this would have been hilarious slapstick comedy, but not under these conditions. While John Thomas again plunged below deck in search of his missing son, sailors put Banoura into a lifeboat.

Anna Turja, 18, inflamed with thoughts of emigrating to America and joining her sister and brother-in-law in Ashtabula, Ohio, shared a steerage cabin in the stern of *Titanic* with two other Finnish women and three children. They were awakened by the shudder of the collision. All of them had dressed by the time one woman's teenage son rushed forward from his quarters with the other single Third Class men at the bow and, exhausted and excited, warned them that the ship was sinking. They started for the boat deck.

◆   ◆   ◆   ◆   ◆   ◆   ◆   ◆

Doctor Frank Blackmarr strolled leisurely along the quiet passenger deck, alone in the crisp darkness, inhaling the April air of the North Atlantic. Awed by the endless expanse of glittering stars above him, he noted that the night was not just dark, but abysmally dark, that, were it not for the ship's lights, he doubted he could even see his hands before his face. The night also felt uncanny and cold. He wore the heavy overcoat which he had had enough foresight to pack in the last minute before leaving Chicago. It seemed absurd, however, taking along this winter garment, since he would soon be basking in the semi-tropical warmth of the Mediterranean Sea. His overcoat would be relegated to the depths of his trunk for the remainder of his vacation. It was just before midnight. His ship was heading east and, unknown to him, he was just over 50 miles from where *Titanic* had just struck the iceberg that Sunday night.

Just after midnight, Frank Blackmarr retired for the night to his berth on board the Cunard Line ship, *Carpathia*, without having any idea of his role in the drama which had commenced on the sinking stage of another ship a scant few miles away.

2 "Lower the Lifeboats!"

There was not a hope in hell of placing 2,234 people into the mere 20 lifeboats that were on board *Titanic*.

Titanic carried 891 crew, 870 male and 21 female. Another two dozen people earned a legitimate living working on *Titanic*, although technically they were not part of the crew: the eight members of the orchestra, five postal workers caring for the 100,000 pieces of mail in 300 bags, nine members of the Harland and Wolff Guarantee staff, plus the two Marconi wireless operators. Many discrepancies exist among *Titanic* head counters, and one reason for this is that the 24 people just mentioned are assumed to be part of the figure for total crewmembers. Other tallies omit the ship's captain and officers, arguing that they are technically not part of the "working" crew.

There were only a few more passengers on *Titanic* than there were crew: a total of 1,343 passengers boarded *Titanic*, which could accommodate a total of 2,433 passengers (and was thus, at 55% full, embarking on her maiden voyage far below capacity) and they were divided into three categories according to location, lavishness and cost of lodgings. In reality, the divisions were based on class structure.

First Class passengers (of whom there were only 337 on board this large ship which could accommodate 735) were the élite on board, occupying the largest, finest, and most elegantly furnished cabins on the uppermost decks. They were the costliest quarters on *Titanic*, closest in convenient proximity to the most spacious passenger decks providing the freshest air, the most ornate dining salons providing the most sumptuous meals, the most comfortable lounges supplying the most ornately carved furniture, including sofas upholstered with the thickest velvet. Everything provided for First Class passengers was physically as distant as possible from the noisy engines and hot boilers at the bottom of the ship.

DIAGRAM OF TITANIC SHOWING LC THIRD CLASS CABINS, CREW

First Class travellers on board *Titanic* included some of the richest men in the world (and it was still a man's world in 1912, with few exceptions). These titans of capitalism bore well-known, highly-respected names such as Astor, Guggenheim, Strauss, and Widener. Their banks, coal mines, steel mills, real estate and railroads fueled an age of opulence in early 1900's America referred to as "The Gilded Age." Their successes, strengths, relationships, and travels supplied newspapers with copy eagerly anticipated by a hero-hungry society in this era before movie stars and sports figures stole the spotlight. Often maintaining lavish homes on both sides of the Atlantic, and sparing no expense or imagination for their extended vacations to Egypt or for their hunting expeditions to darkest Africa, they were the ragtime epoch's version of modern-day jet setters. They jumped at any opportunity that would take them across the ocean faster that usual, so an ocean liner's speed became an important consideration for the moneyed (trans-Atlantic passenger aircraft were still decades away from becoming realities). When these barons of industry travelled, they always went First Class, on *Titanic* paying anywhere from £35 to £300 ($175 to $1500 U.S., in an era when a common laborer earned $10 a week) depending upon the number of cabins required for the entire group: the family itself, plus often a maid, a cook, a butler, and a chauffeur, who, although travelling on the same family ticket, were sometimes housed in Second Class cabins.

Only somewhat less elegant than First Class was Second Class, which represented the newly developing middle class, people who lived comfortably somewhere between the affluence of the "haves" and the poverty of the "have-nots" as a result of greater distribution of the wealth generated by the Industrial Revolution. Many of these were successful shopkeepers who believed in their abilities to improve their lot in life. Second Class on *Titanic,* although socially overshad-

)CATIONS OF FIRST, SECOND AND QUARTERS AND ENGINES

owed by First Class, physically resembled the upper class level: stained glass doors opened to oak-panelled staircases and lounges, while an electric elevator connecting a range of seven decks conveyed those disinclined to confront stairs. Mirrored washstands, oak wardrobes, mahogany beds and electric lights were standard amenities. However, Second Class cabins usually contained berths for four passengers instead of the usual two or three in First Class. On *Titanic*, Second Class accommodations were said to be equal to or better than First Class cabins on most other ocean-going ships. A total of 285 of *Titanic's* 1,343 passengers comprised Second Class (in which class *Titanic* could accommodate a total of 674 people), each paying an average of £15, or $75 U.S. (seven or eight weeks' salary for a manual laborer in 1912) for the one-way trip across the ocean.

Third Class (also called steerage because these people were usually quartered in the bottom portion of the ship's stern area, along with the steering mechanism) dwelled at the bottom of the world's, and *Titanic's,* social hierarchy. This frequently impoverished but adventurous group consisted chiefly of emigrants, ranging from mavericks of the British working class seeking employment opportunities, to Syrian women and children who spoke no English but sought to reunite with the family breadwinner already living in the New World who had sent them passage money. They all had strong dreams of making better lives for themselves in America. Not surprisingly, most Third Class cabins were located at the bottom of the ship, just above the engine and boiler level, at the bow and stern ends, areas of least comfort and stability during heavy seas when the ship tossed and rolled. Different levels of accommodations were priced accordingly. Cheapest was the large dormitory for men at *Titanic's* bow. Women and children were often quartered in cabins containing either two, four, or six berths, in bunkbed or single foldaway berth format, and again priced in direct proportion to degree of privacy (the least private, the cheaper). The average cost of crossing the Atlantic Ocean from Europe to New York City in Third Class was £8, or $40 U.S. (which, in 1912, was several weeks' wages for what today is termed "blue-collar" labor). *Titanic* could carry 1,024 passengers in Third Class, but on her only voyage, she carried 721.

Titanic carried 16 lifeboats, numbered one through sixteen, as well as four collapsible boats, identified by letters A, B, C and D. The odd-numbered boats, as well as Collapsibles A and C, were stowed and ultimately launched on the starboard (right) side of the ship, while the even-numbered boats and Collapsibles B and D were in place and ready for use on the port side. Fourteen of the lifeboats (numbers 3 to 16) had a capacity of 65 persons each; lifeboats 1 and 2 were smaller emergency lifeboats, each with a capacity of 40 people; the collapsible lifeboats were rated to carry 49 persons each. Total lifeboat capacity was 1,186 persons, and *Titanic* carried 2,234 people on board. The problem was far more serious than any mathematics.

◆　　◆　　◆　　◆　　◆　　◆　　◆　　◆

Dressed in appropriate warmth and safety gear, the Bishops waited on deck. Helen observed "tons of ice on the fore part of the ship" while the first lifeboat, number 7, was being readied for loading. Most passengers, including the Bishops' acquaintances, John Jacob Astor, with the new bride less than half his age, gazed down at the dark ocean 65 feet below and expressed their reluctance. "This is all silly. The ship cannot sink," they argued while drawing back from the lifeboat.

Initially, both Helen and her husband claimed that they had been literally pushed into the boat, but later they stated that the officer in command had shouted, "All brides and grooms may board!" Two other newlywed couples stepped into the same lifeboat and the lowering began. The Bishops had delayed their departure from France so they could return on the new *Titanic*, but now they were the first to leave the sinking ship. It was about an hour after *Titanic* hit the iceberg. On board were 24 First Class passengers (12 men and 12 women), a single male Second Class passenger, no one from Third Class, and three crewmen, 28 people in a lifeboat built to carry 65.

John P. Snyder of Minneapolis and Nelle, his bride of eight weeks, obeyed a steward's orders after the collision that they had better go up on deck. There, however, Nelle complained of the cold. They returned to their First Class cabin, reappearing later on the boat deck dressed in heavier clothing and carrying Nelle's jewel case. Still, no one wanted to board the lifeboat.

"The women, after looking over the rail at the water, refused to change their seeming safe position for the more precarious one in a lifeboat. An officer ordered them into the boat, but they still refused to go," recalled John. "Everyone was talking about how the first boat to be lowered from a ship in times of wrecks generally tips over." However, once the first couples boarded, enticed by the words, "All brides and grooms may board," others followed.

Colonel Wick stood on the lifeboat deck, reassuring the four women in his party that everything would work out well. No one around them showed any excitement or fear; it was too early for that. Captain Smith walked to and fro ordering all women and children to be placed in the lifeboats, but the ladies in the group were in no hurry to leave the apparent stability of the large ship.

Finally they boarded Lifeboat 4. George Wick kissed his wife, patted her on the shoulder, and bid them all to keep up their courage. They left, thinking that they would all be together again shortly. The last they saw of Colonel Wick he was leaning over the railing of the deck. He watched with anxious eyes as the lifeboat carried his wife and the other three women away from the sinking ship.

This 1912 print captures many of the emotions which were felt as *Titanic* was sinking. Women and children were ordered into lifeboats and the men stayed behind. In many instances, the separation was forever.   COURTESY OF THE MARINERS' MUSEUM, NEWPORT NEWS, VIRGINIA.

Ida Hippach and her daughter, Jean, noticed people's reluctance to enter the lifeboats. They themselves were in no hurry because they thought they would "be safer aboard the vessel." Conflicting talk circulated among the passengers: the boat was not badly injured, there was no danger of sinking, *Titanic* would stay afloat at least 24 hours, they would be safer on board the ship than in a lifeboat, *Olympic, Titanic's* sister ship, was only a short distance away. In fact, some people claimed to be able to see *Olympic's* lights in the distance.

"Nobody dreamed of such a thing as a shortage of lifeboats," Ida pointed out later. "We passed by Col. Astor when the last boat was being loaded. He told us there was no danger, but advised us to get into the boat in which he had just deposited his bride. Col. Astor was one of the grandest of the hundreds of heroes aboard the *Titanic* ....after assuring his wife that he would follow later, he turned to us with a smile on his face. 'Ladies, you are next,' he said. Jean and I had to clamber out of a window [because the lifeboat had already been partially lowered] and over into the boat in which there were but two sailors, or men whom they called sailors. They didn't know how to handle oars. The women had to take to the oars and row."

Jean recalled later that Col. Astor undoubtedly saved their lives. 'Don't lower that boat until this woman gets in,' he told the officers as the boat was beginning its descent. The officers stated that there was room for only one. When it was apparent that one Hippach woman would not enter the lifeboat without the other, Astor pleaded with the officers to allow both to board, and the men relented.

The lifeboat containing the Hippachs was lowered about 65 feet from B Deck to the ocean.

The Tragedy of the Titanic

AUTHOR'S COLLECTION.

William Silvey placed his wife, Alice, into one of the lifeboats. " I will follow in one of the other ones," he told her as her boat left.

When Walter Douglas placed his wife and their maid into one of the lifeboats, Mahala implored him to join her. "No, I must be a gentleman," he responded, and the Minneapolis millionaire of Quaker Oats fame and fortune stepped back quietly.

Helmina Nilsson, climbing up from steerage, found her way to the upper deck blocked by a number of sailors stationed there to preserve order among the Third Class passengers. But Helmina failed to understand their English commands. Besides, she calculated that her chances for survival were better up in the First Class area. When one of the sailors stepped aside for a moment, she seized her opportunity, climbing over a railing and ascending a small ladder to an upper deck. She found herself in a good position near one of the lifeboats, and she left the sinking ship in what she later claimed was the third boat to leave the larboard, or port, side. She was in lifeboat 13.

Also reaching the boat deck from steerage by means of a ladder, Chicago-bound Irish emigrants, John Bourke, his wife, Katherine, and his sister, Mary Bourke, actually made it into a lifeboat. When John was ordered out of the boat by an officer, both his wife and his sister gave up their seats to remain with him on the doomed ship.

One of the seats the Bourkes vacated was quickly occupied by 21-year-old Anna Kelly, a steerage passenger who was part of the Irish group from Mayo County. By coincidence, she, too, was heading for Chicago. Once positioned in the lifeboat, she stayed put.

Anton Kink, an Austrian steerage passenger bound for Milwaukee, watched as sailors helped his wife, Louise, and their four-year-old daughter, also named Louise, into one of the lifeboats. Then an officer grasped Anton by the shoulder and ordered him back. Mother and daughter cried at the tops of their voices at the thought of their man remaining behind. Anton "ducked down, broke through those standing about and jumped into the boat as it was being lowered." Later, perhaps feeling ashamed about being a man who had survived

The Kink family was travelling to Milwaukee, Wisconsin, when *Titanic* struck the iceberg. From the left, Louise Kink, daughter Louise Gretchen, and Anton Kink.   AUTHOR'S COLLECTION.

the sinking, he told a different reporter that he had jumped into the ocean and was picked up by a lifeboat (many men who survived claimed to have done this save-face-dive into the Atlantic, swimming to a lifeboat and being pulled in by those on board, whereas, in reality, they had entered that lifeboat dry before it even left *Titanic's* side). But Anton was greatly troubled by the fact that, even though he had made it into a lifeboat, in the process he had become separated from his sister, Maria, 22 (who had shared a cabin with Louise and her daughter, and three other women), and his brother, Vincenz, 26, with whom Anton had shared a steerage cabin deep in the ship's bow. His siblings were emigrating to America and travelling with them to Milwaukee, and now, Anton had no inkling as to their whereabouts.

EVERYTHING FOR ENJOYING LIFE BUT NOT MUCH TO SAVE IT.

First Class passengers, dressed in long gowns and tuxedoes while the encroaching ocean nips at their heels, are startled to find a sign, which lists the ship's luxuries, hanging in the davits instead of a lifeboat. This depiction appeared in the *Detroit News* on April 19, 1912.   AUTHOR'S COLLECTION.

Mrs. Catherine Joseph, returning in steerage to her husband in Detroit after a visit with her family in Lebanon, bundled up her children, two-year-old Mary, and Michael, who would turn five within a month. She held her small, helpless daughter tensely in her arms, but could not grab her son.

"Michael," she ordered, at a loss for any other way to keep them together, "Hang on to my skirt tails."

Michael's little fingers clutched tightly, but once on deck, with the chaotic scuffling of large adult bodies, the random yelling of commands, and the endless shrieking of steam noisily escaping from the valves along the smokestacks, the child lost his grip in the confusion and was suddenly separated from his mother.

Catherine, running quickly back and forth along the deck, called out frantically to her son, but he was nowhere to be seen.

Time was running out, and most of the lifeboats had been launched. An officer hastily guided Catherine and Mary into Collapsible C just in time for it to be lowered. It was 1:40 A.M., and the mother reluctantly departed the sinking ship casting her wide, frantic eyes towards the people left behind. Somewhere among that doomed throng was her firstborn.

Two types of men.

This commentary, from the *Cleveland Leader*, April 20, 1912, implied the types of men on board *Titanic*: those who stepped into a lifeboat and those who didn't.   AUTHOR'S COLLECTION.

Borak Hannah, heading to his brother's residence in Port Huron, Michigan, knew that his only chance of surviving the sinking was to get into a lifeboat and stay there. The determined steerage passenger from Syria spoke no English, but he understood the pistol that one officer waved in front of him. His fourth effort to get into a lifeboat succeeded, and he quickly hid under a seat.

Anna Hamalainen, her baby son, and Marta Hiltunen arrived late on deck, having ensured that they were all warmly dressed.

"Stay close to me," Anna warned the nervous Marta, who spoke no English.

"Here's a woman with a baby," shouted one of the ship's officers as Anna came into view. "Hurry and get into the boat," he told her. Anna turned and handed Marta her handbag and stepped into the lifeboat with her baby, fully expecting Marta to follow. But Marta hesitated, and Anna's boat was lowered. It was one of the last. Anna, dropping slowly towards the water, watched Marta standing near a group of men and women on the other side of the ship's railing.

Anna Hamalainen and her son, Viljo, were enroute on *Titanic* to Detroit to rejoin this man, husband and father, John Hamalainen. AUTHOR'S COLLECTION.

Maud Sincock, Agnes Davies and the latter's nine-year-old son, John, shared a Second Class cabin. Agnes' older son, Joseph Nicholls, stayed in another cabin. Both ladies were emigrating from England to new lives with relatives in upper Michigan. Born in Toronto (her mother was Canadian), Maud grew up in England and, at the age of 20, decided to join her father in Hancock, where he had emigrated the previous year. Agnes was relocating part of her family to join another of her sons and his wife at Houghton. From a lifeboat, Agnes last saw her grown son, Joseph, throwing kisses to her and John, from the deck of the sinking ship and shouting reassuringly, "Don't worry, Mother, there's no danger. I'll be saved."

Neshan Krekorian was heading for Brantford, Ontario. COURTESY OF ALICE SOLOMONIAN.

Neshan Krekorian climbed past the human confusion deep below deck in steerage and found comparative calm near the lifeboats. People huddled in small groups and talked, seemingly not concerned about their situation. But *Titanic* was noticeably sinking, and lifeboats were being lowered to the ocean as quickly as possible. With a running start, Neshan leaped into one of the half-filled descending boats, sat on a bench and said nothing. No one else did, either. When the boat hit the water, he immediately helped to row them away from *Titanic*.

Emigrating to the United States and bound specifically for her sister's residence in Milwaukee, but impeded by her club foot, retired nurse Lucy Ridsdale, 50, struggled more than the average passenger to reach the boat deck from her Second Class cabin. Fortunately, she had assistance from her cabin mate, Mary Davis. Both boarded boat 13.

Jessie Trout, returning to the boat deck with her comb and bracelet, was immediately grabbed by a sailor and placed into Lifeboat 9.

First Class passenger Frederick Kenyon of Pittsburgh confidently placed his wife, Marion, in one of the lifeboats with the words, "See you in the morning." She hoped he was right.

Emily Richards, along with her two young sons, her sister, Nellie Hocking, and her mother, Elizabeth, waited for a lifeboat. "We were put through the portholes into the boats," Emily described later, "and the boat that we were in had a foot of water in it. As soon as we were in, we were told to sit down on the bottom. In that position, we were so low that we could not see out over the gunwale...."

Adie Wells and her two children, Joan and Ralph, had strolled casually on *Titanic's* deck earlier in the day with Emily Richards and her boys. The young mothers, in their 20's, each with two small children, were both returning to Akron, Ohio. Dressed and out on deck after the collision, Adie did not grasp the seriousness of the situation, even when an officer brusquely ordered, "Come on here, lively now, this way, women and children." She thought it was a lifeboat drill, not realizing that these actions were in earnest until she and her children were being lowered in Lifeboat 14 to the cold, dark ocean far below.

Adie Wells and her two children, Joan and Ralph, were returning to Akron, Ohio.
AUTHOR'S COLLECTION.

Buffalo, New York Architect Edward Kent, 58, raced up the steps towards the boatdeck. Enroute, he encountered his shipboard friend, also from First Class, Helen Candee, of Washington, D.C. She was despondent, and told him so. Then she suddenly squeezed something solid into his hands. It was an ivory, gold-framed miniature containing a picture of her mother. Kent felt that her chances of surviving *Titanic's* sinking were better than his, but he slipped it into his pocket anyway.

Jennie Howard Hansen, of Racine, Wisconsin, travelling Third Class with her husband Peter, was returning from a visit to his parents and siblings in Denmark. His brother, Henry D. Hansen, was returning to America with them. They awoke when the ship's engines stopped. Noticing people rushing around, they quickly dressed and were told to put on lifejackets. They had to climb up an iron ladder on the outside of the ship to reach the boat deck. An officer ordered Jennie into a lifeboat, but when they blocked Peter, she begged them to let her remain on the sinking ship. Peter quietly spoke to her, "No, you go ahead and maybe one of us will live to tell the story back home. Let the ladies go in the boats. If I went, it would beat a lady out of a chance to live. I would not do that and you wouldn't want me to." He calmly kissed his wife goodbye as an officer yanked her over to the lifeboat. As it was being lowered, Peter threw her pony coat to her, and she caught it. She had heard someone say that the *Carpathia* and the *Olympic* were near and they would rescue everybody, so she felt some reassurance. Yet, as her boat pulled away from the sinking *Titanic,* Jennie hoped that her men would somehow find another lifeboat, and she apprehensively looked back and saw Peter and his brother, Henry, standing on the upper deck where she had left them.

Returning home to Racine, Wisconsin, were Jennie and Peter Hansen.
AUTHOR'S COLLECTION.

Edward Dorking hurried on deck from the Third Class lounge where he had been playing cards and, following several people running towards the bow, found the deck strewn with ice. He gazed seaward, and, on this clear night, saw the iceberg "rising out of the water like a great white spectre, towering above the funnels of the ship....it seemed that the iceberg was at least four or five times as large as the *Titanic*." Assured by fellow passengers and crew that there was no danger, he returned to his card game. It took a while for Dorking and his comrades to notice people streaming towards the lifeboats. He decided to go below deck and don the lifejacket which was under his bunk. Passing the engine room, he noticed Captain Smith, "like a marble statue after a rain" with all the perspiration pouring down his calm face, giving orders to the crew. Dorking's bunk was under water by that time, so he returned to the top deck. Remaining with the ship spelled death, he thought, so he removed his shoes and outer garments, balanced himself as best he could on the angled railing, and jumped into the freezing water forty feet below.

Dagmar Bryhl tightly clutched the hand of her fiancée, Ingvar Enander, as he and her brother, Kurt, led her to a lifeboat. When Ingvar started lifting her into it, she seized both his hands and would not let go. She glanced in the lifeboat and saw that there was room.

"Come with me!" she screamed as loud as she could.

Her scream acted as a signal for an officer to step forward and push Dagmar away from the boat, tearing the lovers' hands apart in the process. Dagmar was soon seated in the lifeboat as it was lowered. At one point, she looked up and saw Ingvar and Kurt, side by side, watching her. As her boat rowed away, they smiled and waved.

Alice Johnson, her two small children in tow, reached the side of what appeared to be one of the last lifeboats, loaded to capacity, just as it was being lowered. She had become separated from her cabin mates; in fact, she never saw Elin Braf "after the first alarm was sounded." But survival ruled. She squeezed the officer's arm and begged for a place in the boat. One man stepped out of the lifeboat and offered her his place*. Alice handed baby Eleanor to outstretched arms, and then she stepped aboard. The boat was lowered.

Suddenly, Alice realized that her four-year-old son, Harold, was still standing at the rail of the ship, crying. She started screaming, "Save my boy! Save my boy!" A man standing nearby seized the child by an arm and a leg, reached over the side of the ship, and dropped him 30 feet into the waiting arms of men in the descending

---

* This man may have been fellow Swede Gunnar Tenglin, who was returning to Iowa. Alice Johnson later told reporters, "I did not see the man who gave me his place again. I hope he was saved." If indeed the man was Tenglin, he was saved; by his own admission, he stepped back into the same lifeboat he had just left because there was still room.

lifeboat. The Johnson family would remain together, and Alice was forever grateful to the stranger who so roughly saved her son's life.

As her lifeboat pulled away from the sinking ship, Alice Johnson looked back and saw one of the tragic scenes that would remain with her forever. A young girl, wrapped in a kimono, stood at the rail and watched her lifeboat leaving. Alice remembered her trying to enter the lifeboat, and the officer claiming that the boat could not stand another passenger. Now, Alice watched the girl, with her head on the rail, crying as the ship sank.

Reverend Harper kissed his young daughter, Nina, goodbye before handing her to a crewman, who deposited her with her waiting aunt, Miss Jessie Leitch, in lifeboat 11. He felt that a repeat of his successful series of sermons in Chicago and elsewhere a few months earlier would have to be delayed.

As soon as the party emerged on deck, Dr. Minahan hurried his wife and his sister to a waiting lifeboat. Other passengers were already waiting there calmly. The doctor took special care to ensure that the ladies' lifejackets were correctly fastened; Lillian did the same for her husband. "No matter what happens, be brave," he said, kissing them both as they entered the boat. He stepped back and the lifeboat was lowered. At one point, Lillian Minahan peered upward and saw her husband near the rail looking down at them. Desperation was taking hold of many of the passengers remaining on the sinking ship. As their lifeboat was being lowered, Daisy noted that "as we reached the level of each deck, men jumped into the boat until the officer [Fifth Officer Lowe] threatened to shoot the next man who jumped."

Daisy Minahan anxiously stared back at the surgeon-brother who had performed an emergency appendectomy on her in Paris just two months earlier. She suddenly remembered the soothsayer who, years ago, had told several peoples' fortunes at a gathering in Fond du Lac. Dr. Minahan was told that he would "lose his life on his second trip abroad." His friends found merriment in the prediction, and ribbed him about it prior to his first voyage across the ocean a few years ago. They reminded him of it when he announced his second trip abroad the previous fall. Lillian and Daisy had each taken out a $5,000 vacation accident insurance policy; Dr. Minahan bought a $30,000 policy for himself. Then he made sure that his business affairs were in order. As their lifeboat rowed away, William Minahan waved farewell.

The Becker family witnessed the beehive of activity around the lifeboats. The two youngest children were placed into lifeboat 11 which was about to be lowered when their mother called out, "I want to go with my children! Please let me in this boat!" Immediately some of the officers picked her up, threw her into the boat, and lowered it to the water. Then Nellie noticed that her daughter Ruth was left standing on deck.

"Ruth!" Nellie screamed. "Get into another boat!"

Nellie watched Ruth disappear into the thick crowd.

Norman Chambers had packed "certain necessities" into his coat pockets. He was an experienced traveller, returning to the States on this trip from Rio de Janeiro by way of Europe, and he liked to be prepared. On deck, he gave his wife, Bertha, a drink from his flask, filled his pipe, and they waited at the rail before entering Lifeboat 5.

"Nearer To Thee!"

From the *Toledo News-Bee*, April 19, 1912.
AUTHOR'S COLLECTION.

Sixteen-year-old Karen Abelseth, emigrating to America and travelling to Minneapolis, Minnesota, shared a steerage cabin with fellow Norwegian, 21-year-old Anna Salkjelsvik, who was heading to Proctor, Minnesota, and several other Scandinavian ladies. After the collision, Karen became very frightened when she witnessed people dragging their trunks and other baggage through the corridor. Karen and Anna were part of a group of Norwegians which included several men, including Olaus Abelseth (no relation to Karen), who saw to it that the women made it into lifeboats. Olaus, who also made Minneapolis his goal, had worked in the Dakotas earlier.

Constance Willard was in no hurry to get into a lifeboat, but when she heard someone yell, "The ship is sinking!", it hit her. "For the first time I had a desire to get aboard a lifeboat---a real desire. Something seemed to hover behind those words which I didn't like, though I was still unafraid." She watched five boats fill and descend to the ocean, but "the eddy of the crowd" pushed her away from any available one. "It was like waiting to get a chance at the cloak room of a crowded opera house," she claimed, yet she still felt no terror at her repeated failures to board a boat. Finally she made it into Boat 10.

Major Arthur Peuchen of Toronto mingled with the crowd near Lifeboat 6. In his onshore life, he mingled business acumen with military activities. Peuchen was President and General Manager of the Standard Fuel and Chemical Company since 1897, and he owned immense lumber interests in western Canada, in the newly-created province of Alberta. Besides being known as a philanthropist who supported a number of charities and donated generously to hospitals' x-ray departments, Peuchen figured prominently in the Royal Canadian Yacht Club and earned recognition as a good skipper while sailing his 65-foot yacht, the *Vreda,* on Lake Ontario. Although he had never seen active service, he was a highly regarded Canadian military figure whom England's King George had decorated with the Victorian Order of the third degree. In Toronto, whenever the Queen's Own Rifles went on parade, Peuchen, usually mounted in the rear of the regiment, was always recognizable as the only officer wearing a beard. As one reporter put it, Peuchen "is an officer of striking appearance."

After *Titanic* struck the iceberg, Arthur Peuchen left his interior cabin, C-104, after pocketing three oranges and a pearl pin, his good luck charm. He left behind the presents for his two children, his other jewelry, and over $200,000 in stocks and bonds.

On deck, the cacophony of escaping steam, the firing of distress rockets from the bridge, and the shouts of officers and passengers loading lifeboats all added to the confusion. Peuchen encountered fellow Canadian Thomson Beattie and shouted what the commotion was all about.

Major. Arthur Peuchen from Toronto.
PHOTO FROM *MEN IN CANADA*, 1901.

"Haven't you heard? The order is for lifebelts and the boats."

Peuchen looked around and, for the first time, noticed that the other passengers, many of them appearing distressed, wore lifejackets.

Second Officer Charles Lightoller had ordered the lowering of Lifeboat 6. Peuchen, leaning on the ship's railing, wondered aloud why the lifeboat was nearly empty. The officer explained that the ropes would not hold a full load. Someone in the small boat yelled up, "We have only one seaman here. Can someone give us a hand?"

Lightoller, gazing straight at Peuchen, asked, "Are you a sailor?"

Peuchen stepped forward. "I am a yachtsman." His bold assertion, assisted by his "striking appearance," saved his life. Lightoller made him an offer.

"If you are as good a sailor as you claim to be, you can get into the boat and join them."

Captain Smith, standing nearby supervising the loading, suggested that Peuchen take the steps and descend one deck, smash a window, and get into the lifeboat at that level. But Peuchen took the most direct route, grabbing a rope, jumping away from *Titanic*, and descending, hand over hand with apparent ease, to the hovering lifeboat 25 feet below him. The seaman already in Lifeboat 6, Quartermaster Hichens, who had been at *Titanic's* helm at the time of collision, remained quiet for the time being, but there was another sailor on board. Lookout Frederick Fleet who had first sighted the iceberg, put Peuchen to work plugging the water drainage hole and preparing the rudder. Peuchen then took one of the oars and they "rowed away like good fellows."

Charles Melville Hays, president and general manager of the Grand Trunk Railway (which, in 1912, boasted "the longest continuous double track railway in the world under one management" -- it ran from 38 miles east of Montreal skirting the St. Lawrence River and the Great Lakes to Chicago, a distance of 876 miles), had been in England securing loans to carry on construction work on his Grand Trunk Pacific Railroad, which ultimately became the Canadian National Railway, the second trans-Canada railroad created to break the monopoly of the Canadian Pacific Railway.

Hays had been in England for a meeting of the directors of the Grand Trunk Pacific Railroad, where he recommended that the company, already greatly in debt, spend its way out of its difficulties. Included in his proposals was a chain of luxury hotels to be built across Canada along the railroad's lines. The first of these hotels, the flagship Château Laurier in Ottawa, was to be opened amidst great fanfare on April 26, 1912. Hays definitely planned to be present. Travelling on *Titanic* with Hays were his wife, Clara, and their maid, Anne Perreault. They occupied First Class suite B-69, as guests of Bruce Ismay, the White Star Line's managing director. Hays' daughter, Orian, and her Montreal stockbroker husband, Thornton Davidson, also accompanied

Charles Hays, President of a railway which ran alongside the Great Lakes. AUTHOR'S COLLECTION.

them, occupying adjoining cabin B-71. This was the young couple's first trip abroad.

The night *Titanic* hit the iceberg, Hays shared cigars, cognac and conversation in the smoking lounge with retired Great Lakes captain Edward Crosby from Milwaukee and Col. Archibald Gracie from Washington, D.C. Hays, aware that Germany was about to launch a passenger ship even larger than *Titanic*, warned that "The White Star, Cunard and the Hamburg-American lines are devoting their attention and ingenuity and vying with one another to attain the supremacy in luxurious ships and in making speed records. The time will come soon when this will be checked by some appalling disaster."

Hays did not know it then, but the time had come when he would take an unwilling part in that appalling disaster.

Yet Charles Hays remained in a relaxed state that showed his disbelief in the gravity of this emergency. Feeling that he had everything under control and that a nearby ship would come to the rescue, he told his daughter, Orian, as he was hustling her into Lifeboat 3, "You and mother go ahead while the rest of us [his secretary, Vivian Payne, and his son-in-law, Thornton Davidson] will wait here until morning. This ship is good for eight hours, so don't worry. Help will arrive long before then." He then told her that he would return to their staterooms and pack two or three small bags of their most vital belongings to take aboard the rescue ship.

Orian, so reassured by her father's earnest words, did not even kiss him or her husband goodbye.

WHEN THOUGHTS TURN TO THE HEREAFTER

[Copyright: 1912: By John T. McCutcheon.]

A dramatic commentary on music and prayer on a doomed ship, this depiction of the passengers' final moments appeared in the *Chicago Daily Tribune*, April 21, 1912. AUTHOR'S COLLECTION.

But the damage to *Titanic* was worse than imagined. Five of the 16 watertight compartments were gradually flooding. Freezing saltwater entered in powerful jets through the slender slits along several hundred feet of hull where rivets had popped from the bent steel plates below the waterline. The double-layered bottom was rendered useless as a safety feature because the point of collision occurred above it where the hull was only single-skinned. With five of her 16 compartments flooded, *Titanic* would sink.

The loading of the lifeboats continued.

Emily Goldsmith and her son, Frank, Jr., entered a boat, leaving the lifebelted Frank, Sr. with the other men on the second deck. "The descent to the water was the most terrifying part of all our experience," recalled Emily. "The lifeboat bumped against the side of the *Titanic,* and once so many people got on one side that it seemed the boat would turn over and spill us all into the sea."

Emily Goldsmith and her son, Frank, Jr., were bound for Detroit, Michigan.
AUTHOR'S COLLECTION.

The initial calm order in the filling and lowering of the lifeboats gradually changed to desperation and chaos as more and more people on *Titanic* realized that the ship was, indeed, sinking, and that there were not enough lifeboats for everyone.

"During the loading of the boats," Nellie Becker stated later, "the Englishmen and the Americans were busily engaged in seeing that the women found places in the boats. I never saw an Englishman or an American make an advance as if they wanted to save themselves and let the women perish. They acted as men. The only trouble was with some of the foreign men. There were about a third of the passengers on the boat from foreign countries. Some of these rushed towards the boats and wanted to get in. It was then that the officers drew their revolvers and told them to stand back and give the women a chance."

Ernst Persson and his older sister, Elna Persson Ström, with her two-year-old daughter, Silma, emerged from the labyrinth of *Titanic's* steerage quarters only to find all the lifeboats gone or the deck so densely crowded that they could not reach any. They had left Sweden together to join Elna's husband, Wilhelm Ström, in Indiana Harbor, Indiana. Now their futures seemed uncertain. As they were being separated by the human scuffle and more and more of the the ship sank, Elna instructed Ernst, "Tell Wilhelm and my parents and sisters if you get rescued."

Dr. Alfred Pain from Hamilton, Ontario.
COURTESY OF THE UNIVERSITY OF TORONTO
ARCHIVES, *TORONTENSIS, 1912*, P. 170.

Alfred Pain, the young doctor from Hamilton, Ontario, stood with his friends Marion Wright, who was on her way to Oregon to marry her childhood sweetheart, and Douglas Norman, a young Scottish engineer bound for Vancouver, on the Second Class promenade deck, watching with awe the lowering of the starboard lifeboats. As the crowd grew in size and emotion, and as distress rockets lit up the clear night sky from the bridge, the small party hastened to the less crowded port side, where they observed an officer having difficulty talking an elderly woman into taking a place in crowded lifeboat 9. Pain gently pushed a reluctant Marion Wright forward to take the woman's place. Wright fully expected that the ship would not sink, that the lowering of the lifeboats was just a precaution, and she looked forward to being back on *Titanic* before morning. She was so certain of the situation that she did not even say goodbye.

Alfred Pain, however, had seen the growing pandemonium and suddenly realized that the ship, its passengers and its crew were all in serious trouble.

Anna Hamalainen observed some of Captain Smith's last actions.

"Captain Smith's only thought was to do what he could toward starting the frail boatloads of humanity on their only chance for life," Anna noted. "After the last lifeboat was lowered, Captain Smith said, 'It's every man for himself now, friends,' He said this as calmly as though he were bidding an acquaintance good morning. 'Each man look out for himself: the last boat's gone.'"

THE LAST BOAT.

[Copyright: 1912. By John T. McCutcheon.]

When the last of *Titanic's* lifeboats left the sinking luxury liner, there were still over 1,500 people on board. This visual commentary appeared in the *Chicago Daily Tribune* on April 18, 1912.
AUTHOR'S COLLECTION.

3 The Cold, Dark Ocean

Many of the survivors in the lifeboats, teeth rattling from the cold, were shaken by convulsive sobs and shivers. The frigid air sent chills to their bones, and their nostrils seemed to freeze. A few wondered what some of the passengers and crew were doing, splashing around in the dangerous sea -- it all seemed so foolish, so unreasonable, so illogical. The immense tragedy of the moment hit them unexpectedly.

Some began to wail, "Oh my God! Oh my God!" *Titanic's* head was bowing deeper and deeper under the water. More of those remaining on board retreated towards the stern like ants swarming to the highest point of land in a flood. The ship's lights, illuminating what could still be seen of her length at several deck levels, spasmodically flickered, then twitched into blackout.

AUTHOR'S COLLECTION.

The initial calm on the ocean felt by those in the lifeboats quickly faded. People's collective breath stopped, and their blood seemed to freeze from something beyond the low temperature. Many grasped the sides of their lifeboat in anxiety, anguish and helpless rigidity.

Lillian and Daisy Minahan observed *Titanic* from their lifeboat which was "the distance of a city block away." The giant vessel had "loomed up through the darkness like a great mountain upon the placid surface of the ocean. The ship was ablaze with lights. Slowly the lights settled lower and lower to the surface of the ocean. Despairing cries could be heard from the decks."

AUTHOR'S COLLECTION.

"The water was like glass," noted Helen Bishop in another lifeboat. "There wasn't even the ripple usually found on a small lake. By the time we had pulled away 100 yards, the lower row of portholes had disappeared. When we were a mile away, the second row had gone, but there was still no confusion. Indeed everything seemed to be quiet on the ship until her stern was raised out of the water by the list forward. Then a veritable wave of humanity surged up out of the steerage and shut the lights from our view. We were too far away to see the passengers individually, but we could see the black mass of human forms and hear their death cries and groans. For a moment, the ship seemed to be pointing straight down, looking like a gigantic whale submerging itself, head first."

"One dining room steward, who was in our boat," continued Helen, "was thoughtful enough to bring green lights -- the kind you burn on the Fourth of July. They cast a ghastly light over the boat, but you know we had no light of any kind. I think all life boats ought to be equipped with lights, crackers and water and compasses. Whenever we would light one of these diminutive torches we would hear cries from the perishing people aboard. They thought it was help coming," she observed naively.

Titanic bowed deeper, then noisily fractured in half with the pandemonious grinding of brittle steel, popping rivets and splintering wood. The unlighted hull rose stern-first straight up to the clear sky and stars, then, to accompanying shrieks rising from the lifeboats as survivors themselves sank emotionally and psychologically, plunged straight down into the black ocean depths in a bubbling fury.

The ship was gone.

◆   ◆   ◆   ◆   ◆   ◆   ◆   ◆

The struggle now began for over 1,500 shouting and screaming people who found themselves desperately treading for life among ice floes in near-freezing water. Death by hypothermia begins with painful numbness within the first 15 minutes, followed by merciful unconsciousness within the next 15. The plunge in body temperature would soon still the flow of life. Within half an hour, most people would have succumbed to icy extinction.

But those thirty minutes after *Titanic's* closing plunge were a nightmare of demented screams and fevered madness as the majority of those carried by the ocean liner grappled in vain for survival. The amplitude of the victims' futile struggles pierced the frightened ears of the survivors.

The cacophonic chaos of so many human beings freezing to death while splashing among the icebergs that night in the North Atlantic Ocean became, for many survivors, the worst memory of the sinking.

"I will never forget those sounds," cried an anguished Nellie Becker. "Screams, yells, cries and curses were mingled with prayers and shouts. It was a terrible din, and the long, last wail spread over the whole ocean, it seemed. Then all was darkness on the spot and the *Titanic* was no more. Even then we did not realize the enormity of the calamity. We even ventured to wonder if any of the poor sailors went down with the ship. We explained that the cries and the yells, even the prayers that were sent up at that instant were uttered because such a giant of the ocean had gone down and that they were offered as a requiem not for the souls that sunk [sic] into the ocean's depths, but because of the passing of this monster of the seas."

"Groans," described Jane Quick, "the most terrible groans, came all about us from the water. They were the sounds of people dying, hundreds of people. Our sailors tried to keep us from knowing that that horrible sound came from those who were about to perish. 'They are cheering,' they told us. Some of the others in the boat may have believed that, but I knew it was the sigh of death."

Daisy and Lillian Minahan recalled, "For many minutes the night air was hideous with with the shrieks and cries of those struggling in the icy waters. It was agony for those in the boats. The cries continued for ten minutes, when quiet descended upon the water, only the wailing of those in the lifeboats being heard at intervals."

Then the dead bodies bobbed in the shimmering waters of the icy North Atlantic in deafening silence.

♦   ♦   ♦   ♦   ♦   ♦   ♦   ♦

Twenty lifeboats of varying occupancy drifted in the darkness on the immense, icy ocean, mere wooden shells, precariously buoyant thin walls separating life from death.

Two weeks after drawing this chilling depiction of the *Titanic* survivors at sea, Homer Davenport, the famous New York City cartoonist, died of pneumonia. Originally in the *New York American*, this copy appeared in the *Grand Rapids* (MI) *Herald* on April 19, 1912.   AUTHOR'S COLLECTION.

Overwhelming grief enveloped the individuals in each lifeboat. Friends had been forced to separate, many never to be seen again by their companions, while wives had been torn from their husbands, and children had been isolated from their mothers. The anguish of not knowing a loved one's fate deadened feelings more than the cold.

Lifeboat 1, one of the two smaller rescue boats with a carrying capacity of only 40 people, was the most underfilled boat, leaving *Titanic's* starboard side at 1:10 A.M. (all times are given as ship's time), with only 12 people, none bound for the Great Lakes region.

Lifeboat 2, the other 40-capacity rescue boat, contained 18 people when it was lowered on the port side at 1:45 A.M. Five of its passengers had Great Lakes destinations: First Class passenger Mahala Douglas and her maid, Bertha LeRoy (Minneapolis, MN), and three members of the Kink family from Third Class, Anton, his wife Louise, and their daughter Louise-Gretchen (Milwaukee, WI).

When *Titanic* actually sank, the wound-up Mahala Douglas finally lost control and shrieked hysterically, "The ship is sinking! The *Titanic* is going down with all on board!" Fourth Officer Boxhall, in charge of Lifeboat 2, commanded her to "shut up!", a response which she later admitted was the right one to give to her outburst. " I had uttered the words instinctively," she confessed, adding in praise, "The Fourth Officer had the presence of mind to supply himself with green flash torches, and it was these that called the attention of the *Carpathia* to us...That is how it happened that ours was the first boat to be picked up, and I was the third woman aboard [the *Carpathia*.]."

Lifeboat 3, capacity 65, contained 38 or 40 people, none of whom was heading for the Great Lakes region. The boat was launched from the starboard side at 1:00 A.M.

Lifeboat 4 left *Titanic's* port side at 1:55, containing only 29 or 30 people, fewer than half the rated capacity. The passengers bound for the Great Lakes region, all from First or Second Class, were: Ida and daughter Jean Hippach (Chicago, IL), Emily Ryerson and her children, Emily, Suzette and John Ryerson (Cooperstown, NY), Victorine Chaudanson (Cooperstown, NY), Grace Bowen (Cooperstown, NY), Anna and Viljo Hamalainen (Detroit, MI), Elizabeth and daughters Nellie Hocking and Emily Richards, the latter with her two small boys, William and George (Akron, OH).

In Lifeboat 4, Anna Hamalainen watched *Titanic's* final moments. "The big steamer was listing badly, we saw as we rowed away from her, and her bows were deep in the water. When we had reached a point about 200 feet away, I should say, the boilers exploded and then the work of destruction was swift. The *Titanic* seemed to heave into the air and split open. The bows settled rapidly and then the whole ship sank. The wave which was thrown up just rocked our boat gently; we were not in danger of capsizing at all."

Her friend and travel companion, Marta Hiltunen, unfortunately went down with the ship. "...the loss of poor little Marta, who started for the strange country with such high hopes, is hard to think of," Anna would sigh later back in Detroit.

In the lifeboat, her thoughts drifted to other acquaintances who died with *Titanic*. "I saw many cases of women refusing to leave their husbands for the lifeboats," Anna recalled later. "The case of the

Lahtinnens was particularly pathetic. Mrs. William Lahtinnen, whose husband was pastor of a Lutheran church in Minneapolis, and I had become acquainted on the voyage. Reverend and Mrs. Lahtinnen had been visiting in his old home, Finland, for several months, and last January their daughter died there. When the time came for Mrs. Lahtinnen to get into a boat, she refused, choosing to die in her husband's arms to living without him."

Ida and Jean Hippach recalled when their lifeboat left *Titanic*. "We rowed and rowed and expected to be sucked right into the whirlpool. The suspense was fearful. At first, we saw the lights of the ship winking out one by one, then they all went out except a flash in the mast. Then that became dark. We heard a fearful cry from the people on the ship. O, I can never forget it! We expected to be sucked into the ocean in the wake of the *Titanic* and I closed my eyes. I waited and waited. Finally I opened my eyes and the *Titanic* was gone. The boat listed so to one side that I felt sure we would be swamped."

Most of the Ryerson family from Cooperstown, New York, were on Lifeboat 4, feeling the effects of a double tragedy. The family, in Europe enjoying a motorcar vacation, had decided to return to America as quickly as possible when they learned of the death of their eldest son, Arthur Ryerson, Jr., in an automobile accident. It was coincidental that the earliest, fastest ship on which they could book passage was *Titanic*. When the new vessel sank, Arthur Ryerson, 61, perished, but not before ensuring that his family was placed in a lifeboat. Saved were his wife, Emily Borie Ryerson, 48, daughter Suzette, 21, another daughter, Emily, 18, and son John, 13. Travelling with the Ryerson family, and saved

Arthur Ryerson of Cooperstown, New York. AUTHOR'S COLLECTION.

with them in Lifeboat 4 were John's governess, Grace Bowen, and Victorine Chaudanson, the Ryerson maid.

The Hockings and the Richards in Lifeboat 4 were also impacted by tragedy. Richard Hocking, (Elizabeth's son, Ellen Wilkes' nephew, Nellie and Emily's brother, George and William's uncle, and the male leader of this family exodus), had gone down with *Titanic*, the only family member to perish. The watchman at the Diamond Rubber Company in Akron had stood his last watch.

Lifeboat 5, with a capacity of 65, carried only about 35 people when it was launched from the starboard side of the sinking ship at

The Cold, Dark Ocean *69*

12:55. The only Great Lakes area people saved on it were Norman and Bertha Chambers (Ithaca, NY).

Lifeboat 6 had been launched from the port side at 12:55 A.M. Those Great-Lakes-bound persons on board were First Class passengers Major Arthur Peuchen (Toronto, ON), Martha Stone and her maid, Amelia Icard (Cincinnati, OH); one seemingly out-of-place Third Class passenger, Syrian Philip Zenni (Dayton, OH), completed the list.

Major Peuchen and Quartermaster Hichens played power games. Peuchen attempted to take command of the lifeboat, but Hichens held his ground by clinging tightly to the tiller. Peuchen was the only First Class male among the 19 First Class Women in this lifeboat. Two male and two female crewmembers of *Titanic* were also on board. Lifeboat 6, with a capacity for 65, had left *Titanic* with 25 people.

Martha Stone was indignant that she, a 62-year-old woman, should be given the task of standing on the lifeboat's plug all night.

Phillip Zenni explained matter-of-factly how he, the only steerage passenger in Lifeboat 6, ended up there. "...I walked up to this [the first lifeboat] and tried to get in, but the officer on duty there said, 'Stand back, women and children go first.' I did so. But as there seemed to be no great desire on the part of many of the favored ones to get into the boat, I tried again. This time the officer said, 'Try that again and I'll blow out your brains.' The sight of a revolver made me think that he meant business and so I took his advice....the boat was not full to its capacity by at least ten.... The *Titanic* was sinking so rapidly that I could feel it settling under me. I feared that we were going to the bottom and I determined to get away if possible. As the second lifeboat was being filled, the officer turned for a moment to attend to a woman and child. At that moment I took a desperate chance and leaped across the few intervening feet into the boat. No one saw me; at least there was raised no objection and I was soon safe under one of the seats. I felt pretty uneasy for some time until we were let down to the water and a few rods away. Then there was raised the cry for assistance at the oars....I crawled out and presented myself, and soon laid to the oars...."

Lifeboat 7 contained only 28 people, less than half its capacity of 65, and was lowered from the starboard side at 12:45. On board were six First Class passengers bound for the Great Lakes: Dickinson and Helen Bishop (Dowagiac, MI), Catherine and daughter Harriette Crosby (Milwaukee, WI) and John and Nelle Snyder (Minneapolis, MN).

The first boat launched, Lifeboat 7 had only three crewmen on board, so passengers took turns rowing. But the 13 male passengers apparently were not enough. A phony German nobleman who called himself Baron von Drachstedt (but who was really named Alfred

Nourney, the only Second Class passenger in this lifeboat), refused to help row, according to Helen Bishop, opting instead to sit and smoke. Other men also felt that manual labor was beneath their social class dignity, and the newly-pregnant Helen felt obliged to take a turn at an oar. French aviator, Pierre Maréchal, proved an exception, and his image lingered in Helen's memory because he never once removed his monocle from his eye, even when rowing.

After *Titanic* disappeared from view and the screams and cries of those in the freezing ocean ceased, all was quiet. Slowly, conversations started up in various parts of the lifeboats for relief or distraction. Helen Bishop related a tale of her recent experience in Egypt.

"A fortune teller told me that I would survive a shipwreck, and I would survive an earthquake, but an automobile accident would end my life. So we have to be rescued," she announced cheerfully, "for the rest of my prophecy to come true."

"Although we were the first boat to leave the *Titanic*, we were about the fourth picked up by the *Carpathia*. The scenes on that little craft adrift in midocean with little hope of rescue were most heart-rending," lamented Helen Bishop. "Still, the characteristics of the individuals [in our lifeboat] appealed to me."

Lifeboat 8, capacity 65, carried only 28 people when it was launched from *Titanic's* port side at 1:10. All those heading for the Great Lakes were from First Class: Elizabeth Bonnell (Cleveland, OH), Caroline Bonnell (Youngstown, OH), Marion Kenyon (Pittsburgh, PA), Mary Wick and her stepdaughter, Natalie Wick (Youngstown, OH), and Sarah Daniels, the Allison maid (Chesterville, ON).

Lifeboat 9, capacity 65, contained from 45 to 48 people when it was launched from the starboard side of *Titanic* at 1:30 A.M., but only four of them had connections to the Great Lakes: Second Class passenger Ellen Toomey was bound for Indianapolis; also in Second Class, Jessie Trout was returning home to Columbus, Ohio; Juho Stranden, a Third Class passenger from Finland, was emigrating to Duluth, Minnesota; and, from *Titanic's* crew, William Ryerson, who had been born on the shores of Lake Erie at Port Dover, Ontario, and was distantly related to the Cooperstown (New York) Ryersons who were aboard the doomed ship.

Ellen Toomey noticed that most of the women in her boat were thinly clothed, probably because some of them had been told to go back to bed after the collision, and had done so, only to be aroused later "when it was too late to dress." To Ellen, the weather was bitter cold and there was much suffering in Lifeboat 9. "One French woman who had lost her husband* became frantic in her grief, but we calmed her. This was the only confusion in our boat," she stated.

Lifeboat 10 contained 30 to 32 people, only half its rated capacity of 65. It was launched from *Titanic's* port side at 1:20, and only three of its occupants made the Great Lakes area their destination: Constance Willard from First Class (Duluth, MN), Neshan Krekorian from Third Class (Brantford, ON), and Florence Thorneycroft from Third Class (Clinton, New York).

Percival and Florence Thorneycroft, travelling from England to Clinton, New York, had been married for almost a dozen years when *Titanic* parted them. Percival's body was never recovered, and Florence returned to England.

Lifeboat 11 contained from 55 to 60 persons, almost reaching its capacity of 65. It was launched from the starboard side at 1:35. The Great-Lakes-bound passengers on this lifeboat were baby Trevor Allison and his nurse, Alice Cleaver (Chesterville, ON), Mildred Brown, the Allison cook (Chesterville, ON), Alice Silvey (Duluth, MN), Nellie Becker and two of her three children, Marion and Richard (Benton Harbor, MI), little Nina Harper and her aunt, Jesse Leitch (Chicago, IL), Jane Quick and her daughters, Winifred and Phyllis (Detroit, MI), Maude Sincock (Hancock, MI), Theodor De Mulder (Detroit, MI), Julius Sap (Detroit, MI), Jean Scheerlinckx (Detroit, MI), and Jennie Hansen (Racine, WI).

Jane Quick and her two daughters had been hastily placed into Lifeboat 11, which now dipped slowly away from the sinking ship. Winifred was hysterical, but Phyllis slept the entire time, unaware that she was in the greatest maritime disaster known to mankind.

Jane Quick noted that the people in her lifeboat at first prayed, some quietly, some aloud, and then they tried to cheer one another up. They talked about different incidents and about impending rescue. "And this helped," Jane said. "By talking to one another and by trying to help someone else be brave, we became braver ourselves." Others also offered the Quicks assistance. One lady gave Jane a golf cape for Phyllis, into which the small child was wrapped for warmth. Winifred, high-strung, nervous, and frightened, began to

---

* The only French women in Lifeboat 9 were Mlle. Leontine Aubart, 24, and her maid, both from Paris and both unmarried. However, Mlle. Aubart was reportedly the mistress of married American millionaire Benjamin Guggenheim, 46, who had paid for her and her maid's passage, and who went down with *Titanic*. Guggenheim's famous last words to a steward were: "...Tell my wife that I played the man's game out straight and to the end. No woman shall be left aboard this ship because Ben Guggenheim was a coward." Mlle. Aubart was likely grieving over him in Lifeboat 9.

cry until the soothing arm of another woman next to her wrapped the child in part of her own coat and kept her warm against her body. Jane quick also observed that a woman was taken aboard their lifeboat from the water once they had left the sinking *Titanic*.

"The four sailors were rowing and made slow progress," noted Nellie Becker, "although the sea was calm and the stars were shining. The officers kept telling us that that the boat would not sink."

They were wrong, and Nellie later described the sinking: "I will never forget the sight of the *Titanic* as she sank. It seems even now a horrible nightmare. We had left the boat for some time and were about a mile away. When we left the orchestra was playing 'Nearer My God to Thee' and other similar songs. As our boat proceeded, the sounds continued until finally they died down.

"We were watching the *Titanic* and noticed that the bow of the boat seemed somewhat lower than the stern. As we watched we could see one row of lights and then the other go out. This continued until most of the rows of lights were gone.

"Then suddenly there was a terrible explosion and the boat hesitated for an instant. She seemed to hang on the balance and the officer in our boat said, 'She is going to float? She is going to float?' But at that instant the middle of the boat seemed to rise up and the bow lowered a bit, then the stern. Then the boat sank to the bottom."

Mrs. Nellie Becker hugged her two youngest children in Lifeboat 11 and grieved all night long for her twelve-year-old daughter, Ruth, whom she had last seen on the deck of *Titanic*.

Jennie Hanson later commented that, "The night was the most beautiful of the whole trip. The sea was calm and the only bad feature was the cold....There were three oarsmen in the boat, but there was not food nor water nor blue light, three things every lifeboat is supposed to be equipped with. There was only one boat in the whole bunch that had a blue light, and we were forced to burn handkerchiefs and clothing all night so that any rescue ship might sight us...."

A lamp trimmer later admitted that there were no lights in some of the lifeboats. After four boats had cleared the doomed vessel, he went to the store room and discovered the lamps, flares and oil there. Captain Smith immediately ordered him to equip as many of the remaining lifeboats as possible.

Lifeboat 12 left *Titanic's* port side at 1:30 with 28 people, far short of its capacity of 65. The only two Great-Lakes-bound passengers in it were both in Second Class: Dagmar Bryhl, bound for Rockford, Illinois, and Lillian Bentham, heading for Rochester, New York.

Lillian Bentham, a good friend of Peter McKain and William Douton, who were lost with *Titanic,* admitted later that she wanted to "forget the whole thing": she had witnessed people crowding to enter too few boats, officers threatening to shoot men who jumped into life-boats, people on their knees in prayer, and lifejacketed passengers jumping over the side of the ship. For her, it was a night to forget.

Lifeboat 13 carried 60 to 62 people, near its capacity of 65, and was launched from the starboard side at 1:40. Its Great-Lakes-bound passengers were Edward and Ethel Beane (Rochester, NY), Ruth Becker (Benton Harbor, MI), Albert, Sylvia and Alden Caldwell (Roseville, IL), Lucy Ridsdale (Milwaukee, WI), John Asplund (Minneapolis, MN), and Helmina Nilsson (Joliet, IL).

Edward and Ethel Beane had been married in England only a few days before *Titanic's* maiden voyage commenced, and they were one of several honeymoon couples on board the star-crossed ship. Fortunately, they both survived and were heading for Rochester, New York, where Edward had emigrated a number of years earlier.

Albert and Sylvia Caldwell, missionaries returning in Second Class from Bangkok to Roseville, Illinois, with their ten-month-old son, Alden, huddled together in Lifeboat 13 and watched the people on the luxury liner scrambling to keep alive. Albert thought of the people worshipping God at that evening's hymn service, and now many of them were on the verge of meeting Him. Sylvia, in a quick flashback, remembered asking as she boarded at Southampton, "Is this ship really unsinkable?" and a deck hand responding, "Yes, lady. God Himself could not sink this ship." She now caught the irony of that blasphemous statement unknowingly made by a crude sailor to a missionary's wife. She turned to watch *Titanic* sinking.

Albert Caldwell wrote years later, "...The lights of the *Titanic* burned until a few minutes before she sank. She tipped, headfirst, lower and lower into the water, until all that we could see was the stern of the boat outlined against the starry sky. She hung as if on a pivot and then, with a gentle swish, disappeared from sight. For a moment, all was silence and then, across the waste of waters, wafted a sound that will ever ring in my ears, the cries of those perishing in the icy water. They did not drown for they could not withstand the cold water and died, one by one, from exposure...."

Helmina Nilsson estimated that Lifeboat 13 "carried over 60 people, ten or 12 of them men, and only two of those men were sailors." One woman helped row the heavily-loaded lifeboat. Helmina, raised near a lake in her native village in Sweden, longed to help at the oars, "but so heavily loaded was the boat that the occupants were forbidden to stir." In fact, "the gunwales were less than six inches above the icy water in which immense cakes of ice were floating." Helmina recalled noticing that "the sea was like glass and a death-like calm prevailed. The bright stars alone lighted the terrible scene, while there was a reflected light from the iceberg with which the ship had collided, which aided somewhat in dispelling the darkness....I could distinctly see *Titanic* as the stern lifted into the air and as it settled prow first into the ocean. I was unable to distinguish the tune which was being played by the musicians, but I could plainly hear the strains of what I later learned was 'Nearer My God to Thee*.'"

Helmina Nilsson cringed when her ears filled with the terrible screams of both those doomed to go down with the ship and those who had been thrown into the icy water when, she claimed, two lifeboats in close proximity to hers capsized.

Third Class passenger from Sweden, John Asplund, 23, could only think of surviving and reaching his brother in Minneapolis.

Unknown to her family, 12-year-old Ruth Becker was safe in lucky Lifeboat 13, which she had entered shortly after seeing her mother and siblings safely launched in Lifeboat 11. Ruth, despite her youth, had learned responsibility and observation. Unlike her mother, she had strength of character which allowed her to talk freely in later years about her experiences that night. She recounted that her lifeboat "was filled to standing room with men and women in every conceivable condition of dress and undress. It was bitter cold, a curious, deadening, bitter cold. And then with all of this, there fell on the ear the most terrible noises that human beings ever listened to, the cries of hundreds of people struggling in the icy cold water, crying for help with a cry that we knew could not be answered...."

---

* One is left with the distinct impression that the hymn, "Nearer My God to Thee" was so associated in people's Victorian minds with the concept of death that, had *Titanic's* band not played that song on the decks of the doomed ship as it sank, many people would have heard it anyway! In the 1912 era, the melody and lyrics of "Nearer My God to Thee" represented the most suitable music for funerals. The *Titanic* survivors on board the *Carpathia* had almost three days' time before facing the journalistic onslaught in New York (16 reporters from the *New York Times* alone!) to reach agreement on what melody they deemed most appropriate for the sinking of *Titanic*, although this hymn might have been played to provide soothing deceit to dull the fear of death. In the Great Lakes region, "Nearer My God to Thee" had long been associated with maritime memorial services. The *Detroit Free Press* of May 31, 1903, the day after Memorial Day, wrote (in what must surely be one of the longest sentences ever published in a newspaper), "With the sweet strains of 'Nearer My God to Thee,' softly played by the Letter Carriers' band, wafted across the shimmering waters, while gray-haired survivors of the struggle of '61-'65, the veterans of the Spanish-American war and the naval reserves, many with uncovered heads, stood reverently about on the deck of the *Yantic* yesterday morning, 150 pupils of the Amos school, under direction of Principal James Mandeville, went through that beautiful and impressive ceremony which has come to be a distinctive feature of the Memorial day observances in Detroit, the strewing of flowers upon the water, a silent but none the less eloquent tribute to the gallant men of the navy, who gave their lives in behalf of their country and the memory of whose deed will always remain...."

Lifeboat 14, capacity 65 people and launched from the port side at 1:25 A.M. containing about 45 people, including several Great Lakes passengers from First and Second Class: Daisy Minahan (Green Bay, WI), Lillian Minahan (Fond du Lac, WI), Agnes and John Davies (Houghton, MI), Amelia Lemore (Chicago, IL), and Adie, Joan and Ralph Wells (Akron, OH).

Miss Amelia Milley Lemore, 34, who had shared cabin F-33 with three other ladies, including Mildred Brown, the Allison's cook, knew she was going to make it back to Chicago once her boat pulled away from the sinking *Titanic*.

Daisy and Lillian Minahan felt the night cold through the nightgowns, kimonos, and light blankets they wore. They worried that if a wind came up and disturbed the ocean calm which prevailed, many of the lifeboats which were heavily loaded would be swamped.

Lifeboat 15 consisted mainly of Third Class passengers, including many men, and was filled to capacity (65 people). It was launched form the starboard side at 1:40. Passengers in this lifeboat bound for Great Lakes destinations were Harry Haven Homer (from First Class, bound for Indianapolis, IN), Elin Hakkarainen (Monessen, PA), Borak Hannah (Port Huron, MI), Helga and Hildur Hirvonen (Monessen, PA), Ivan Jalsevac (Galesburg, IL), Alice, Harold and Eleanor Johnson (St. Charles, IL), Erik Jussila (Monessen, PA), Franz and Manca Karun (Galesburg, IL), Eino Lindqvist (Monessen, PA; interestingly, all five of the survivors from Monessen ended up together in the same lifeboat), Nicola Lulich (Chisholm, MN), Karl Midtsjo (Chicago, IL), Ernst Persson (Indianapolis, IN), Anna Turja (Ashtabula, OH), Hedvig Turkula (Hibbing, MN), and David Vartanian (Brantford, ON).

Karl Midtsjo, a 21-year-old heading to Chicago, related that he had been allowed by First Officer Murdoch to climb down the line from the davits into Lifeboat 15. He later wrote to his brother in Norway, "....Well, it was no fun to be in a little boat out on the Atlantic. It was pretty well in the middle of the Atlantic. We sat in the lifeboats and thought now it is their turn and soon it will be ours. It is no joke when such a big ship is sinking...."

Franz Karun, concerned that his little daughter, Manca, did not have her cap, held her close to keep her warm on the boat. He later said, "...There was a lifeboat lowered and I think it was the last one put down. They put my little girl down first, letting her down with a rope. Then they let me down. I do not know why they did this. Perhaps it was because it was the last boat, and there was still room for somebody....I think that I was the last man to get off the ship...." Continuing, he described the sinking. "I heard two big booms. I think it was the boilers exploding. I did not see the ship break in two. An awful scene followed, people drowning and crying for help. I shall never forget the sight. I did not feel the suction from the ship when it went down...."

Carl Jonsson, returning from Sweden to Huntley, Illinois, had been travelling with fellow Swedes Paul Andreasson, Albert Augustsson and Nils Johansson who were also heading for Illinois. As he caught occasional glimpses of other lifeboats from his position in Lifeboat 15, he wondered which of those boats carried his friends.

A young Croatian in Lifeboat 15, Nicola Lulich, thought about the mining work to which he was returning in Chisholm, Minnesota.

Hedvig Turkula, 63 years of age, had been helped into Lifeboat 15 by fellow Finn Eino Lindqvist (who was also in this boat). Undoubtedly Hedvig's six children and 30 grand-children, scattered all around Minn-esota where she was heading, were later grateful to him.

Anna Turja recalled that "After we left our ship, it was so dark that the men and women had to burn their hats, coats, or anything else they could spare so that the other boats could see and keep together."

David Vartanian hoped to reach Canada, but not by swimming. He later described how he jumped off the sink-ing *Titanic* just before it went under and swam hard towards a crowded life-boat. Initially, the occupants tried to

Nicola Lulich, Duluth, Minnesota.
AUTHOR'S COLLECTION.

keep him out, even going so far as to hit his hands with an oar.

Each time, he persisted in returning to the lifeboat until they let him hang onto the side. He moved around considerably and kicked nonstop in the freezing water to maintain his circulation. Finally, two people pulled him into the boat. This and the arrival of the rescue ship later that morning became the best parts of David Vartanian's mem-orable 22nd birthday.

The lifeboat locations of several survivors, particularly regarding Lifeboats 13 and 15, have left modern researchers confused. Both boats were, or almost were, at full capacity (65), and both were launch-ed successively from *Titanic's* starboard side at about 1:40 A.M.

Alice Johnson described an experience in her lifeboat: "....It was awfully cold. A woman with a little babe wrapped in a shawl gave part of the shawl for protection for little Eleanor, my baby, and both babies, the only two in our boat, were wrapped in the one shawl until we were picked up by the *Carpathia....*"

If Eleanor Johnson was indeed in Lifeboat 15, then she, at the age of 20 months, was the youngest on board. The only other babe in arms in Lifeboat 15 would have been 26-month-old Hildur Hirvonen. If Eleanor were in Lifeboat 13, there would have been TWO other babies on board, 10-month-old Alden Caldwell and 20-month-old Beatrice Sandström (who was heading to San Francisco with her mother and sister), and it has been argued that Alice Johnson, due to the kinship that young mothers have with one another and their helpless offspring, would have observed the presence of any and all babies besides her own in her lifeboat. Besides, Alice Johnson and her children had shared a steerage cabin with Helmina Nilsson, who was in Lifeboat 13, and Alice surely would have recognized Helmina had they been in the same boat. Helmina later claimed that in her lifeboat, she did not even get her feet wet, while Alice declared that her "lifeboat was half full of water." So that would place the three Johnsons in Lifeboat 15.

Alice claimed to witness a rescue from their lifeboat, and she later told a journalist the tale: "We were being rowed away from the sunken *Titanic* rapidly as it was feared the suction of the sinking vessel would swamp our loaded boat. A foreigner* , an Italian I believe, was swimming after us crying, 'Save me, save me,' at the top of his voice. He gained on our boat and on getting within speaking distance, panted, 'Save me. I've got a quart of whiskey.'" He was taken aboard. "The liquor was the only stimulant the men at the oars had for the five long hours before we were taken aboard the *Carpathia.*"

Lifeboat 16, with a capacity of 65 persons, was launched from *Titanic's* port side at 1:35 with about 40 people in it. In that group were these five people heading for Great Lakes destinations: Lyyli Silven (Minneapolis, MN), Karen Abelseth (Minneapolis, MN), Mary Davison (Bedford, OH), Annie Kelly (Chicago, IL) and Ellen Wilkes (Akron, OH).

In Lifeboat 16, Lyyli Silven, the chilly air stinging her face, felt pleased with herself for having taken the time to dress warmly.

Collapsible A, capacity 49, carried 17 people, some of whom died. The boat was swamped throughout the night, and was later set adrift. The only people bound for the Great Lakes to emerge from

---

* It has been conjectured that this "foreigner" might have been David Vartanian, who admitted to swimming over to a boat which, in all likelihood, was Lifeboat 15. But he himself never made reference to having any bottle of liquor with him.

this boat were Olaus Abelseth (Minneapolis, MN) and Oscar Olsson Johansson (Manitowoc, WI).

Norwegian Olaus Abelseth put his seafaring experience to work for him. Seeing that all the lifeboats had gone, he was one of the many who decided that it would be best to stay with the sinking ship for as long as possible. Hanging onto the ropes dangling from a lifeboat davit until he was only a few feet above the ocean, he finally let go --- only to find himself entangled in the ropes in the water! He worked his way out of these, but saw that the two male relatives who went into the water with him had disappeared. Swimming around for a few minutes, he found himself next to Collapsible A. Greeted with antagonism from the occupants, he waited a while before he took a chance and pulled himself into the lifeboat. Two men died from hypothermia while Olaus was doing all he could for them.

Collapsible B had floated off *Titanic* upside-down before it could be righted, and about 30 men tried to survive by balancing themselves upon the barely-floating hull. Those with Great Lakes destinations were Edward Dorking (Oglesby, IL), Ernst Persson (Indianapolis, IN), and Victor Sunderland (Cleveland, OH), all three from steerage.

Edward Dorking had cast himself into the cold sea just before *Titanic* sank, and, after the initial shock of the freezing water hit him, he began swimming away with all his strength, worried that the suction from the sinking ship would pull him under water. He was only about 60 feet away from the steel hull when it suddenly tipped up on its nose, lifted its rear end out of the water exposing the propeller blades, and slid gently forward into its watery grave. Much to Dorking's surprise, the sinking caused scarcely a ripple on the ocean's surface.

Dorking soon clung to overturned Collapsible B, fighting off desperate people who were also struggling in the water grasping his arms and legs. Men on the boat pulled him up just as his strength ebbed, and he drifted in and out of consciousness.

Ernst Persson had been pulled underwater a fair distance when *Titanic* sank, but when he regained the surface, he clung to some wreckage before swimming to overturned Collapsible B. He was allowed some room on this crowded hull which floated to a height of only three feet above the water. Much of the time, a fair portion of his body was in the icy water. He was later taken into a lifeboat when the rescue ship approached. But his sister, Elna Ström and her daughter, Silma, perished.

Victor Sunderland watched Second Officer Lightoller and others try in vain to launch Collapsible B. Just before *Titanic* sank, Victor jumped clear of the ship and started to swim away, but soon found himself right next to this lifeboat, so he pulled himself onto the hull with all his strength and helped balance it throughout the long night.

Collapsible C was almost at full capacity of 49 persons when it was launched from the starboard side at 1:40 carrying 40. Almost half of them were passengers with Great Lakes destinations: Marianna Assaf (Ottawa, ON), Banoura Ayoub (Columbus, OH), Shanini George (Youngstown, OH), Emily Goldsmith and her son Frank (Detroit, MI), Hilda Hellstrom (Chicago, IL), May Howard (Albion, NY), Catherine Joseph and her daughter, Mary (Detroit, MI), Fatima Masselmany (Dearborn, MI), Velin Öhman (Chicago, IL), Anna Salkjelsvik (Proctor, MN), and Hanna Touma and her children, Maria and George (Dowagiac, MI).

A young Swedish woman, Velin Öhman, heading to Chicago for a visit with her uncle, Henry Forsander, sat in the slightly bobbing boat, gazing at the clear night sky and the millions of bright stars, wondering if she would live to reach America. To sooth their frayed nerves, she shared her small bottle of brandy with fellow Swede, Hilda Hellstrom, also 22, who was bound for Evanston, Illinois, to visit her widowed aunt, Johanna Erikson.

Also in Collapsible C (placed there, according to later reports, by Captain Smith himself) was a young Syrian woman, Hanna Touma, and her two children, Maria, 9, and eight-year-old George. Her husband awaited them in America, where, in 1911, he had purchased the E.F. Howe farm northwest of Dowagiac, Michigan, and who, in February, 1912, had sent the family the funds to join him. Hanna and her children had been enroute since February 26, 1912, travelling overland and boarding *Titanic* at Cherbourg. Now, bobbing in the ter-rifying total darkness of the cold North Atlantic night, Hanna hoped against hope that she and the children would see her husband again.

Shanini George, returning from Lebanon to Youngstown, Ohio, was travelling with several male cousins, all of whom she feared were lost in the sinking. In Collapsible C, she put her arms around young Banoura Ayoub, also a relative, to comfort the both of them.

May Howard, 24, was travelling from Southampton, England, to visit her sister, Mrs. Henry Hewitt, in Albion, New York. She wanted to cross on one of the smaller ships that was scheduled to depart before *Titanic,* but owing to the coal strike, she ended up taking passage on the new ship. She shared a cabin with her friends, Emily Goldsmith, her husband and her son, who were heading for Detroit.

She and the Goldsmiths struggled through thick crowds to reach the lifeboat deck. "One of the ship's officers grabbed Mrs. Gold-smith and myself and pushed us to the edge of the ship where the lifeboat was being filled with women and children. An officer there shouted, 'All men back, women come first.'....Those in our boat did not understand that the ship was in danger, but we believed we were to be taken in the small boats for about two or three hours and after the *Titanic* had been repaired and made ready to continue her journey, we would be returned to the *Titanic*....My friend, Mrs. Goldsmith, and her son, left the *Titanic* in the boat with me and were saved. Her husband was one of those who stood back to make room for women passengers in the lifeboat and was drowned." May looked around Collapsible C.

A young mother's heart languished in misery all night long in Collapsible C. Catherine Joseph had lost her son, Michael, somewhere in that desperate crowd on *Titanic's* deck, and now, *Titanic* was gone. Bobbing on the freezing waters of the North Atlantic, she squeezed her little daughter, Mary, closer for warmth and comfort.

A young steerage woman, Mrs. Fatima Masselmany, 17, bound for Dearborn, Michigan, seemed intent on keeping quietly to herself.

Even more quiet and trying his utmost to be inconspicuous in the midst of so many Third Class passengers in Collapsible C was J. Bruce Ismay, head of the White Star Line.

Collapsible D, capacity 49 people, contained only 24 when it was launched from the port side at 2:05. The two who were Great-Lakes-bound were Joseph Dequemin (Albion, NY) and four-year-old Michael Joseph (Detroit, MI).

Steerage passenger Joseph Dequemin, 24, heading for Albion, New York, froze his legs so badly in Collapsible D (he claimed that he had to swim to it) that they troubled him for the rest of his life.

On board *Titanic* late that night, four-year-old Michael Joseph realized that he had become separated from his mother and sister in the swirling fury of adult confusion on the deck of a sinking ship. He stood frozen in terror, but he showed no panic. After what seemed an interminable length of time, he felt a guardian angel grab his hand and he was placed into a lifeboat. It was Collapsible D. He was unaware that his mother and baby sister were nearby in Collapsible C.

Somewhere in one of those 20 lifeboats was survivor Maria Osmon, heading for Steubenville, Ohio.

◆   ◆   ◆   ◆   ◆   ◆   ◆   ◆

As the first subtle sunrise glow broke the horizon, Jane Quick in Lifeboat 11 saw that "there was no *Titanic*, only water, ice and pieces of wreckage."

After a while, the shocked, cold lifeboat occupants saw the lights of a large ship in the distance, and they hastened to row and steer towards her. Ellen Toomey in Lifeboat 9 described the approach of the ship as "the grandest sight that mortal eyes ever witnessed."

4 The *Carpathia*

The 13,555-ton Cunard line passenger steamer, *Carpathia,* under Captain Arthur Rostron, left New York City on April 11, 1912, bound for Naples, Italy, and other Mediterranean ports. The ship carried American tourists when she sailed east across the Atlantic Ocean, and returned with them plus hundreds of emigrants when sailing west-bound back to the United States. Rostron, an experienced, able officer, had been given this command less than three months earlier. On this trip, he was carrying 125 First Class, 65 Second Class and 550 Third Class passengers to the Mediterranean.

The Cunard Line passenger steamer, *Carpathia.*
COURTESY OF THE MARINERS' MUSEUM, NEWPORT NEWS, VIRGINIA.

When the steamer, *Virginian,* first received *Titanic's* "C.Q.D." distress message over the wireless, she said that she could not reach the stricken liner until 10 A.M., about eight hours after *Titanic* sank. The

Parisien, which had also picked up the distress call, was even further away. The "mystery ship" which appeared to be sitting for the night on the edge of the ice field only a few miles away from *Titanic* failed to turn her attention to both the wireless emergency messages and to the distress flares being fired.

It was up to the *Carpathia,* 57 miles away, to rush to the disaster site, even though it took almost four hours cruising at full speed.

Titanic sank two hours and forty minutes after hitting the iceberg. An hour and a half later, the *Carpathia* arrived at the scene. In those 90 minutes, over 1,500 lives were lost, but the rescue ship saved more than 700 who had been at the mercy of the icy elements in small, open boats on the unforgiving North Atlantic Ocean.

◆   ◆   ◆   ◆   ◆   ◆   ◆   ◆

There was a loud shout of joy from Lifeboat 9 as the rescue ship approached. All of the lifeboats kept as close together as possible under the circumstances and in spite of the current, and several of them were tied together to keep them from getting separated and lost.

Sketch of the rescue scene after the *Carpathia* arrived. AUTHOR'S COLLECTION.

Jane Quick described the ordeal of boarding the *Carpathia* from a lifeboat at sea: "They lowered a sort of swing to us, and we had to climb into this. Then I found my hands were so stiffened and frozen that I could not put my children into this, so one of the crew did it for me. Then I tried to get in myself. I thought I could not close my hands and hold onto the rope, but I had to, so I shut my eyes and was swung upward."

Adults had ropes tied to their waists and held by sailors on deck in case they slipped or fell while ascending the steel side of the ship. Babies were hoisted to the decks of the *Carpathia* in bags. The human cargo took hours to load.

Titanic's Collapsible D lifeboat approaching the *Carpathia* the morning after the sinking.
COURTESY OF THE MARINERS' MUSEUM, NEWPORT NEWS, VIRGINIA.

Jean Hippach was relieved to see the rescue ship at dawn. "...when we were nearly dead with cold, we saw the *Carpathia*. It stopped to pick up lifeboats about two miles from where we were, and we rowed the distance over to the ship and were taken up in swinging seats. My, but it was good to be taken aboard and nursed."

And nursed they were. Captain Rostron had seen to it that hot drinks and food were prepared for the arrival of the survivors. Every blanket on the ship that had not been issued to a *Carpathia* passenger was made available for the guests which fate had transferred from one trans-Atlantic passenger ship to another.

Ellen Toomey lauded their *Carpathia* reception. "We were treated with all of the consideration that could be shown us. They were very kind and good to us. Men gave up their rooms and women passengers shared their rooms with the *Titanic* survivors. They gave us clothes. They gave us hot brandy and coffee, and took the best of care of us...."

"The officers gave up their state room to us and the women with children were given the best to be had," recalled Nellie Becker.

Lifeboat 6 heads straight for the *Carpathia*. COURTESY OF THE MARINERS' MUSEUM, NEWPORT NEWS, VIRGINIA.

"Brandy, blankets and proper food were waiting for us on our arrival and everything was done for our comfort. There have been statements issued that we were asked not to say anything about the accident, but these were untrue. We had to sign several papers, but they related to our destination, our condition and were prepared for the purpose of helping us to reach relatives or to assist those of us who needed assistance. We have no complaints to register against the officers of the *Carpathia* nor of the *Titanic*. They did all in their power to aid. But for the stewards on the *Titanic* who gave their lives to the women on board, there would have been more lost."

Franz Karun recalled, "When we got aboard *Carpathia,* people cried and took [sic] on terribly over the shock. Oh yes, I felt it too. I never had been through anything like that. They got the doctors for us and did everything they could for us. The experience made me sick, affected my head, too much sea, I guess, and it made my little girl sick, too. Many who were rescued were hysterical when they were taken aboard."

The final survivor boarded *Carpathia* at 8:45 A.M. from the 20th lifeboat to be unloaded; it was Second Officer Lightoller, the highest-ranking officer from *Titanic* to survive.

Many survivors later admitted that, when they stepped into the lifeboats and left *Titanic*, everyone seemed cheerful and had no idea of the horrible disaster that was soon to follow.

"All of us expected to hold a reunion on the *Carpathia,*" recounted Nellie Becker, "and the real piteous scene was when the women who left their husbands realized that they were now widows. Every one was grief stricken and their wail was 'If we had only known we never would have left them there to die alone.'"

Nellie's daughter, Ruth, added, "That was the saddest time of all... So many of the women who had been put into lifeboats by their husbands, and told they would meet each other later, realized that they would never see each other again...."

Jessie Trout, widowed for seven months and aware that her life was no longer what it had been before her husband's death, stated, "While I am thankful I was saved, gladly would I have given up my life to have prevented the separation of any husband and wife...."

On the *Carpathia*, survivors mingled in hopes of identifying family and friends. When Catherine Joseph found her son, Michael, she was overtaken by surprise, intense relief, and uncontrollable emotion. Running to embrace him, she lost her balance and both of them fell to the deck. But it was a joyous tumble, and no one was hurt.

Maude Sincock, heading to Hancock, Michigan, turned 21 on April 17, 1912, while on

Titanic survivors boarding the *Carpathia*. COURTESY OF THE MARINERS' MUSEUM, NEWPORT NEWS, VIRGINIA.

board the *Carpathia*. She and Lyyli Silven, three years her junior, had become acquainted on board *Titanic* before the collision, and now, on the *Carpathia*, they shared a table for meals. Friendship came easy for them, even though Lylli spoke no English, and after they landed, they travelled together to Hancock.

Olaus Abelseth, tenderly unfolding the precious blanket he had been handed when he boarded the *Carpathia,* curled up on the open deck and slept in the same clothes that he had put on just after *Titanic* struck the iceberg, the same clothes he wore when he plunged into the freezing ocean, the very same clothes he wore as he shivered in a half-swamped collapsible lifeboat throughout the night that he thought would never end.

Over 700 *Titanic* survivors were picked up by the *Carpathia*. With 740 of her own passengers already on board, the unexpected addition taxed the ship's space and supplies. Captain Rostron felt that returning to the port he had just left was the best choice. After circling once in the remote possibility that he might find more survivors, he ordered the *Carpathia* turned west to New York City.

Above: Rescued *Titanic* passengers being supplied with blankets aboard the crowded *Carpathia.* *Below:* Mr. and Mrs. George Harder, *Titanic* survivors, console Mrs. Charles Hays, whose husband perished.   BOTH COURTESY OF THE MARINERS' MUSEUM, NEWPORT NEWS, VIRGINIA.

A total of 705 survivors and one body, which had been in Collapsible A, were taken aboard the _Carpathia_. Three of the survivors who were in critical condition (they had found their way into lifeboats after some time in the icy water) succumbed within hours. Rostron delivered 702 people from _Titanic_ alive to New York City.

A controversial news blackout was imposed until the _Carpathia_ reached New York City. However, the following message did get sent from the wireless room on board the rescue ship on the morning of Wednesday, April 17, 1912: "_Carpathia_ picked up seven hundred _Titanic,_ mostly women. Over two thousand lost. Ice berg [sic] continuous mass twenty five [sic] miles. Chicagoans this ship well." It was signed "Dr. F. H. Blackmarr, 8:35 a. m." The doctor himself wrote on his receipt for this telegram, "I had to bribe the operator to get this out." The information was certainly sent out without Captain Rostron's knowledge or consent. The vacationing doctor had become the self-appointed publicist.

Chicago newspapers were delighted to have received this exclusive information, particularly since it came from a Chicago native, and, needless to say, the information was promptly printed. More than one newspaper, however, added a caution about part of the telegram: "His estimate of the number lost is probably in error, as there were not so many as 2,700 on board the _Titanic_." Another Chicago newspaper printed a photograph of the doctor next to the words of his telegram.

Dr. Blackmarr, with his keen sense of observation, recorded as much information as he could about the sinking and the subsequent rescue. He requested and received written descriptive statements signed by several of _Titanic's_ survivors, and he compiled photographs and drawings in a scrapbook. He lectured on the sinking of _Titanic_ when he returned to the Chicago area, presumably using his scrapbook to visually enhance his talks.

Blackmarr died some time in the 1940's. By that time, his scrapbook had disappeared.

♦   ♦   ♦   ♦   ♦   ♦   ♦   ♦

Captain Arthur Henry Rostron, a 42-year-old Englishman with 29 years of seafaring experience already behind him when the _Carpathia_ rescued the _Titanic_ survivors, enjoyed a magnificent maritime career for almost two more decades after that fateful night in 1912. From the people who lived through the _Titanic_ tragedy he received a gold medal, presented to him by survivor Molly Brown. Honors were sent by President Taft, culminating in the the Congressional Medal of Honor being conferred upon the captain. Various British organizations heaped more medals upon him. He was given command of the _Lusitania,_ but not long enough to go down with the ship when she was torpedoed in 1915. When World War I broke out, he commanded the

Captain Arthur Rostron, *Titanic* hero.   COURTESY OF
THE MARINERS' MUSEUM, NEWPORT NEWS, VIRGINIA.

steamer, *Aulania,* which transported the first Canadian troops to England. Later in the war, he was captain of the *Mauretania,* which had been converted to a hospital ship. After the war, he was still in charge of the *Mauretania,* now reconverted to passenger ship service crossing the Atlantic Ocean. In 1919, he formally became "Sir Arthur Rostron." In 1928, he became commander of the steamer, *Berengaria,* which was formerly the German Hamburg-American ocean liner, *Imperatur,* and he was made Commodore of the Cunard fleet that same year.

In the spring of 1931, as his 62nd birthday present to himself, he retired from the sea and subsequently wrote his autobiography. He died of pneumonia in England on November 4, 1940, at the age of 71. His tombstone clearly marks the role he played in the *Titanic* rescue as his greatest maritime and personal lifetime achievement.

◆　　◆　　◆　　◆　　◆　　◆　　◆　　◆

The steamer, *Carpathia*, failed to fare as well as Captain Rostron. Half a dozen years after the *Titanic* experience, the 16-year-old, British-built *Carpathia*, part of a Boston-bound convoy, was torpedoed by a German submarine on July 17, 1918, near the end of World War I, and sank, with the loss of five crewmembers' lives (the remainder of the crew and over 50 passengers escaped in lifeboats), in about 520 feet of water 120 miles south of Fastnet, Ireland. On May 22, 2000, documentary film company Eco-Nova Productions located and filmed the upright shipwreck.

5 The Loved Ones Back Home

White Star Lines offices in England, the United States, Canada, Ireland, Sweden, Norway, France, and elsewhere were inundated with telephone calls and personal visits from people asking about the welfare of their friends and relatives who had sailed on *Titanic*. Others read of the disaster in the newspaper and waited at home with various degrees of patience for word from their loved ones. Even the public waited. The shocked world seemed busy trying to recuperate from the disaster. Flags flew at half mast in most Great Lakes towns and cities. The *Minneapolis Sunday Tribune* of April 21, 1912, spoke for all Great Lakes communities when it began its "Society" page with the words, "On account of the recent *Titanic* disaster, there will be a noticeable decrease in entertaining during the coming week...."

Mr. James Borebank, who lived at 285 Euclid Avenue, Toronto, wondered about the safety of his son. John James Borebank had left Toronto about 15 years earlier for Winnipeg, where he made his fortune in real estate, but had moved back to Toronto in 1910. In 1911, when he was 41, he packed up his family and went on an extended vacation to the British Isles and the continent. His wife and eight-year-old daughter were still in England, where the child was attending school, when John James booked passage for himself on *Titanic*. James Borebank Senior tended to his modest grocery store, wondering if his son's millions had helped him survive.

Lebanese immigrant Harry Boulos worked long hours as a bus driver for the Rankin Hotel in downtown Chatham, Ontario, and had saved enough money to bring his wife, Sultana, and their two children, Laura, 9, and Akar, 6, to Canada from Mt. Lebanon, Assyria. He sent his wife the passage money in early March, 1912, and presumed that the family was underway, but precisely how they were travelling or when the would arrive, Harry did not know. In fact, he was daily expecting news from them announcing their imminent arrival. When tales of the tragic loss of *Titanic* filled the newspapers, Harry anxiously scanned the lists for his loved ones' names in the odd chance that they had been on board, but they were not listed. Then he received a telephone call from his nephew in Detroit asking him to come to that city. There was some information that could not be given out over the telephone.

Impatient, Harry Boulos felt that the noon Grand Trunk train on Monday, April 22, 1912, would never reach Detroit, a mere 60 miles away. Once there, he wished it hadn't. His family had gone down with *Titanic,* he was told as someone handed him a list of the lost. Harry was shocked, but soon he convinced himself that the list was erroneous. Through an interpreter (Harry's English was bad), he telephoned and apprised his employer, John Pleasance, of the situation and received a few days' leave of absence. Harry then telegraphed an Assyrian newspaper in New York City, requesting that they contact the White Star Line office to determine what had happened to his family.

The news was not good. Harry's family had, indeed, perished on *Titanic,* as had several of his other relatives.

Harry returned to Chatham on Thursday evening, April 25, 1912, feeling as if caught in an inescapable bad dream. Two days later, hearing that an Assyrian survivor had arrived in Detroit, Harry once more asked John Pleasance for a few days off work, a request which was compassionately granted. An hour later, the train carried Harry westbound towards Detroit.

The Lebanese woman verified that Sultana and the two children had been passengers on the ill-fated vessel, but were not among those who had been picked up by the rescue ship.

At this point, Harry definitely lost all hope. His family was gone. But then he thought about his oldest son, the firstborn that he and Sultana had had over 21 years ago. He was working in Brazil as a dentist.

It is not known if Harry Boulos ever returned to Chatham.

George M. Eitenmiller, a telegraph operator in the Postal Telegraph office in Detroit (who, with pride, displayed a picture of the inventor, Thomas Edison, signed and inscribed "To George Eitenmiller, star operator of the seventies") worked with feverish diligence at the wireless key in hopes of receiving the news that his 23-year-old son, George Floyd Eitenmiller, had survived *Titanic's* sinking. The good news never came. The son, an engineer with Cleveland's Schacht Motor Car Works, had been sent to England to demonstrate the company's cars, and was returning on *Titanic.* The despairing father, whose wife had died two years earlier, now lost his only child in whom all of the pride and hope and love of his 70 years had been directed. Ironically it was the elder George who had persuaded his good friend, Captain Inman Sealby, after the loss of his ship, *Republic,* in 1909 "shattered his nerve for a life on the main," to come to Michigan to attend law school. Sealby had planned to meet the returning son at Detroit's train station.

George F. Eitenmiller and Alfred Rush: both were bound for Detroit.   AUTHOR'S COLLECTION.

Detroit families sent money to their relatives in England so they could join them in America. Alfred Rush, only 16 years of age, longed to join his older brother, Charles, and his wife, who had lived and worked in Detroit since 1904. Alfred had quit school and taken a job at 14 to save money for the trip, but he was out of work in the winter of 1911-1912 and despairingly spent his savings. His brother and sister-in-law* sent him the necessary funds, making him the happiest young man in London. Alfred, the last child to leave home, waited to book passage on the first ship after his mother's birthday. That ship happened to be *Titanic*. Alfred was lost in the sinking.

Alfred Rush had been travelling with others bound for Detroit: the Goldsmith family. The parents and several siblings of Emily Gold-

---

* Ironically, Mrs. Charles Rush had experience with a ship striking an iceberg. In June, 1909, she and a lady friend took the *Empress of Ireland* out of Montreal for a crossing to England. "At 10 o'clock on the Sunday night following our departure, we awoke with a start to find we had been tumbled out on the floor....when we scrambled up on deck amid the noise and confusion that followed, we found that the ship had a large hole in her side following a collision with a berg....the officers informed us that while there was some danger, it was not imminent. Our wireless operator got in touch with a passing ship and she kept near us all the way into port...." No lives were lost.

smith had lived in Detroit for some time and encouraged her, her husband, Frank, and their nine-year-old son, Frank Jr., to move to America. They had sent them the money to do so in 1910. However, Frank Sr. feared water and dreaded the thought of an ocean crossing. Finally, with his work situation in England bad and opportunities in America good, the family dared to go. Goldsmith's dread of seasickness compelled the family to book passage on the vessel they felt most likely to cause him the least discomfort: *Titanic*. Ironically, Frank Goldsmith did not survive.

WAITING

The loved ones back home, regardless of race, color, creed, or social status, grieved together for the relatives and friends who perished on *Titanic*. A society belle and a beshawled lady of foreign origin suffer together. This is from the *Detroit News*, April 17, 1912.   AUTHOR'S COLLECTION.

Thomas Davies, of 67 Foot Street, Pontiac, Michigan, and a successful mason contractor there, had returned to West Bromwich, England, the previous December for a visit and encouraged more of his family (his brother, Richard, was already there) to come to America. Four took him up on his offer: his three brothers, Alfred, John and Joseph (ages 24, 22 and 17 respectively) and his 39-year-old uncle (his mother's sister's husband), James Lester, all machinists who expected to take up their professions in some of the automobile factories. The brothers' parents and younger sisters, as well as the uncle's family, were to follow when funds became available. All four were lost in the sinking. Portions of their final enthusiastic and affectionate letters to their brother in Pontiac were published by the local press.

Thomas Davies, the oldest brother, was devastated. "I am afraid the shock will kill our mother back home. All she has left now are the three little girls...," he lamented. "I persuaded the folks to let the boys come and feel as if I was responsible for their deaths....It's so hard to believe they are gone and we won't ever see them again."

William and Alice Silvey caused great concern about their safety, not only to people in Duluth where they had lived as man and wife for 20 years (with him working in real estate), but also to Mr. Silvey's mother and sister back in Washington, D.C., where he was born. His mother anxiously said, "They went over on board the *Olympic*, a sister ship of the *Titanic*. The *Olympic* met with some trouble, and my daughter...feared all along that something would happen to the *Titanic* on their return." The Silvey's 18-year-old daughter, attending college in Farmington, Connecticut, planned to meet them in New York when they arrived on *Titanic*.

In Manistee, Michigan, Mrs. Otto Peterson of 408 Sibben Street was also grieving. Her sister, Ida Andersson, coming over from Sweden, had written to her that she would be crossing on *Titanic*. Ida was initially listed among the survivors, but Mrs. Peterson thought it strange that her sister did not wire her. The hope remained that she had landed on the *Carpathia* in New York but, not knowing English, she may have been afraid to request any financial assistance with which to contact her sister on Lake Michigan's shores. There was even the chance that Ida had not even boarded *Titanic,* but had taken another ocean liner instead. With no news reaching her as time went by, Mrs. Peterson feared the worst and sobbed, "She must be dead."

Ida Andersson was travelling to Manistee, Michigan, to visit her sister.
AUTHOR'S COLLECTION.

The missing name.

The grief was intense when the husband or the father failed to survive the sinking. This emotional artwork appeared in the *Cleveland Leader* on April 18, 1912.   AUTHOR'S COLLECTION.

John and Ellen Lingane had emigrated to America in the late 1800's from County Cork, Ireland, with their five sons, and settled on a farm just northwest of Chelsea, Michigan. John yearned for the old country, and plans were being made for such a return when his wife died in 1911. In an attempt to overcome his grief, John visited Ireland alone in late 1911, and was returning to Michigan on *Titanic* when the ship sank. Described as "a prosperous farmer" (*Manistee Daily News*, April 30, 1912), John Lingane was never recovered, but his four sons still living in 1912 added his name to the family headstone in Chelsea.

On another Michigan farm to the west of Chelsea, Darwis Touma received a telegram on Saturday, April 20, 1912. It was from his wife, Hanna, who had left Syria (Lebanon) weeks ago to join her husband. She relayed the message that she and the children were safe, having just landed in New York City on the *Carpathia*, and that they were about to leave by train for Dowagiac. This was the first that the shocked husband knew that his family had been travelling on *Titanic*.

Claus Benson, who had anglicized his name, lived at 200 Ridgewood Avenue, Joliet, Illinois, and worried about his brother, Ernest Aronsson, and his cousin, Gustaf Edvardsson. They had never been to the United States before, but Claus had written to them in Sweden about the opportunities in America, and, before long, they planned to make Joliet their new home. They booked passage on *Titanic*.

The only thing to arrive at Claus Benson's home was a telegram from the White Star Line: "Lost on *Titanic,* Ernest Aronsson and Gustaf Edvardsson, enroute from Sweden to Joliet."

Another telegram of happier note arrived in Joliet at Edwin Lander's home. Sent by St. Luke's Hospital in New York City, it read, "Helmina Nelson ["Nilsson" anglicized], *Titanic* passenger, from Sweden, booked Joliet, Ill. ---Safe--- Will leave for your city in few days. Unusual escape." Edwin immediately contacted his two brothers, Albin and Emile, and their sister, Mrs. Freda Benson, all of whom had settled in Joliet, with the jubilant message that their sister was alive.

They had been apprised of their sister's possible departure date from home in Sweden, but did not believe that she would have sufficient time to catch *Titanic's* maiden voyage. Edwin spoke in joyful, broken English to the press, "I feel so good over her being saved that I can not express myself as I would like to and I feel sure that she will have a wonderful story to tell when she reaches this city." A letter from Helmina settled any possible fears over her health. She stated that she had recovered rapidly from the shock and exposure and that she would reach Joliet in the near future, travelling as far as Chicago with Swedish people who were also on the steamer.

Her brothers immediately departed for Chicago to meet all passenger trains from the east. After a day and a half, their initial enthusiasm for train-meeting growing thin, the Landers returned to Joliet and talked John Carlson, who ran the local White Star Line agency from his drug store at the corner of Cass and Collins Streets, into wiring a request for information to St. Luke's Hospital, her last known location. The hospital promptly replied that the young woman had left yesterday and would reach Chicago at 5:00 P.M. that very day.

Off to Chicago the brothers went again. This time, they returned home with the Swedish package.

Two sisters in Pittsburgh had received a letter from another one of their sisters in England, informing them that she would soon surprise them. They received their surprise as they glanced over a list of *Titanic* survivors and found the name of Maude Sincock, their sibling.

A young married couple in Cleveland was shocked to discover that each of them had lost a younger brother when *Titanic* sank.

Albert Stanley had invited his 21-year-old brother, Roland, from England to visit them in America, and his wife, Jessie Crease Stanley, had done the same for her brother, Ernest Crease, only 19 years old. The two young men, who first met only 40 minutes before *Titanic* departed Southampton, were travelling together. Neither body was found.

ROLAND STANLEY   ERNEST CREASE

AUTHOR'S COLLECTION.

Mrs. Louise Logsdon in Indianapolis received a letter from her favorite brother, Harry, telling her that he had survived the *Titanic* sinking. The brief letter stated only that he "was suffering much from the nervous shock occasioned by the disaster," and that he planned to go directly to San Antonio, Texas, for his health before returning to Indianapolis. He related nothing of the details of the shipwreck. Louise had not heard from him since he wrote to her from Cairo, Egypt, several weeks earlier. She and her brother had been almost inseparable since childhood, and she hated the work he did because it kept him away for such long stretches of time. She did not know exactly what he did for a living, other than what he had told her: he travelled for a land company in Texas, and his duties carried him to all parts of the country as well as to Europe. This trip from which he was just returning was his fourth abroad in the past year. Her brother was well-liked by others, too. The newspaper had printed that "...On his short visits here, he made many friends and acquaintances."

Other people thought less of "Harry Haven Homer." Reportedly he was one of the best and most notorious cardsharps in the business, and he supposedly crossed on *Titanic* to separate some of the rich male passengers from their cash. He knew that such a heavily publicized maiden voyage would surely offer sheep ripe for fleecing, in spite of the White Star Line's warning that professional gamblers might be on board. He had booked passage under the name "E. Haven" to escape detection and, of course, he travelled First Class.

It was not Harry Haven Homer's intention to ever let the world know what became of him.

Harry Haven Homer of Indianapolis.
AUTHOR'S COLLECTION.

The *Toledo News-Bee*, on April 30, 1912, printed a tongue-in-cheek account of how the "heroic" gamblers on *Titanic* really behaved when the ship sank. . AUTHOR'S COLLECTION.

Other gamblers were on board *Titanic* as well, or, after the sinking, were reputedly on board. The story of how gambler Jay Yates from Findlay, Ohio, tried to con the world, and in particular the police who were searching for him, into believing that he had gone down with

Titanic has been oft-told. Some contemporary newspapers were conned, and they hailed the late Yates as a hero ("Goes to His Death With Sinking *Titanic* After Helping Women and Children to Safety--- Sends Good-By to Mother"). In truth, he had never left dry land.

One Ontario newspaper in 1912 described professional gambler Charles "Harry" Romaine, travelling in First Class and working the wealthy on *Titanic*, as being "formerly of Toronto" and "well known in Toronto and Guelph." The same article states that card-sharps Harry Homer, Harry Romaine, and "Boy" Bradley (George Brereton), although helping load women and children into lifeboats, furtively entered a lifeboat with 12 stokers to save themselves.

Albert Silven, a professional photographer in Hancock, Michigan, had entertained his sister, brother-in-law, and their newly-adopted daughter, all from Minneapolis, for a week the previous fall at his home, just before they departed to visit relatives in Finland. In early April, 1912, Albert had received tragic news from Finland that the adopted daughter had passed away suddenly, and that the bereaved adoptive parents would return home right after the funeral. In late April, 1912, Albert opened another telegram, this one from the White Star Line, informing him that his sister and her husband, Rev. and Mrs. Lahtinnen, were not among the survivors of *Titanic*. The only light for Albert Silven at this dark time in his life was the visit from his cousin, Lyyli Silven, who had been travelling with the Lahtinnens and survived the sinking.

Thirty-one-year-old Swede Karl Johansson was not as fortunate. He had emigrated to the U.S.A. earlier and had worked in the construction trade at Duluth, Minnesota. On a return visit to Sweden in 1911, he became engaged to Berta Olsson, his childhood sweetheart. Both planned to cross to the U.S.A. on the *Olympic* later in 1912, but Berta's brother, Oscar, and their friend Samuel Niklasson persuaded him to travel with them on the new liner, *Titanic*, in April. Berta would follow on the *Olympic* in the fall, a plan which fell through when her financé died in *Titanic's* sinking. His body was not recovered. Her brother, Oscar Olsson, survived.

Oscar Olsson, an experienced sailor in Sweden, had made his way to the Great Lakes at the age of 24 in 1904 and signed on aboard the steamer, *Bulgaria,* at Detroit. Claiming that people had difficulty pronouncing "Olsson," he changed his name to Johansson (since he was the son of Johan). This complicated things later, more for researchers than for anyone else. Not only was his sister's fianceé named Karl Johansson (and he died on *Titanic*), there was another Oscar Johansson on *Titanic* who survived, and this latter Oscar

Johansson, who headed for Bridgeport, Connecticut (where he ironically drowned in a shallow pond 13 years later), had initially told authorities that he was bound for Milwaukee! Little wonder that compiling an accurate list of *Titanic* passengers became a confusing journey through a complicated maze.

The Great Lakes Oscar Olsson, now Oscar Olsson Johansson, worked on the *Bulgaria* for six years, residing with Norwegian-American Captain John Peterson and his family at 897 Vinewood Avenue, Manitowoc, Wisconsin, during the shipping off-season. He became greatly attached to the Peterson family during those years. In 1910, Johansson returned to Sweden to visit his parents in a small village outside Stockholm. He was married there in 1911, but work was hard to find. Early in 1912, he wrote to Captain Peterson, asking if he could have his old job back on the *Bulgaria*. "You can start work if you're here for the breaking of the ice," came the captain's response. Johansson promised to report for duty on April 15, 1912.

Oscar Olsson Johansson was returning to Manitowoc, Wisconsin for lake work. AUTHOR'S COLLECTION.

That was the day that *Titanic* sank, and Johansson happened to be on board, but he survived. However, somewhere between New York City and Detroit, the hearty sailor was lost. His whereabouts drew such a blank that both the mystified Captain Peterson and the puzzled press wondered what had happened to Johansson. Peterson had wired New York, offering to send the survivor funds, but received no response.

Oscar Olsson Johansson, upon his New York arrival, sent his wife in Sweden a two-word telegram ("Saved, Oscar"), and then, forgetting to contact his Great Lakes friend and employer, spent time assisting other survivors who seemed lost in their new foreign world.

The Manitowoc, Wisconsin press optimistically reported that if Johansson showed up before the *Bulgaria* cleared port, efforts would be made to book him for an appearance at the Crystal Theater to tell his story of the most terrible sea disaster in history. "He doesn't speak English fluently, but he is a bright boy," warned Peterson.

Oscar Johansson arrived in Manitowoc on April 24, 1912. Sick and nervous from the ordeal, and tired after a week of bombardment by reporters' questions, he spoke sparingly to the locals. With " a strong Swedish accent," he addressed a group in a south side hotel. "I hope none of you will ever have to go through what I went through ten days ago. I would rather die than see those terrible sights of fear and hear those pitiful cries again...." Someone asked him if he now feared the water as a result of the disaster, "No, on the freight boats there are lifeboats and men who know how to man them, instead of palm gardens....I thank God it is all over for me."

Sick and nervous from the ordeal, observers could see that the small man was far from well. He did not appear at the Crystal Theater, and he did not sail on the *Bulgaria*, opting instead to take some time to recuperate and sail on another of the company's ships.

Oscar thanked God too early, because it was not over for him, and his confidence in Great Lakes freight boats would soon be shaken. The ship he signed on grounded and sank, with Oscar surviving in his underwear. His days as a sailor were numbered.

"Sailing on *Titanic*."

Such was the terse telegram received by Mrs. Peuchen at 599 Jarvis Street in Toronto from her husband, Major Arthur Peuchen in Southampton just prior to his return voyage. This came as no surprise to her, as he had stated prior to his departure from Canada a month earlier that he would endeavor to book return passage on this largest and newest steamer.

When *Titanic* sank and the Toronto newspapers bulged with padded speculation, all they could initially write was that the major's rescue was "decidedly indefinite," a description guaranteed to infuriate any loved ones. Mrs. Peuchen and her two children, a 15-year-old son and a daughter who was six, spent a sleepless Monday night, April 15, 1912, eagerly awaiting a telephone call from the White Star Line regarding her husband's situation.

By Tuesday morning, no word had yet been received. Peuchen's fellow officers in the Queen's Own Rifles were seriously considering postponing their annual reunion banquet for all past and present officers at the Toronto Club that night. Such was the esteem in which they held their missing compatriot.

In mid-day, Mrs. Peuchen received a telegram from the White Star Line office: her husband was among those rescued and was presently on board the *Carpathia*, due to arrive in New York on Thursday evening. She hastily packed some clothing and necessities into a travel bag, arranged for the care of the house with friends and neighbors, and purchased tickets for herself and her two children for the evening train to New York -- but not before sharing this good news with her husband's colleagues in the military.

The Queen's Own Rifles proceeded with their annual dinner in good spirits that night. A formal toast was made: "This day in Toronto has been one of great anxiety and trial, and it is with great thankfulness that we have learned that through the mercy of heaven, one prominent officer has been saved to return to the regiment and to his family." They drank to Peuchen's health in silent thanks.

After dinner, the officers watched moving pictures of their regiment's visit to Aldershot, England.

A 59-year-old metallurgical expert from Sault Ste. Marie, Ontario, Ernest Sjostedt, had also sent a telegram to his wife, informing her that if he finished his business (for his employer, the Lake Superior Corporation, as well as studying mineral extraction methods for the Canadian Department of Mines) in his native Sweden in time, he would catch *Titanic*. Unfortunately, he was a man respected for his efficiency. Mrs. Sjostedt, upon hearing of the ship's loss, headed to her daughter's residence at 98 Kendall Avenue in Toronto to await word of her husband, but he was not among the survivors. The Great Lakes region lost the creative man who ran an assay office at 807 Queen Street in the Sault, and who had invented an electric smelting furnace and a sulphur roaster.

Across the St. Mary's River in the Michigan Sault Ste. Marie, Mayor Short attentively read a newspaper account of the disaster. He had never heard of 17-year-old steerage passenger Petar Calic from Croatia, whose destination had been the Michigan Sault, but who was lost in the sinking. However, skimming a long list of victims, Short recognized an acquaintance, "a wealthy Chicago jeweller," Edwin Lewy. "It was during several trips that I made to Hot Springs that I became friendly with Lewy," he later told the local press. "I met him and several of his friends there numerous times and it was just recently that I heard he was touring abroad. He was to leave on the *Titanic*, I know, but I never thought to look for his name in the list of those drowned until I ran across it by accident."

In Chicago, M. D. Lewy and J. B. Lewy, the brothers of missing jeweller Ervin G. Lewy, who had booked passage in First Class on *Titanic*, worried about their sibling's safety. Ervin, 30, unmarried, and zealously devoted to the family company, was returning from his annual overseas diamond buying expedition, a habit in which he happily indulged since 1907. The two brothers waited patiently at 5628 South Park Avenue, the home they shared with Edwin, for glad tidings. They had received an early message from a friend in Halifax reporting that the steamer, *Californian,* had rushed to the aid of *Titanic* and was on its way to Halifax with more of the survivors. "I hope that the message is true, and that Ervin will be among those on

Ervin G. Lewy, Chicago. AUTHOR'S COLLECTION.

board," stated one brother optimistically. As it turned out, nothing in that report could have been further from the truth. Edwin Lewy never came home to his brothers. Neither did his diamonds.

Speaking of diamonds and Great Lakes connections to *Titanic,* a man named W. Wattles, "one of the leading jewelers in Pittsburgh, dropped dead...when he read of the sinking of the *Titanic,* which was bringing him a large consignment of jewels from Paris."

Titanic diamonds were also front-page news in the *Milwaukee Free Press* of April 17, 1912, reporting that "Mrs. John Jacob Astor had with her on the *Titanic* diamonds of the value of 15,000,000 francs, or $3,000,000, which she bought from Cartier, a Paris jeweler."

In Hamilton, Ontario, at the eastern end of Lake Ontario, many family members and friends were profoundly affected by the loss of 27-year-old Dr. Alfred Pain. His father, Captain Alfred Pain, a well-known commission merchant in that city, was broken-hearted, while his mother, once passionately devoted to her son and his ambitions (she had travelled with him to Quebec the previous autumn when he had left for Europe), was prostrate with grief over the fate of their boy. The joy of anticipating Alfred's early homecoming was changed to sorrow at the news of his death.

Pain's on-board friend, Marion Wright, wrote to his grieving family from Oregon the day after she was married there. "...though I knew him for but three days, I felt he was a friend. He said I was the first lady he had ever spoken to.... We had several meals together and he told me how much he had enjoyed his stay in England.... It is such a grief to me that I did not say goodbye to him, but I thought, as everyone else did, that we would be back on the *Titanic* before long.... how I wished your son had been among the 700 [survivors]. It all seems so sad and overwhelming...."

In Niagara Falls, New York, Mr. and Mrs. Thomas Goodwin of 520 25th Street received a telegram from the White Star Line on the morning of April 17, 1912, which read, "Fred Goodwin and Family on list of *Titanic*." This message left Thomas Goodwin confused, wondering if his brother, an electrical engineer who planned to work at the big power station there, and his family, emigrating to America from England in Third Class, had survived the sinking. By April 22nd, having heard no more, they assumed the worst about their relatives: Frederick, 40; Augusta, 43; and their children, Lillian, 16; Charles, 14; William, 11; Jessie, 10; Harold, 9; and Sidney, 2. The Goodwins likely had occupied two four-berth cabins at *Titanic's* stern, where most steerage families and single women were quartered. Also likely was that they refused to be parted when the ship began to sink, explaining why not so much as a single member of the family survived. By the time this large family made it to the boat deck, no lifeboats were left. Tragically, they all perished, and no bodies were ever found.

The Goodwins, an entire British family wiped out in the *Titanic* sinking, were heading for Buffalo, New York. . AUTHOR'S COLLECTION.

Other families were also decimated. Four young Belgians were bound for Fremont, Ohio, where Jules Vanderplancke, 31, had been offered a position as a foreman in a sugar plant. With him came his new wife, Emily, and two of his siblings, Augusta, 18, and Leo, 15. The latter two were going to visit relatives in Detroit before joining their older brother and sister-in-law at their new home in Fremont. All perished in *Titanic's* sinking, and no body was recovered.

Heading to Coal Center, Pittsburgh, Pennsylvania, most of the Panula family was returning from Finland. Maria Panula and her hus-band, John (originally Juha), had lived in the Pittsburgh area earlier, but had returned to Finland. Before long, they decided that it would be best for their family to live and grow up in America. John went ahead in February, 1912, and bought a house, while Maria sold their farm in Finland. With part of the proceeds, she purchased steerage passage on *Titanic* for herself and her five sons. Ernesti, 16, and Jaako, 14, the two oldest, were quartered with the other unmarried Third Class men in the ship's bow, while Maria and the three young-est, Juha, 7, Urho, 2, and Eino, 1, shared a cabin in the stern with Anna Turja and Sanni Riihiivuori. Sanni, 22, was a neighbor of the Panulas in Finland, and she embraced the chance to emigrate to America and work as their maid. But their situation was desperate. Maria panicked; she had lost a teenaged son by drowning in Finland, and now, in her anguish, she asked, "Do we all have to die by water?" As it turned out, the entire Panula family on *Titanic,* and Sanni Riihiivuori, perished; no bodies were recovered. John Panula was left with a new-ly-furnished home ready to receive the family that would never arrive.

Many *Titanic* passengers were bound for the Pittsburgh area, and many of them reached their destination. The Monessen *Daily Independent* of April 22, 1912, reported that "This morning on the 9 o'clock express, Mrs. Hilda Hirvonen and daughter Hilgur [sic], accompanied by Matt Hirvonen, the husband and father, and Mrs. Elin Hakkarainen, a bride of but three months, Erik Jussila and Eino Lindquist [sic] arrived here, the former two and last three are survivors of a party of seven who were passengers on the ill-fated *Titanic*...."

Eino Lindqvist told how he survived: "...Going out on the deck, we saw the sailors lowering the lifeboats away, filled with women, with men at each end and in the middle to guide and row. My friend, Jussila, was called upon to help row one of the boats and I was left alone on the deck. Not realizing the extreme danger I was in at the time, I wandered around for about half an hour and came upon Mr. Hakkarainen who had just aided in putting his bride of three months into one of the boats. Together we watched until the last boat put off....we began to look around for some avenue of escape, when suddenly with a deafening sound the boilers blew up, the ship gave one final heave and sank slowly....Being on the third deck, our section reached the level of the sea before that of the first and second cabins, and the waves washed Mr. Hakkarainen and I into the ocean and the last words he said were, 'Good Bye.' Being a fairly good swimmer, I exerted myself to the utmost and was able to reach the last lifeboat which was about 200 yards from where the ship went down and was taken on board...." By some suspicious coincidence, it was Lifeboat 15, which also contained Lindqvist's sister and niece, Helga and Hildur Hirvonen, and his friends Elin Hakkarainen and Erik Jussila. Modern theorists suggest that Lindqvist entered the boat from *Titanic*.

Mary Phyllis Miller married Percy C. Corey in August, 1911, in their home town of Pittsburgh. Corey was the superintendent of the English Oil Company in Upper Burma, and his new wife joined him there. Claire Bennett, 22, of Pittsburgh, married Frank Karnes, an employee of the English Oil Company in Upper Burma, at about the same time, in the autumn of 1911, and joined him at his work. Both Percy Corey and Frank Karnes were friends. Both young brides were returning by way of England and *Titanic* for a visit with their families and friends in Pittsburgh when they died in the sinking. Mary Corey had earlier been a school teacher at the Westlake school in Pittsburgh. Coincidentally, in Burma, Percy Corey stood watch over the sickbed of Frank Karnes, who died of smallpox four days before *Titanic* sank. It was Corey who later cabled word of his friend's death to Pittsburgh and asked that the news be broken to Mrs. Karnes gently. Simultaneously, a cablegram was dispatched to Corey informing him of the death of his wife and Mrs. Karnes on the ill-fated *Titanic*. The German page appearing daily in the *Pittsburg Leader* newspaper told this story under the heading "Driefache Tragödie" ("Threefold Tragedy") closing with the words, "Diesen Sommer wollte [Frau Corey] bei ihren Eltern zubringen und überredete ihre Freundin, Frau Karnes, sie zu begleiten. Beide solten das Ziel ihrer Reise nie erreichen.* "

MRS. P. C. COREY

AUTHOR'S COLLECTION.

These two ladies were among the few (only 14) Second Class women who died in the sinking. Neither body was recovered.

George Allison, a brother of Montreal millionaire Hudson Allison, and his uncle, George Johnston, both connected with Hudson's firm in Montreal and both under the impression that the Allison family on board *Titanic* had survived, left for New York to meet *Carpathia*. They were grimly disappointed to learn that the only family member to survive the sinking was one-year-old Trevor.

Nurse Cleaver had boarded a lifeboat with baby Trevor. Apparently the rest of the Allison family was not aware, for whatever reason, that this took place. One imagines them scouring the decks of *Titanic* frantically searching for their missing baby. By the time they realized that he was probably in a lifeboat with the nurse, there were no lifeboats left for themselves. Lorraine Allison was the only child in First Class who perished.

---

* Translated: "[Mrs. Corey] planned to spend this summer with her parents, and talked her friend, Mrs. Karnes, into joining her. Both were destined never to reach the goal of their trip."

The Allison family, from Chesterville, Ontario (but Bessie Allison was born and raised in Milwaukee) perished, except for their baby boy. An artist imagined the family's final moments on *Titanic*. AUTHOR'S COLLECTION.

The other Allison brother, Percy, remained in Chesterville, Ontario, managing Hudson's 400-acre purebred stock farm. In late June, 1912, more than two months after *Titanic* sank, he received two dozen Clydesdale horses that his late brother had ordered and shipped on a slow boat from Scotland. Ironically, as Percy drove the herd from the train station to the farm, they passed Maple Grove cemetery and the towering obelisk that marked the grave of Hudson Allison.

The police chief of Berlin (later, in 1916, during a spurt of patriotic fervor and anti-German sentiment during World War I, this city in southwest Ontario was renamed Kitchener) lost his nephew, J. J. Flynn, on his way to the New World from Ireland, in the sinking.

George E. Graham, buyer for Canada's Eaton Company in Winnipeg, but born in St. Marys, Ontario, was remembered in a packed Toronto memorial service on Saturday, April 20, 1912. In attendance were his aging father and most of his siblings. One brother, the Reverend William Graham, simultaneously conducted a similar service in St. Marys, Ontario, with other family members and friends present. The Toronto and Winnipeg stores of the Eaton Company were closed on Saturday afternoon as a tribute to George Graham.

◆　　◆　　◆　　◆　　◆　　◆　　◆　　◆

The *Titanic's* late Captain Edward Smith was known and mourned by many marine men in the Great Lakes.

"Captain Smith of the *Titanic* was a very able navigator," proclaimed an assured William Livingstone, President of the Lake Carriers Association. "I had known him about 27 years. I first met him in Liverpool and have seen him a number of times since. He made the first trip on all the large steamers of the White Star line."

"He was regarded by the White Star line," added Detroit steamship agent Christian Leidich, "as one of the most capable commanders on the seas. Since 1892, the company had placed him in charge of each new vessel it brought out."

Hindsight being blessed with 20/20 vision, this author, if placed in Captain Smith's predicament, would have fired up *Titanic's* engines after the collision and set a beeline course towards the steamer, *Californian,* which was sitting still on the edge of the icefield, waiting out the night. *Titanic's* officers knew that some vessel was nestled near their sinking ship, for its lights were within unaided viewing distance, and since that ship failed to respond to wireless distress signals, a signal lantern on deck and a series of rockets fired high into the air, desperation should have prompted the officers to make every effort possible to place the doomed *Titanic* closer to this sleeping vessel. One recent writer has argued that *Titanic's* engines were restarted, but that Smith continued heading for land hundreds of miles away, and that this movement only increased the volume of water leaking into *Titanic's* bow, thus sinking her faster. The few testimonials that mention this restarted movement give a time of only about ten minutes that the ship would have been underway again after the collision. They should have been underway longer, but heading towards the *Californian.* The final wireless message from *Titanic* went out at 1:45 A.M. ship's time, fully two hours after the impact, stating "Engine room full up to boilers." Smith surely had time to move his ship into a more visible, more favorable position towards that nearby floating succor. But it was his call, and he opted for speedy evacuation.

◆　　◆　　◆　　◆　　◆　　◆　　◆　　◆

William Thomas Stead, a famous British caller to Toronto, made an unusual observation there in 1906. Visiting his friend, Dr. Goldwin Smith, for typical English afternoon tea, served in the quaint and richly stocked library at the Grange, he and his host discoursed on world figures and events with rare and intimate knowledge.

Suddenly, Stead, physically signaling a dramatic pause as he sat next to the fireplace, announced, "There has come to me the assurance that I shall live every moment of my days. I shall be wiped out at the end -- sometimes it is borne upon me that I shall be kicked and beaten to death by a mob on the streets of old London, at other times I seem to realize my end as one of the victims in a great disaster which will wipe out hundreds."

"Strange idea," was Dr. Smith's only quiet comment.

Six years later, William Stead perished in *Titanic's* sinking, fulfilling one of the possibilities he predicted about his demise.

William Stead.
AUTHOR'S COLLECTION.

William Stead, publisher and British radical, proponent of world peace, controversial writer (his article, "If Christ Came to Chicago," had them talking for years), publisher of the *Review of Reviews* magazine, and zealous spiritualist, was described by a Toronto newspaper as being "the best-known man aboard [*Titanic*]."Another Toronto newspaper man, who had once worked as an editor under Stead and was familiar with the many times he had reputedly heard from dead people in the afterlife, fully expected that Stead would send messages to those who survived him after he died on *Titanic*.

A message from Stead in the afterlife arrived almost immediately. A delegate at the Pennsylvania state Spiritualists' convention in Pittsburgh, which Stead was to have addressed had he lived, recounted his appearance "from the other world" to her with the message that he "was very busy now, but that he would be with us later." Psychic communications with Stead were also reported by Chicago spiritual- ists, his basic report being, "I was ready." He allegedly sent similar messages to several more of his fans in the supposedly real world.

But the remainder of *Titanic's* dead did not communicate with the living world.

6 Silent Cargoes

More than 1,500 people perished when *Titanic* sank, and some of the bodies were recovered for a respectful but sad homecoming. Two cable ships, the *Mackay-Bennett* and the *Minia,* with embalmers and a minister on board, sailed out of Halifax for the express purpose of picking up *Titanic* bodies.

The pursuit of body recovery, already a difficult task emotionally, was made physically more challenging by unfavorable weather and rough seas. A dense fog prevailed for days and hampered operations.

The Canadian cable ship, *Mackay-Bennett,* sailed out of Halifax searching for *Titanic* bodies.
COURTESY OF THE MARINERS' MUSEUM, NEWPORT NEWS, VIRGINIA.

When the *Mackay-Bennett* arrived at the latitude and longitude given as the site of *Titanic's* sinking, the searchers found absolutely nothing. They began to cruise in a large pattern, finally locating the first *Titanic* body 40 miles from the alleged doom site. Two fully-manned boats, working in relays from dawn until dusk, scoured the area. Suddenly they came upon a floating cluster containing 30 bodies, including many women. Nearby was an empty lifeboat with a woman's red skirt attached to an oar. Speculation ran rampant among the search crew, who felt that this boat had originally held all of the people whose cadavers bobbed together. The red skirt, they surmised, must have been used as a distress signal. The boat had evidently capsized, spilling all of the occupants into the deadly cold ocean. In reality, only Collapsible B had capsized (while leaving *Titanic*), but only 13 of the total of 20 *Titanic* lifeboats had been retrieved by the *Carpathia*. The others were purposely set adrift after removing the survivors. This boat had undoubtedly been orphaned on the bitter Atlantic.

The next day, Monday, April 22, 1912, the *Mackay-Bennett's* lookout on the bridge sighted another large cluster of bodies, this one containing about 50. Among the bodies taken on board was that of a lightly clad, light-haired boy about two years of age. His little body floated face upward alongside the searchers' boat. Many of the hardy sailors had tears in their eyes as they tenderly cradled the lifeless form over the side into their vessel.

A recovery crew from the *Mackay-Bennett* pulls a life-jacketed corpse away from the ocean's grasp.   COURTESY OF THE PUBLIC ARCHIVES OF NOVA SCOTIA, N0716.

Numerous half-clad bodies gave the impression that these people had had little time to get dressed. Some wore shoes, while others were in their socks and stockings. Some wore one boot while the other was missing. Some of the female bodies wore only nightclothes beneath their coats. Bodies were found in various positions; some face upwards, others floating face down.

Some of the recovered bodies were so horribly battered and mutilated as to be beyond recognition, and there was nothing on the bodies by which they could be identified. The finders guessed that these victims must have been in a powerful explosion on board. The arms and legs of some of them were broken. The features on others were cut badly. It might have been a stretch of the imagination to say that the sea and the ice caused such bodily damage.

Embalming was done immediately on board the *Mackay-Bennett,* until the chemicals were all used up. Many bodies were buried at sea.   COURTESY OF THE PUBLIC ARCHIVES OF NOVA SCOTIA, N 215.

Of the several hundred bodies recovered, many were of crew-members that included stewards, waiters, firemen and engineers. Not one was a ship's officer.

All the bodies, excluding that of the little boy, wore life preservers. Some of the men were identified by letters, cards and other papers found in their possession. Virtually every watch worn by a man had stopped at 2:10 or 2:15 o'clock, approximately the time that *Titanic* slid beneath the lightly rippling ocean surface in the early morning of Monday, April 15, 1912. Most of the First Class passengers' bodies were found in clusters, class solidarity to the bitter end.

SHOWS WHERE THE MACKAY-BENNETT IS NOW SEEKING BODIES

The *Mackay-Bennett's* crew observed a gigantic iceberg which they supposed was the one that had sent *Titanic* to the ocean bottom. Floating around it was an enormous debris field of deck chairs, fittings, and a few bodies. Reportedly a mysterious wedge-shaped blade projected from the side of the iceberg, which some of the crew immediately concluded (incorrectly, in all likelihood) had been responsible for the tearing open of the ship's side.

Two more drifting lifeboats were sighted between 50 and 60 miles from the disaster site, while another one had moved 170 miles during the interlude since the tragedy. No bodies, however, were nearby.

♦   ♦   ♦   ♦   ♦   ♦   ♦   ♦

The recovery ships lacked enough embalming chemicals and materials for the unexpectedly many bodies they found. Out of necessity, 116 of the 306 bodies recovered were buried at sea.

Some First Class passengers were buried at sea, along with many of the unrecognizable bodies. Most of the cadavers, however, were in a remarkably good state of preservation after several days' immersion in salt water. The finders attributed this to the freezing water temperature. The corpses which were buried at sea were wrapped in canvas, weighted, sewn up, and consigned to the deep. On Sunday, April 21, 24 bodies were buried at sea. On Monday, 15 more were sent over the ship's side, one by one. On Wednesday, as the men again stood on the deck with bared heads and the ship's bell tolled for each victim, the bodies of 77 more were buried. Reverend Canon Hind held a special service for each body as it was consigned to its ocean grave. Several of those were of people who had been heading for the Great Lakes.

Nineteen-year-old Joseph Nicholls, travelling in Second Class to reach Houghton, Upper Michigan, went down with *Titanic*. He had helped place his mother, Agnes Davies, and nine-year-old stepbrother, John Davies, into a lifeboat, asked permission for himself to board, and was refused, with the threat that he would be shot if he attempted to get in. He stayed on board *Titanic*. His body was recovered by the *Mackay-Bennett*, but because he was not immediately identified, his remains were buried at sea. When his pocket possessions were later studied at Halifax, his identity became known.

Vassilios Katavelas, 18, a Greek immigrant whose destination was Milwaukee, never made it. His body was recovered and buried at sea. The personal effects in his pockets (key, comb, pocket mirror, two memo books) a train ticket from New York to Milwaukee, and a purse with ten cents in it, were sent to his siblings in Greece.

The body of Thor Olsvigen, 20, who had been heading for Cameron, Wisconsin, was recovered and buried at sea. He carried with him a gold watch and chain, a pocket knife, a bundle of photos, a comb and $24.50 in cash, all of which was sent to his parents in Norway.

Croatian steerage passenger, Josef Drazenovic, 33, never made it to his destination of Niagara Falls, New York. The effects removed from his body before it was buried at sea on April 21, 1912, reflected his simple lifestyle: a pipe, a passport, a set of beads, and a few dollars.

Edward Lockyer, 21, was emigrating to the town of Ontario, New York, on the shores of Lake Ontario, but instead, his body was buried at sea on April 24, 1912. His simple personal effects were forwarded to his father in England.

Mary Mangan, 32 years of age, was part of the group travelling from Mayo County, Ireland, to Chicago. The amount of gold found on her floating body belied the fact that she was a steerage passenger: a gold watch engraved "M. Mangan," a gold locket engraved "Mary," a gold bracelet engraved "M. M.," a gold chain, a wire gold brooch, and a diamond solitaire ring. She was buried at sea, but her effects were returned to relatives in Ireland.

The 81st body recovered by the *Mackay-Bennett* was that of a fair-haired man, estimated age 35, with the following items in his pockets which indicated that, in all likelihood, he was not a steerage passenger: a gold watch and chain, with fob, a gold pin, a silver match box, a Masonic button, a knife, keys, a photo, and a purse containing £11 (pounds sterling) 9 shillings and 8 pence, and a U.S. dime. He also carried a check drawn on the Dominion Bank, payable at Windsor, Ontario, for the sum of $243.12, and he wore a gold ring marked with the initials "P. S." This was Second Class passenger Phillip Stokes, a London bricklayer who was on his way to Detroit. His body was buried at sea on April 24, 1912.

Thomas Theobald, who was travelling to Detroit with the Goldsmith family was buried at sea on April 24, 1912.

Philip Stokes was heading for Detroit.
AUTHOR'S COLLECTION.

On his person were a pipe, a tobacco pouch, a razor, a memo book, a silver watch and chain, a gold ring bearing the initials "C. T.", and four shillings. A waterstained Third Class menu dated April 12, 1912, and his passenger ticket were stuffed into the pockets on his shoeless body.

Reginald Hale, a 30-year-old who had been living in Auburn, New York for a decade, decided to spend Christmas, 1911, with his newly-widowed mother in England. Returning home on *Titanic,* he died in the sinking, but his body was recovered. When a White Star Line agent in England, upon the mother's request, crossed the ocean to claim the body in Halifax, he was informed that it had been necessary to bury it at sea. Reginald Hale was doomed to have no homecoming.

◆   ◆   ◆   ◆   ◆   ◆   ◆   ◆

One of the "funeral ships," the *Mackay-Bennett*, returned to Halifax with 190 bodies, 106 of which were embalmed. No time was lost in removing the bodies from the ship after reaching port. The bodies which had been embalmed and laid in caskets were the first to be carried ashore by the ship's crew and stacked in covered horsedrawn wagons which hastily conveyed them to the temporary morgue at Mayflower Rink.

Body transfer from the *Mackay-Bennett* to the skating rink was still done the old-fashioned way in 1912: horse-and-buggy.   COURTESY OF THE PUBLIC ARCHIVES OF NOVA SCOTIA, N0332.

Other bodies on board the recovery ships were wrapped in canvas and sewn up. As each of these covered cadavers was removed from the ship's hold, it was carried ashore on a stretcher by four of the crew. Under two special marquees set up on the pier to frustrate the eyes of the curious, undertakers placed the bodies into coffins waiting on the wharf, fastened down the lids, and transported them to the morgue as quickly as possible, with minimal confusion and pedestrian rubbernecking. In fact, very few people were allowed near the ship.

Friends and relatives of the deceased waited at the Mayflower Rink for the hearses' arrival. As each vehicle conveying bodies left the harborfront, sailors and police stood at attention and saluted the departed. As one newspaper described the scene, "The absence of throngs of people was remarkable, and the utmost respect was shown the dead on all sides."

Frank Walsh, who travelled from Milwaukee to Halifax to identify and claim the body of Captain Edward Crosby, described what he saw:

"When I arrived in Halifax the day after the death ship *Mackay-Bennett* arrived with the bodies, there was still a crowd of the morbid curious gathered around the skating rink in which the bodies had been placed. The bodies were placed in a row, there being about sixty bodies left when I reached there. The bodies were in coffins, only the faces being visible. Most of them were in good condition and were easily identified by relatives who had made the trip to Halifax to claim those who met death in the disaster.

"The purser of the ship [*Mackay-Bennett*] had an excellent system of taking care of the bodies that were found. When a body was picked up, the clothing taken from the body, and also the valuables, were wrapped in a canvas bag and numbered. The same number was placed on a tag, which was tied to the wrist of the body from which the clothes were taken. When a body was identified by a relative, the clothing, valuables, and everything that was taken from the body was handed to the claimant, with an itemized list of everything taken...."

The *Minia* had recovered the body of Charles Hays, President of the Grand Trunk Railroad, but adverse conditions made it impossible for his body to be transferred to the *Mackay-Bennett* at sea. The *Minia* returned several days later when she retired from the search.

The recovery of the body of the wealthiest man on board *Titanic*, John Jacob Astor, was the talk of the town, especially as $2,500 in cash was found in his pockets. Waiting relatives and friends quickly identified and claimed the body --- and the money.

The corpse of George Graham, Eaton Company buyer, was identified by J. W. Graham of St. Marys, Ontario, and Dr. Jackson of Winnipeg, both of whom travelled to Halifax to identify and pick up the remains. Arrangements were made to have the body shipped to Toronto and then to Harriston, Ontario, for interment.

Hudson Allison's body (but not those of his wife and young daughter) was recovered and identified, and original plans were to have his body conveyed home on board the same train as that carrying Charles Hays. However, the *Minia,* with Hays' body on board, was still at sea concluding its search. Allison's body was sent directly to his old home at Chesterville, Ontario, where he was buried.

William Berriman, 23, and his 19-year-old brother-in-law, William Carbines, were travelling in Second Class to Calumet, Michigan, where two of William's brothers had already emigrated. Both men on *Titanic,* however, perished in the sinking. Berriman's body was not found, but Carbines was recovered and brought to Halifax, where the brothers from Michigan's upper peninsula identified the body and sent it back to St. Ives, England, for burial in the family plot.

The difficult homecoming of the corpse of travelling salesman Stanley H. Fox of Rochester, New York, returning from a two-month business trip to England, France and Germany, was confusingly described in the Toronto *Globe* on May 2, 1912. No sooner was the ink dry on his death certificate, issued at Halifax, than his sister-in-law, Mrs. Lydia Fox, arrived to claim the body and the personal effects (which amounted to two watches and $70) on behalf of Stanley Fox's widow, Cora Fox. Cora, Lydia claimed, was too ill and grieving at her Rochester home to make the trip herself. The body was placed on a train for Rochester. Then Halifax authorities received a telegram from Cora Fox, requesting that her late husband's body, as well as his personal effects, be retained by the authorities and not forwarded in the care of Lydia Fox. So the remains and the effects of Stanley Fox were removed from the train at Truro, Nova Scotia, returned to Halifax, and then shipped directly to his widow at 38 Gregory Street, Rochester, New York. Whatever communication failure transpired, or whatever fraud was attempted, has remained a family secret.

Secrets from family featured in the story of William Harbeck, 44, of Toledo, Ohio, one-time deputy sheriff of Lucas County. His fame as a documentary filmmaker growing, he was crossing Europe selling his films when he wrote to one of his two teenaged sons from Berlin that his work was done, that he had booked return passage on *Titanic* and that he would soon be back home at 733 Michigan Street with the boys and their mother. When his body was recovered, his locked arms were clutching the purse of a 24-year-old French woman named Henriette Yrois. Inside the purse was, among other items, Harbeck's wedding ring. Henriette, who also perished in the sinking but whose body was not recovered, was apparently crossing the Atlantic as Harbeck's wife. The real Mrs. Harbeck was not impressed. She had the White Star Line ship her husband's body to Toledo and had it buried without a marker in the Harbeck family plot in Woodlawn Cemetery (his sons, John, a reporter, and Stanley Harbeck, later added one).

A young farmer named Albert Wirz was emigrating to America , specifically to Beloit, Wisconsin, where he had an aunt. When he left Switzerland, his stepmother and father had a premonition that some awful disaster would overtake him. In fact, his stepmother had written to her sister in Beloit that she was afraid to have Albert make the trip, as she felt that she would never see him again. Her fears proved correct. Albert's body was recovered by the *Mackay-Bennett* on April 24, 1912. The dark-haired, mustached corpse wearing a dark suit, woolen socks and buckle shoes carried two watches, a brass chain, a knife, an ink pot, keys, a passport, a Third Class ticket and a purse containing 36¢. Albert Wirz was transported to Beloit and buried in the local cemetery on May 12, 1912. His parents never saw him again.

Sigurd Moen, 25, originally bound for Minneapolis with other Nowegians, was recovered and forwarded to Norway for burial.

The body of First Class passenger Edward Kent was recovered by the *Mackay-Bennett*. The gold frame miniature that fellow traveller Helen Candee had given him for safekeeping was still in his pocket. It was returned to Helen in Washington, D.C., and Kent's body was transported home to Buffalo, New York, for burial.

Recovered by the *Mackay-Bennett*, the body of Dr. William Minahan from Fond du Lac, Wisconsin, was identified by his gold watch, his name engraved on it. His other personal effects immediately established his First Class passenger status: diamond ring, gold cuff links, $380 U.S. collars and over 16 British pounds in gold. He also carried a tool of his profession, a clinical thermometer. Attorney Victor Minahan sojourned from Green Bay to Halifax to identify and claim his brother's body. The human remains of the beloved doctor were interred in a crypt in Green Bay's Woodlawn Cemetery near his parents.

◆   ◆   ◆   ◆   ◆   ◆   ◆   ◆

Many unfortunate people who were heading for the Great Lakes but died in the *Titanic* disaster were recovered, identified, and buried in Halifax for a number of reasons, predominantly cost. Many relatives, particularly those of lost steerage passengers, could simply not afford that expense of having a body shipped home. The sympathetic residents of Halifax gave the victims the best homecoming that they could receive under these black circumstances.

Two young Swedish women, cousins Jenny Henriksson, 28, and Ellen Pettersson, 18, travelled in steerage with friends from home, the Skoog family, who were returning to Iron Mountain, Michigan. Wilhelm Skoog, a mining engineer, and wife Anna had packed up their four children, Karl (10), Mabel (9), Harald (4) and Margit (2), and returned to Sweden in late 1911, but they soon decided that they preferred the conditions in Michigan's Upper Peninsula mining region. All six members of the Skoog family, as well as the female cousins, perished, and the only body recovered and much later identified was Jenny's. Only a glove was missing from her fully clad remains. One brooch was the extent of possessions found with her body, which was taken to Halifax and buried in Fairview Cemetery. "Probably Third Class" was the only identifying notation. The red initials, "J. H." on her chemise, although noted at the time of recovery, were not used to identify her until many years later.

The English baker, Harold J. Reynolds, only 21 years old and crossing the ocean on *Titanic* in steerage, wished to follow in the footsteps of an encouraging colleague who had opened a successful bakery in Toronto. Instead, Reynolds was interred at Fairview Cemetery, Halifax, Nova Scotia. His body, one of the last to be recovered (#327 in the official list of recovered bodies) by the final search of yet another Halifax ship, the *Montagny*, had been afloat in the ocean for almost a month when found on May 10th. Little wonder that the coroner estimated his age to be twice what it actually was.

Frederick Charles Sawyer, 23, a young Englishman heading for Halley, Michigan, was recovered by the *Mackay-Bennett*, identified by the Third Class ticket in his pocket, and ultimately buried at Fairview Cemetery in Halifax.

Twenty-two-year-old Achille Waelens was part of the annual influx of migrant workers from Belgium toiling in the sugar beet fields of Michigan and Ohio. A Third Class passenger bound for Stanton, Ohio, his body was recovered and buried at Fairview Cemetery in Halifax. His personal effects included a watch, knife, pipe, trouser clips, $25.00 and some foreign coins.

Malkolm Johnson, 33, had done well for himself working in Minneapolis for several years in the construction business, but he hoped to buy a farm in his native Sweden when he returned for a visit. When that deal fell through, a disappointed Johnson decided to return to America. He booked passage on *Titanic*. When his body was found by the *Mackay-Bennett*, his personal effects did not reflect the fact that he was travelling in steerage: a gold watch and chain, a gold tie pin, a diamond set, a diamond solitaire ring, $165.00 in notes, a couple of $20.00 coins, a check for $1,200.00 (at *Titanic's* average Third Class fare, he could have crossed the Atlantic Ocean 30 times on this amount!), plus miscellaneous coins. All of his clothing was intact, even his boots, except, oddly enough, for the fact that his socks were missing. Johnson was buried in Halifax's Fairview Cemetery and his effects were mailed to his brother in Sweden, who repeatedly sent letters asking about his late brother's socks. Apparently, Johnson had sewn over $2,000.00 into his socks before leaving Sweden. The mystery of Malkolm's missing socks will likely never be solved.

Malkolm Johnson, who was on his way to Minneapolis, was instead buried at Halifax. Alma Pålsson, pictured here with one of her children (all of whom died in the *Titanic* sinking). was also recovered and buried at Halifax. She had planned to meet her husband in Chicago.   AUTHOR'S COLLECTION.

Malkolm Johnson's headstone at Fairview Cemetery, Halifax.   PHOTO BY CRIS KOHL.

The *Mackay-Bennett* recovered the body of a light-haired woman, about 30, and in her pockets, they found simple tokens of steerage immigration: a mouth organ, a purse containing the small sum of 65 Swedish kroner, and a letter from her husband, Nils Pålsson, of 94 Townsend Street in Chicago. The body was that of Alma Pålsson, who was crossing the ocean with her four small children to join her husband. He had saved enough money and sent it to her so she and their family could join him in America. Instead, she was buried in Halifax, Nova Scotia, Canada.

The unidentified light-haired boy about two years of age was buried in Fairview Cemetery in Halifax with a large grave marker dedicated to "The Unknown Child," paid for by the affected crew of the cable ship, *Mackay-Bennett*, which had found his tiny corpse. Years later, researchers established that the child's body was likely that of Gösta Pålsson, None of the other three Pålsson children was recovered. None of the family ever rejoined the despondent father in Chicago.

The grave of "The Unknown Child" is that of a young Swedish boy who was enroute to Chicago with his mother and siblings. Purely by coincidence, his mother was buried nearby (the background grave marker to the right).   PHOTO BY CRIS KOHL.

7 Homecomings

Two young British men arrived at their new homes in Calumet, Michigan on April 26, 1912, with the story of having crossed the Atlantic Ocean from Liverpool to St. John's, Newfoundland, on board the steamer, *Lake Erie,* and having witnessed the new leviathan, *Titanic,* race past them "like a fast flying express train passing a slower freight." The two men felt that it was possible that their ship's passengers were the last ones to see *Titanic* before she struck the iceberg. With vast fields of ice slowing her down, the *Lake Erie* took 12 days to make the passage, twice as long as *Titanic* would have taken.

The *Titanic* survivors were in a better position to arrange the final leg of their homecomings when they disembarked from *Carpathia* on the dark, cold, rainy night of Thursday, April 18, 1912, in New York.

Lillian and Daisy Minahan were among the first to come ashore from *Carpathia* at New York. Dr. John R. Minahan of Fond du Lac, Wisconsin, brother of the lost Dr. William Minahan, waiting for them, whisked them away in a taxicab to the Hotel Astor, where, within 20 minutes, "every attention was given them." John telephoned the manager of the Altman store, an establishment similar to the Marshall Field store in Chicago, explained who he was, outlined the plight of the two ladies, and asked him to attend to having outfits of clothing secured. Within a short time, the women were newly attired. The party arrived by train in Chicago, where an army of newspaper reporters besieged them and were kept at bay by Dr. Minahan. At Milwaukee, reporters were awaiting the train, but the doctor absolutely refused to permit any to see the ladies.

Alice Silvey left the rescue ship at 10:00 P.M. and immediately retreated to a room at the Hotel Gotham. The pain of her broken ankle was nothing compared to the agony of losing her husband, William, without whom she would have to return home to Duluth.

The story of *Titanic's* loss and Duluth residents William and Alice Silvey's experiences received artistic coverage in the April 21, 1912, issue of the *Duluth News Tribune*.   AUTHOR'S COLLECTION.

Helmina Nilsson and Alice Johnson with her two children spent a few days recuperating in St. Luke's Hospital in New York before travelling to the Chicago area together, their friendship cemented by the most ghastly experience in maritime history.

Albin Lander immediately whisked his sister, Helmina, away to his home at 115 Cedar Slip, Joliet, Illinois. Since a small, inquisitive crowd, most of whom had never before seen or heard a shipwreck survivor, let alone a *Titanic* shipwreck survivor, had gathered around the home of brother Edwin, Albin acted in the belief that Helmina would be less annoyed by the curious at his house than if she stayed at the abode of another brother, Edwin Lander (the three brothers had, for some reason, agreed to change their name from Nilsson to Lander when they first arrived in America), at 315 Garnsey Avenue, where Helmina eventually took up residence. However, upon her arrival, more than 20 friends gathered and a happy reunion was held among the members of the family, with no ill results. In fact, an almost constant stream of visitors called at the home of Albin Lander to express their best wishes the day after his sister arrived safely from Sweden by means (or in spite) of *Titanic*.

Alice Johnson and her two children were met back home at the St. Charles Chicago Great Western station by a large number of friends and relatives when they arrived at 7:30 P.M. on April 24, 1912. Baby Eleanor was still ill from exposure to the cold winds off the Atlantic's field of ice in which *Titanic* sank. Four-year-old Harold, who had perhaps come closest to death by almost being left behind at *Titanic's* rail, was quite spirited, "the peppery one of the party," upon his arrival home. Oscar Johnson had gone by train to pick up his family in New York. Now, friends beseiged Alice for a recital of her experiences, and she told and retold her tales until she "almost fainted."

Seven members of the Wick family of Youngstown, Ohio, took a train to New York to greet their family survivors on the *Carpathia*. The 14-year-old son of Col. George Wick thought that both of his parents had been lost in the sinking, but when he encountered his mother on the pier, tears of joy were plentiful. The experience of the Wicks at this dock reunion underscored a "ghastly feature" of the scramble for tickets that would admit relatives to the pier. When the seven *bona fide* family members requested tickets at the surveyor's office, they were told that 27 dock passes had already been issued in the Wick name. Curiosity seekers had manifestly requested them.

Estates and wills of the wealthy were the domain of the press in 1912. Col. George Wick's estate, valued at over $2,000,000, was reportedly held long-term for the family, daughter Natalie receiving $3,000 annually, son George, $10,000 a year, and widowed wife Mary, $10,000 annually, for 15 years, when the remainder would be divided.

But if Mary remarried within 15 years, she would lose all her income. Earthly love affairs could be controlled even from the Great Beyond.

IN MEMORIAM

Regardless of the provisions in his will, Colonel Wick was a highly-respected businessman in the steel industry. They city mourned when he passed away, as indicated by this artwork from the *Youngstown Telegram*, April 24, 1912.   AUTHOR'S COLLECTION.

Adie Wells and her children were greeted in New York by her husband, Arthur, and her brother, who had both come from Akron.

Ida and Jean Hippach found warm greetings in New York from the two men in their family, Louis Hippach (the husband and father) and Howard Hippach, the only remaining son and brother. Two other sons, Robert, 14, and Archibald, 11, had been among the 600+ people who perished in the dreadful Iroquois Theater Fire of December 30, 1903, in Chicago. In fact, Ida went on this vacation to Europe with Jean in an effort to help overcome her still-troubled emotions from this tragedy. Louis, a partner in the Tyler & Hippach Glass Company, could not take time from work to accompany them, since this was the era of incredible boom in the building industry in Chicago. Indeed, his company's glass adorned famous structures such as the Field Museum, the Civic Opera Building, and what was then the largest building in the world, the Merchandise Mart. Now the men were ecstatic to have the Hippach women back.

An irate Ida felt that she and Jean had been tricked into buying passage on *Titanic*. "We decided that we would take the *Titanic* if the passenger list was fairly large. We wanted to test the traveling public's confidence in the new boat, so I told my daughter that we would find out if there were any staterooms left. At the White Star office in Paris, we were told that there was only one stateroom left in the First cabin. We bought our ticket and considered ourselves lucky. When the *Titanic* left Cherbourg, there were scores of staterooms unoccupied. Scores of passengers had felt the same way we did about embarking on the *Titanic* on her maiden voyage, and all of them had been induced in the same manner to sail."

Annie Kelly, 21, and Annie McGowan, 15, were both hospitalized in New York upon their arrivals. During that time, the younger of the two claimed, she had visitors from the White Star Line. "Four men came to my bed in the hospital and told me to sign something. I couldn't write." Her hands and arms were purple and swollen. "So one of them held my hand while I wrote. I was so very tired, even that seemed an effort. Then one of the men pinned something on my clothes lying on the bed. I asked them if I would get to Chicago to my sisters and cousins, and they said, 'Oh, you'll get there all right.'" Annie fell asleep for a while and, upon awakening, found $25.00 pinned to her underwear. She claimed that the men had her sign a waiver releasing the company from further liability. "But I didn't leave [the hospital] as soon as I thought I would. It seems there was some misunderstanding about the steamship company paying the sisters of St. Vincent's hospital where I was taken, for attending to me."

Several days later, both young Annies were released, and, wearing hospital nightgowns, coats, and shoes, they reached Chicago. Annie McGowan recalled, "When I finally left, I felt so embarrassed I huddled into a seat on the train. It was awful to start on a journey sick, but to be almost without clothes was worse...."

Upon arrival in Chicago, Annie Kelly, went to 303 Eugenie Street, the home of her cousin, Mrs. Daniel Garvey (to whom she had written recently, "I am coming to America on the nicest ship in the world...."), but she was suffering from after-effects of the sinking. Still physically ill from hours of exposure in the lifeboat, she also experienced insomnia, haunted by the wild scenes on *Titanic* just before it sank. "Miss Kelly is a nervous wreck," diagnosed Dr. Thomas J. O'Malley (likely unaware of his bad pun). "I doubt if she ever will completely recover her normal condition. Unless she can overcome her awful fear and terror at every sound, I fear for her life."

Dagmar Bryhl wrote to Oscar Lustig, in Rockford, Illinois, from her hospital bed in New York City the day after the *Carpathia* landed: "Dearest Uncle -- As uncle has, of course, read in the newspaper, the *Titanic* has gone down....I would have been glad if I had been permitted to die, because life no longer has any value for me since I lost my beloved [both her fianceé, Ingvar Enander, a promising graduate of agricultural engineering, and her brother, Kurt, had perished]. I feel myself so dreadfully alone in this land. These people are certainly good, but nevertheless do not understand me. Could uncle possibly come here, if it would not be too difficult or expensive?...With the heartiest greetings to all relatives. Uncle's affectionate, Dagmar."

Oscar Lustig did not receive the letter. He was in New York City searching for his niece. Although she was listed as a survivor, no one seemed to know what had happened to her.

Uncle Oscar was not happy with the White Star Line office in New York. When he appeared there inquiring about his niece, he was met with icy looks and chilly courtesy. The manager even refused to talk to him. When the irritated uncle threatened to go to the newspaper office and tell the press about the treatment he was receiving, the effect was electrical. The manager suddenly found time for him. Although he had no information about Dagmar, he did let the uncle know where he could continue his search. After striking out at the Swedish consul and the Scandivanian Emigrant Home, Oscar went to the *New York Tribune* offices, where a reporter remembered having seen a Swedish girl who had lost two brothers (he thought) and who spoke French (which Dagmar did, as well as German and enough English to be communicative). The journalist thought she had caught a train for Montreal. Oscar prepared a telegram to the *Montreal Gazette*, asking that newspaper to try to intercept the girl, and was on the verge of sending it when he received a telegram from his sisters in Rockford. The place where Dagmar was staying in New York had telegraphed them. It seems that a well-meaning survivor on board the *Carpathia* had taken Dagmar under her wing, and, instead of registering her with the Relief Committee in New York upon arrival, she had whisked her away by automobile to the Hospital for Deformities and Joint Diseases. And Uncle Oscar wondered why he couldn't find his niece!

Oscar Lustig had the highest praise for the staff of the hospital where he found Dagmar. The wealthy director of that hospital took a liking to both niece and uncle, and toured them around the New York Stock Exchange and other sites. Oscar and Dagmar shopped for new clothes for her, since the only things she had taken from *Titanic* were the clothes she wore and a watch, given to her by her fiancée and worn on a chain around her neck for safekeeping.

She had survived, yet Dagmar Bryhl was grief-stricken. She confessed to her uncle repeatedly between sobs that if she had thought that her brother and her sweetheart would be lost, she would never have allowed them to put her into the lifeboat. She would rather have died with them than to live with the memory of all that took place graven into her mind for all the subsequent days to come. She felt that this blow fell heaviest upon her father in Sweden.

Her brother, Kurt Bryhl, had worked as a sailor and had ventured all around the world in that capacity. He had lived for a time in Paris. One newspaper report summed up his life with the words, "He is said to have been a carefree young man who had seen much and who was preparing to settle down and put his wide experience to use in the calmer affairs of life." But he never lived long enough to settle down.

The heartbroken Dagmar Bryhl, sole survivor from their *Titanic* trio, unhappily reached Rockford, Illinois, with her uncle and went right to bed, disappointing a number of waiting reporters.

Anton and Louise Kink, along with their young daughter, Louise, travelled by train to Milwaukee with tickets purchased using funds sent by an uncle from that city, and in early May, 1912, the three spent a week appearing on the vaudeville stage of the Crystal Theater at every performance, with a well-known lecturer named Frank Cook giving the talk of their *Titanic* experiences, as told by Anton Kink in his native German, "as he has not had time to learn English since landing in New York."

Jennie Hansen's history of poor health and the terrible ordeal of *Titanic* landed her in a New York hospital upon arrival. Dazed and in shock over the loss of her husband, she lamented, "Oh! Why didn't they let me die with Peter? I begged and begged to be allowed to stay with him, but an officer just threw me into the boat. I thought Peter had been saved too, or I would have jumped into the ocean instead of going on board the *Carpathia*." After a few days in the hospital, Jennie travelled by train (First Class, and accompanied by a White Star Line nurse, all paid for by the company) to Chicago, where she was met by members of her family who took her by train the rest of the way to Racine. At Kenosha, two reporters and a lady attendant (to care for her just in case she was alone) boarded the train and received her story of the disaster. In Racine, a waiting car took her to her brother, Thomas Howard's, residence on Center Street. In February, she had reportedly told this brother, "I dread taking this trip to Denmark, for I have a feeling that I will never return alive," and she went on to detail the kind of funeral she wanted. Yet she was the one who survived. "I still believe that Peter is safe and I can't get anything else into my head," she told the reporters. But her husband and her brother-in-law had indeed perished and their bodies were never found.

Aaron Willer, 37, was a poor tailor returning to Chicago from a desperate fund-raising trip to his relatives in England. Apparently he had been successful, for he wrote to his wife, "I am coming home with lots and lots of money, and I am bringing presents for you and the kiddies. We shall never want again." Feeling reassured by her husband's words, yet pressured by all the overdue bills, she pawned the few remaining pieces of furniture that were in the house. Their rent was long overdue and the landlord was acting edgy. Then arrived the bad news that her husband had perished in the *Titanic* sinking. Gone also were the presents and the money. A sympathetic Chicago reporter found the family in a tiny, bare flat and described the pitiful scene: "...the four children were grouped on the floor, hungry-eyed, about the weeping form of their mother. Mrs. Willer occupied the only chair in the room---all the others having gone for food...." A portion of Chicago's relief fund for the *Titanic* victims was given to the destitute widow. Mrs. Willer later became the first person in the Great Lakes region to prepare a lawsuit against the White Star Line, seeking $10,000.00 in damages. The lawsuit was unsuccessful.

A distraught Mrs. James McCrie waited at her home on North Christina Street in Sarnia, Ontario, for word of her husband, a Second Class passenger returning from an 18-month stint in Egypt, his contract having just expired, as an oil rig operator ("one of the best known oil drillers in Lambton county," according to one journalist). Apparently in no hurry to return, he had written his wife a letter from England indicating his plan to remain there for a week so he could make the ocean crossing on the new *Titanic*. He perished and his body was not recovered. Conflicting reports indicate that either McCrie's wife or one of his children was extremely ill, prompting his return from overseas.

Another Sarnia-area connection was *Titanic* survivor, First Class passenger Mary Hughes Smith, 18. She and her father, West Virginia Congressman James A. Hughes, reportedly spent many summers at the family cottage on Stag Island in the St. Clair River because Mr. Hughes was "a former Corunna [Ontario] boy," Corunna being the closest Canadian town to Stag Island. Mary Smith had married 24-year-old Lucien Smith on February 8, 1912, and they were returning from Egypt on board *Titanic*. Like matching teenage wife Madeline Force Astor, Mary Smith, widowed on her honeymoon, soon became a mother, and both women bore high-profile sons whom they were carrying on *Titanic*. Coincidentally, Mary Smith later married fellow survivor, Robert Daniel, but the marriage did not last. When she died in 1940, she was gathering material for a book on the *Titanic* sinking.

Awaiting Richard Otter of the Cleveland suburb of Middleburg township was his young wife and their 12-year-old son, both of whom went to Cleveland to be closer to sources of information. But the husband and father would not be returning home. His widow later stated, "It is hard to lose him, but it is fine to think he went as he did. I think it is right the men should stand back. It will be a wonderful thing for our son to remember his father died a hero. My husband was an Englishman, and I should want him to meet his end bravely."

RICHARD OTTER.

AUTHOR'S COLLECTION.

Mrs. William Douton, steadfastly disbelieving that her husband could be among the lost, left for New York City from her home in the town of Holley in upstate New York on Wednesday, April 17, 1912. She stood at the dock when the *Carpathia* landed the next evening, but Mr. Douton did not disembark. He was definitely among the lost.

First Class passenger Marion Kenyon returned alone, brokenhearted, to her home in Pittsburgh. Her husband, Frederick, perished in the sinking and his body was never located.

"Don't worry. I am home again."
These were Ellen Toomey's consoling remarks to the score of relatives and friends who met her with tears of joy streaming down their faces at the Union Station in Indianapolis at noon on April 24, 1912. Some people were surprised at her appearance, expecting to see signs of the hardships she had experienced. Instead, Ellen emerged from the train walking swiftly, her ruddy cheeks glowing with pleasure at her reception. She had spent a few days in a New York hospital recovering from her ordeal.
"...A number of Sisters of St. Vincent were there [at the dock] and took about 150 of us to St. Vincent's Hospital to rest," Ellen recounted to her family and the press. "Only a few were sick, but we all went along. I was in the hospital until I started for home."
Now, back home, so many people kissed and embraced the little woman that she found it necessary to straighten her hat and readjust her clothing. The returning celebrity boarded a carriage to the home of her sister, Mrs. Richard Haney, at 911 Bates Street, where she told

and retold her tale to dozens of well-wishing visitors who punctuated the afternoon. She later repeated the performance at the home of another sister, Mrs. Michael Delaney. Ellen Toomey didn't mind. She was a survivor.

This is the first photograph taken of Anna Turja after she survived the *Titanic* disaster. She was with family in Ashtabula, Ohio.   COURTESY OF ETHEL RUDOLPH.

Miss Maria Osmon returned to Steubenville, Ohio, from a visit to her native Austria-Hungary. Her plans at home reportedly included visiting her brother, Meli, who was serving a life sentence for murder.

In another part of Ohio, Anna Turja, eyes a-twinkle, stepped off the Nickel Plate train at Ashtabula right into the outstretched arms of her waiting brother, Matti Turja, who had travelled there from his home in nearby Conneaut. Within a minute, he whisked her away to their sister and brother-in-law's house at 81 Oak Street. Friends and neighbors soon crowded into the home of Mr. and Mrs. John Lundi to see the *Titanic* survivor and to extend their greetings.

Edward Dorking, given a new outfit of clothing when he left the hospital in New York, felt a jolt when he went to purchase passage to Illinois and discovered that someone had relieved him of 20 of the 25 dollars given to him at the hospital. Fortunately, "through the generosity of New Yorkers," Dorking was able to buy his train ticket. He arrived at his uncle's residence in Oglesby, Illinois, on Saturday, April 27, 1912. The immigrant from England soon found himself a local celebrity in the midst of Illinois, appearing on stage to recount his *Titanic* experiences in such venues as opera halls and vaudeville stages. Then he drifted into obscurity.

Up in Michigan, the Calumet/Hancock/Houghton region of the Keweenaw Peninsula on Lake Superior welcomed four *Titanic* survivors on April 25, 1912. Normally refined and appealing, the twice-widowed Agnes Davies was distrought and emotional, not only due to her shocking shipwreck experience, but also because she had lost her 19-year-old son (from her first marriage), Joseph Nicholls, her main means of support. Her nine-year-old son, John Morgan Davies, survived with her and, along with an older son and his wife who had previously settled at Houghton, provided consolation. Lyyli Silven, 18, from Finland, visited a cousin in Hancock, unsure if she would continue to Minneapolis since her other cousin from there had died on *Titanic*. Lyyli spoke no English, but through an interpreter, she gave an account of her shipwreck experiences to the local press. Maude Sincock, greeted by her father, Frank Sincock, at a jubilant reception upon her arrival with a large crowd of well-wishers at the depot, also regaled the journalists with her tale.

Sadly, four young Englishmen bound for the upper peninsula of Michigan planning to take employment in the Isle Royale mine, perished on *Titanic*. John Banfield of Houghton would never see his brother, Fred Banfield, again. George Fillbrook of Hurontown, Michgan, would miss his 18-year-old nephew, Charles Fillbrook. James Andrew would mourn the loss of his distant relative, Frank Andrew. Samuel Sobey, alone in the group with no relatives in the Houghton area, was returning to the U.S.A. after visiting family in England.

Stephen Jenkin, a steerage passenger, did not survive the sinking to return to his mining job in Houghton, Michigan. He had emigrated from England with his brother in 1903 and became a U.S. citizen. He was returning home after a visit with his parents in Cornwall, England.

A 16-year-old Belgian man named Alphonse De Pelsmaeker was in steerage on board *Titanic* planning to join his older brother, Gustave, in Gladstone, Michigan, but he was lost in the sinking.

Twelve-year-old Banoura Ayoub arrived in Columbus, Ohio, but her cousin, John Thomas, of 160 North Fifth Street and his son, Tannous, had perished. Both Banoura and Tannous had been attending the American school in Syria, but John wanted the youngsters in the USA so they could receive a better education and learn American ways faster. John had lived in Columbus for 12 years (hence his anglicized name) where he tried his hand at running a women's garments factory and, later, the Princess Theater. Also in company with John Thomas was his wife's brother, Tannous (Thomas) Daher, a male cousin named Gerios Yousseff (Joseph), and a female cousin named Shanini George; only the latter of these three survived *Titan-*

ic's sinking. The men had planned to find work in America, possibly in the steel mills at Youngstown.

Also arriving in Columbus was Jessie Bruce Trout, only to find that her parents and her sister, Mrs. George Findlay of 184 North Princeton Avenue, had no idea that she had even been on board *Titanic*. Jessie had originally booked onto the *Oceanic* for May, but, wanting to return home sooner, she switched to the new ship. She and her parents had come to America in 1905 from Scotland and settled in Columbus, but her parents were on the verge of moving to Winnipeg, Manitoba, and Jessie felt lost. "I am not sure what I will do now," she admitted. "I am all alone, and it matters little where I live."

Franz Karun spent two or three days in a New York City hospital before he and his little girl reached Galesburg, Illinois by train, tickets paid for by the White Star Line, at ten o'clock on Monday evening, April 22, 1912. Franz was wearing the same suit that he had put on in his steerage cabin the night *Titanic* sank. It was an emotional family reunion when his overjoyed wife and four other children surrounded them the moment they reached the train platform. Accompanying Franz Karun was fellow Austrian-Hungarian and *Titanic* survivor, Ivan Jalsevac, who stayed as a guest at the Karun home.

David Vartanian spent several days in a New York hospital recuperating, but his legs had suffered immeasurably from the cold, and he walked with a limp for the rest of his life. Even without the limp, David would be reminded regularly in later years of his connection to the most famous shipwreck in the world, because visiting relatives and friends in Detroit nicknamed him *"Titanic* David."

Helen Bishop's parents, the Waltons, had driven from Florida, where they had spent the winter, to New York City to meet their children. Arriving a week before *Titanic* was due, they stayed at the Waldorf Astoria Hotel. There they first heard about the ship's loss.

"I suppose," said Mrs. Walton, "that we bought one thousand newspapers in our anxiety to get assurance that our children were among the ones rescued."

Upon the *Carpathia's* arrival, the Waltons whisked the Bishops, who were among the first to leave the rescue ship, to a room booked for them at the Waldorf Astoria. In New York City they purchased entire new wardrobes and other personal belongings to replace those lost on *Titanic*. Dickinson sent a telegram to Earl Patterson, their chauffeur, to pick them up in their Lozier car and drive them home to Dowagiac, Michigan. In the end, the Bishops took a train to Dowagiac because the roads were too muddy to drive.

But the first *Titanic* survivors to reach Dowagiac were not the well-known, long-established and press-pampered natives who had been travelling as First Class passengers. Instead, a Third Class immigrant mother and her two small children who had never before breathed fresh Michigan air or ever trod on fertile Great Lakes soil stepped off the train and into new lives at the un-First-Class-like hour of 5:40 A.M., Thursday, April 25, 1912. Even the local press took note, printing, "...Little did the people locally think that others than Mr. and Mrs. D.H. Bishop on the doomed ship, were destined for Dowagiac." Darwis, Hanna, Maria and George Touma were overjoyed at being reunited as a family. Darwis whisked the fresh arrivals to their new farm home where they were "united and happy." Adding to that joy, Hanna Touma received a check for $90.00 from the Ladies' Relief Committee of St. Vincent's Hospital in New York two weeks after she arrived. Hanna's name had been among those registered with the New York Society of Women as needy passengers. She assuredly put the money to good use for her family.

Frederick Quick had journeyed from Detroit to New York to find his wife and daughters when the *Carpathia* landed. He struggled in the immense dockside crowd to catch a glimpse of his wife. " I thought I saw her on the boat as I waited there on the dock," he later related. "Then I gave the old whistle just like I used to whistle when we were sweethearts back in England. But it was another woman."

"But then I saw her," he continued, "and I called to her and she heard me and came running toward me. I grabbed all three of them. Then a reporter came and took her away from me."

Newspapers wanted their story. On a train passing through southwestern Ontario enroute to Detroit, pausing in London, the Quicks were assailed by a city reporter, since the family had lived in East London for a time until May, 1911, when they moved to Detroit. Mr. Quick was employed by the Grand Trunk Railroad carshops while in London, later transferring to the Grand Trunk in Detroit.

Later in Detroit, extremely composed and coherent after their long trip from New York, the Quicks and their two young daughters were on a streetcar when suddenly, there was a sharp report as the overhead switch was thrown and the other passengers jumped, startled. "Another iceberg," Jane Quick calmly remarked with a smile, and continued with her conversation. Such controlled behaviour prompted a Detroit journalist to describe Jane Quick as "no ordinary woman."

Her husband agreed. "My missus is the most wonderful woman in the world," he stated admiringly. "And these two children are the finest you'll find....And my missus brought me a souvenir," He unfolded a small bedraggled flag with a white background, black bars and an insignia in the corner. This was a White Star Line flag from *Titanic.* "I believe it was the only one saved," Frederick Quick noted.

"Mine," said Phyllis Quick, her pudgy baby hands closing about it. The sight of a baby waving a flag attracted absolutely no attention on that Detroit streetcar. If only those passengers knew....

Jane Quick agreed to tell the story of the *Titanic* tragedy on the Vaudeville stage, signing an agreement with the National Theater in Detroit to appear "for seven consecutive days and to tell how she was saved and also to tell as nearly as possible how the ship went down." Her daughters made silent guest appearances. Jane Quick did this only long enough to recoup her family's financial loss in the wreck.

DARING LITTLE ENGLISH WOMAN AND HER FAMILY NOW UNITED IN DETROIT; SOME OF THE SCENES THROUGH WHICH SHE LIVED

MRS FRED QUICK

THE PICTURE IN THE CENTER SHOWS MR. QUICK AND THE QUICK CHILDREN.

In Detroit, the joyous return of Jane Quick and her two daughters, plus her exciting story about their survival, compelled the artists at the *Detroit News Tribune* to go to work drawing vignettes of her tale for the April 21, 1912, issue.   AUTHOR'S COLLECTION.

Three members of a Belgian party, travelling in steerage with most of them planning to work on farms in the Detroit area, took a train which passed through southwestern Ontario. At Chatham, Ontario,

Bank of Montreal manager H.A. Dean boarded and soon struck up a conversation in French with Theodore De Mulder. Dean was ecstatic when De Mulder gave him a saltwater-stained memento, the last supper menu card of the steerage passengers on *Titanic.*

Three *Titanic* survivors arrived together in Detroit shortly after their landing in New York City. From left to right, Julius Sap, Theodore De Mulder and Jean Scheerlinckx. AUTHOR'S COLLECTION.

At the Detroit train station, the three survivors were welcomed by Belgian-Americans who helped them translate their stories for the waiting press. "I shout so much in water Sunday night I have no more throat," described Theodore De Mulder in his broken English before surrendering to the linguistic assistance of his fellow nationals. De Mulder, along with companions Jean Scheerlinckx and Julius Sap, claimed to have survived the sinking by jumping off the ship just as it went down and swimming to lifeboats which picked them up "just after the big *Titanic* had disappeared beneath the waves." Since other survivor accounts make no mention of retrieving these three men from the sea, it has been postulated that they really survived by stepping into lifeboats as they were being lowered, but made up the dramatic story of swimming for their lives in order to save face. They praised the generosity of the White Star Line in New York City, which had provided them with the funds to reach Detroit and purchase some necessities. Several of their less lucky Belgian travelling companions on *Titanic* -- Philmn Van Melkebeke, Victor Vandercruyssen, Camille Wittevrongel, Leo Hampe, René Lievens, all Detroit-bound -- perished.

Borak Hannah received initial assistance from New York's Syrian community. Its members contacted his brother in Port Huron, who immediately took a train to New York and fetched his sibling home.

Mrs. Albert Alexander of 6 West Ave., Albion, New York, expressed thanks to "all kind people of Albion who extended sympathy for the loss of her dear brother [William Alexander] on the *Titanic*."

George and Percy Allison, two uncles of one-year-old Trevor Allison, journeyed to New York from Ontario to claim their nephew, the only survivor from his immediate family. Trevor was staying at the Hotel Manhattan in the care of the family nursemaid, maid and cook.

Major Arthur Peuchen stepped off *Carpathia* into the welcoming arms of his wife and children. Their plan was to immediately carry him off to the privacy and comfort of a hotel room. Peuchen, aware that he would have to explain why he survived when others perished, put the onus squarely upon himself. He had requested and received from Officer Lightoller a written statement attesting to the fact that Peuchen had been sent by Lightoller into Lifeboat 6 because he was an experienced sailor who could help man the boat. Feeling that this was not enough, Peuchen assumed a defensive posture as soon as he emerged from the *Carpathia*. Confronted by the press, he transferred any attention paid to the fact that he survived to his thundering allegations of negligence and irresponsibility on the parts of Captain Smith, the crew and the White Star Line. Only when he was done letting off steam to the reporters did he rejoin his indulgent family. His wife and two children allowed the survivor that liberty. It was, after all, the Major's 53rd birthday.

◆   ◆   ◆   ◆   ◆   ◆   ◆   ◆

Charles Hays, born on May 16, 1856 at Rock Island, Illinois, began his railroad career at the age of 17. He worked his way up and across various railroad companies, until finally, on January 1, 1910, he was made president and a member of the board of directors of the Grand Trunk Railway Company, for which he had worked since 1895 and which also operated the subsidiary lines of Central Vermont, Grand Trunk Western, Detroit, Grand Haven and Milwaukee, and several other smaller railroads, all of which carried industry to the Great Lakes. In that same year, he had refused a knighthood because he would have had to renounce his U.S. citizenship. The *Toronto World* called him "one of the greatest railroad men in the world."

Hays travelled extensively around the Great Lakes region fulfilling his duties for the Grand Trunk Railway. Years earlier, he had visited the small town of Wiarton, Ontario, near the base of the Bruce peninsula which separates Georgian Bay from Lake Huron. This important man's visit became the year's highlight for this small town. The weekly newspaper, *The Wiarton Echo*, dated June 16, 1904, made Hays' visit their front page story, praising him and his "magnificent [railroad] coaches,...everything about them was spick and span...."

In memory of the late railroad President, Charles M. Hays, there was announced "an absolute cessation of work in every department of the Grand Trunk and Grand Trunk Pacific Railways in Canada, Britain and the United States at 11:30 A.M., Thursday, April 25, 1912." This appeared in the Toronto *Globe* on April 24, 1912.   AUTHOR'S COLLECTION.

Unfortunately, Charles Hays left Wiarton from that 1904 visit before the newspaper came out. He would have enjoyed the praise and humor in the article about his visit. He might even have flipped it over and read what was printed on the backside of the front page:

WORST OF OCEAN PERILS
Icebergs Are a Great Menace to North Atlantic Vessels.

The perils most dreaded by navigators of the North Atlantic Ocean are the icebergs that, released from their arctic moorings, float southward until the warm rays of tropical suns dissolve them into their first element. These gigantic masses of ice are found in the north Atlantic east of Newfoundland, the whole year round. They are most numerous in the spring, when they are carried south over the Grand banks in the midst of the mighty frozen fields, which are torn from their arctic home and sent careering [sic] across the wide waste of waters from Greenland to Labrador.

Last season bergs were unusually numerous on the Grand banks, and nearly a score of ships were damaged by striking against the crystal islands....

Hays' motto was, "Do a thing, and do it quick." Perhaps he died on *Titanic* the way he lived.

The body of Charles Hays was recovered by the steamer, *Minia,* on April 26, 1912, and was returned to Montreal for burial in what had been his private railway car.

♦   ♦   ♦   ♦   ♦   ♦   ♦   ♦

John B. Thayer of Philadelphia was well-known in the Great Lakes region. He relished his position as President of the Anchor Line of steamships, although that role was usually overshadowed by his title as Second Vice-President of the Pennsylvania Railroad. The shipping line was the smaller of the two large transportation companies.

Just two years earlier, Thayer had travelled to Detroit for the launching of the new Anchor Line steamer, the 372-foot steel freighter, *Allegheny*. Accompanying him were his wife, Marian, his two sons, John ("Jack") Jr., who was 15, and Frederick, who would turn 14 in a week, and one of their two younger daughters, Margaret, whom everyone called "Peggy." The youngest, eight-year-old Pauline, stayed at home in Haverford, Pennsylvania.

The Thayers had taken the train as far as Buffalo, New York, where they boarded one of the Anchor Line ships, the *Juniata,* for the upbound cruise across the length of Lake Erie to Detroit. Upon arrival on July 9, 1910, they proceeded to the yards of the Detroit Ship-building Company in Wyandotte.

There, daughter Peggy had the honor of "neatly" breaking a bottle of champagne on the bow of the new ship at the launching and her father and mother proudly watched this maritime moment.

A Detroit newspaper described the event: "At the same instant the craft began to slide and in a few seconds it was all over but for a few rebounding swells. All launchings that are successful are beautiful, but it really seemed as though the *Allegheny* made her debut a little more gracefully than any predecessors built in the big yards...."

Less than two years later, the parents and their eldest child, Jack, were on board *Titanic*. John Borland Thayer, Sr., was the only family member there who did not survive the sinking. Although he displayed courage by remaining on the doomed vessel, it was a maritime moment he undoubtedly would have preferred to miss. His body was not recovered.

Five members of Pennsylvania's Thayer family (including all three who were on board *Titanic* less than two years later) comprised part of the launching party for the new Anchor Line freighter, *Allegheny*, on the shores of the Detroit River on July 9, 1910. AUTHOR'S COLLECTION.
Inset, young Peggy Thayer christened the new ship while wearing her sailor's outfit. AUTHOR'S COLLECTION.

Within four days of *Titanic's* loss, the Anchor Line ships *Delaware* and *Conemaugh* (the latter being the sister ship to the *Allegheny*), in harbor at Duluth on Lake Superior, flew their flags at half mast, as did all the other ships of the line, out of respect for the company president who would never see the Great Lakes again.

◆   ◆   ◆   ◆   ◆   ◆   ◆   ◆

Some *Titanic* passengers heading for Great Lakes communities were totally deprived of any kind of a homecoming. They perished in the sinking and their bodies were never found. Among them were Daniel Coxon, 39, who had been travelling to Merrill, Wisconsin; Kalle Makinen, a 29-year-old who had hoped to reach Glassport, Pennsylvania, but left behind a young widow in Finland instead; First Class passenger Albert Stewart of Gallipolis, Ohio, who was the New York representative of the Stowbridge Lithographing Company of Cincinnati (he had left his family on vacation in France to return quickly to the U.S.A.); Swede Albert Augustsson, 23, who was on his way to Bloomington, Illinois; William Elsbury, 47, a respected farmer from Gurnee, Lake County, Illinois, who was returning from England after settling his late father's estate (later, his widow, seeing suits against the White Star Line started by widows in Chicago, tried to do the same. They all learned that they could file only for the value of the fare that was paid by the deceased, and claim a share in what was salvaged from *Titanic*, namely lifeboats which the company valued at about $4,500. However, the White Star Line had received a monition from a New York court, requiring any claims against the company to be filed in no other place but New York City. This deterred many potential lawsuits from being filed); Carl Carlsson, 24, who was on his way from Gothenburg, Sweden, to visit relatives in Huntley, Illinois; Alfred Gustaffson, 20, who was returning to Waukegan, Illinois, after a stay with relatives in Finland; William Beavan, 18, who was bound for Russell, Illinois; Jeso Ecimovic, a young Croatian who was heading for Hammond, Indiana; John Bengtsson, 26, who was travelling from Sweden to his brother's residence in Monee, Illinois, near Joliet; Nils Ödahl, 23, the Swedish agricultural student who planned to further his studies in America but did not survive to visit the uncle in Peoria, Illinois, who had sent him his ticket; August Carlsson, 28, who had left his wife and two small sons behind in Sweden to visit his brother in Fower, Minnesota, and be the vanguard of the family's emigration to America; Peter Soholt, 19, who was travelling to Minneapolis with a group of fellow Norwegians; Karl Salander, 24, who was emigrating from Sweden, heading for his brother's residence in Red Wing, Minnesota; Second Class passengers Peter McKain, 46, and William Douton, 54, who were travelling together to Rochester, New York, where the latter lived; Second Class passengers Percy Bailey, 19, who had secured a position in Akron, Ohio, where he could complete his apprenticeship as a butcher, and one of his cabin mates, Henry Cotterill, 21, also heading to Akron; Third Class passenger Anthony Abbing, 42, who was returning to his home in Cincinnati, Ohio; Austrian siblings Maria and Vincenz Kink, who were heading for Milwaukee with their older brother, Anton, who survived; John Craftam, 59, who was returning home in a First Class cabin to Roachdale, Indiana, from a vacation in Europe; Howard Case, 49, from First Class, who was returning to Rochester, New York, from yet another business trip to England; Richard Rouse, 50, who set sail on *Titanic* against his wife's wishes (she felt the ship would never make the crossing) to visit his married daughter in Cleveland and see about finding work there; Croatians Milan Karajic, 30, and Stefan Turcin,

36, who were on their way to Youngstown, Ohio; and Third Class passenger William Alexander, 26, heading for Albion, New York;

Englishmen John Garfirth, 22, and his friend, George Patchett, 19, were both emigrating to Canada, planning to live and work in Berlin (renamed Kitchener), Ontario, where George's brother had done well for himself. Originally booked to cross the Atlantic on board the *Empress of Britain,* their train was late and they missed the boat. But they felt genuinely lucky when they were able to exchange their tickets for passage on the new *Titanic.* Fate dealt them a bad hand. Both men were lost in the sinking and their bodies were never found.

Two men made Elmira, New York, their destination, although they were not travelling together. They undoubtedly did not even know each other. William Botsford, a 25-year-old architect in Second Class, was returning to his home state after studying architecture in Egypt. Arthur Ford, 22, was emigrating from England. Both perished and their bodies were never found.

A group of four male Finnish emigrants, bound for the mining city of Sudbury in northern Ontario, were lost when *Titanic* sank: Isak Aijo-Nirva, 41; Nikolai Kallio, 17; Matti Maenpaa, 22; and Matti Rintamaki, 35. No body was ever recovered.

Heading for Ottawa, Ontario, a group of 13 Syrians met with almost total disaster when *Titanic* sank. Only one, Mariana Assaf, who was returning from a visit with her two sons, survived to reach her destination. Those lost were Mariana's cousin, Gerios Assaf, 21; Catherine Barbara, 45; Saude Barbara, 18; Hanna Boulos, 18; Joseph Caram, 28, returning to his shop in Ottawa, and his new bride, Marid Elias Caram, 18, along with her brothers, Joseph Elias, Jr., 17, and Tannous Elias, 15, and their father, Joseph Elias, 39; Betros Khalil, 25, and his wife, Zahie Khalil, 20; and Solomon Khalil, 27, Mariana Assaf's nephew. None of their bodies was ever recovered.

Brantford, Ontario, served as the destination for five young men fleeing persecution in their Turkish-occupied homeland of Armenia. Neshan Krekorian, 25, David Vartanian, 22, Arsun Sirayanian, 22, Artun Zakarian, 27, and Maprieder Zakarian, 26, were emigrating to Canada, a country of greater freedoms and more opportunities than they could ever imagine back home. Unfortunately, religious harassment of Christians by Moslems took a distant second place in the priority of their concerns when *Titanic* struck an iceberg. The friends were parted during the sinking, and only the first two survived. The last named was recovered and buried at Fairview Cemetery in Halifax.

All three passengers on *Titanic* who were heading for St. Paul, Minnesota, were emigrating from Sweden. They all perished and their bodies were never recovered: August Nilsson, 21; Olof Vendel, 29; and Elina Olsson, 31, who planned to stay with her brother in St. Paul, at least until she and her fiancé, fellow *Titanic* voyager, Thure Lundstrom, were married (Thure survived and went on to Los Angeles).

The city of Chicago, destination of numerous emigrants, lost dozens of prospective residents when *Titanic* sank.

Several Irish emigrants perished in the sinking and not only never reached Chicago, but were never recovered: Robert Nemaugh, 26, from County Wexford; John Bourke, 28, his wife, Katherine McHugh Bourke, 32, and John's sister, Miss Mary Bourke, 25; Bridget O'Donoghue, 21, from County Mayo; Joseph Foley, 26, en route to join his brother, Thomas; and Katherine McGowan, 36 (her niece, Annie McGowan, survived).

A number of Swedes aimed to emigrate to the Windy City, but died on *Titanic*: Paul Andreasson, 20, was going to live with his brother; travelling with Paul, but heading for his uncle's residence, was Nils Johansson, 29, who had also talked his fiancée, Olga Lundin, into coming along to visit her sister in Connecticut; unlike Nils, she survived the sinking; Johan Petterson, 25, was crossing the ocean bound for Chicago with his sister, Johanna Ahlin, 40, who was returning to Akeley, Minnesota, but both perished in the sinking; Miss Gerda Dahlberg, 22, from Stockholm, hoped to join her sister, Signa Dahlberg, in Chicago, but *Titanic's* loss ended that plan; and Per Fabian Myhrman, 18, had looked forward to joining his aunt and uncle in Chicago.

A large group of laborers from Bulgaria made Chicago their goal, but all perished and none was recovered: Minko Angheloff, 26, and Khristo Dantchoff, 25, were friends from the same village; Guentcho Bostandyeff, 26, was also lost; Peju Colcheff, 36, Marin Markoff, 35, and Stoytcho Mionoff, 28, had been potters in the old country; Fotio Coleff, 24; Yoto Danoff, 27; Lalio Jonkoff, 23; Kristo Laleff, 23; Penko Naidenoff, 22; Minko Nankoff, 32; Nedeca Petroff, 19; Pentcho Petroff, 29; Alexander Radeff, 27; Todor Sdycoff, 42; Ivan Staneff, 23; Ilia Stoytcheff, 19; and Lalio Todoroff, 23.

Young emigrants from Croatia (then part of the Austro-Hungarian Empire) bound for Chicago all died on *Titanic* and no body was recovered: Luka Cacic, 38; Miss Manda Cacic, 21; Miss Marija Cacic, 30; Grego Cacic, 18; Miss Jeka Oreskovic, 23; Miss Marijo Oreskovic, 20; Luka Oreskovic, 20; Mate Pecruic, 17; Tome Pecruic, 24; and Ivan Strilic, 27.

8 "Read All About It!"

Newspapers were at the heyday of their golden era in 1912. That was one of the final years before electronic media hell broke loose with the development of commercial radio (early 1920's), popular television (late 1940's), satellite communication (1960's) and the Internet computer information highway (1990's).

Newspapers in 1912 were enjoying their virtually exclusive media peak as unique barometers of their times. As such, they recorded the climate of the society from which they sprang. Simultaneously, people grew up relying on the newspaper for all their knowledge of the rapidly changing world.

So the reliability of the responsible press depended upon the integrity of an army of journalists and their sources of information. The predominant serious newspaper, the *New York Times,* popularized its slogans, "All the news that's fit to print," and, lesser known, "It will not soil the breakfast cloth," to counterbalance the "yellow journalism" style (epitomized by William Randolph Hearst's NY *Morning Journal,* with many imitators both then and today) which focused on scare headlines, sensationalistic writing, pseudo-scientific articles, a downplaying or omission of certain truths or facts, a shortage of news interpretation and an abundance of photographs.

◆　　◆　　◆　　◆　　◆　　◆　　◆　　◆

Newspapers indulged in a feeding frenzy when things failed to go smoothly on the maiden voyage of the largest ship in the world.

Initial reports in virtually every newspaper, Great Lakes and otherwise, indicated that *Titanic* had struck an iceberg, but that the ship was heading to Halifax either under her own power or in tow of another ship. Every passenger was reported to be safe or to have been safely removed. This, of course, proved to be tragically incorrect.

Great Lakes newspapers reported the bad news with a wide range of inaccuracy. Sources for these numbers are not known, but that a single event could be reported with such diversity is frightening:

"At Least a Thousand Souls Go Down" --- *Dayton* (OH) *Journal,* April 16, 1912

"...Loss of 1,200 Souls" --- *Chatham* (ON) *Daily News*, April 16, 1912

"...Not Less Than 1,200" --- *Hamilton* (ON) *Spectator,* April 16, 1912

"1,234 Lives Are Lost" -- *Evening Record,* Windsor (ON) April 16, 1912

"1,241 Missing...from *Titanic*" --- *Detroit News*, April 16, 1912

"1,264 Are Drowned" --- *Sault* (St. Marie, ON) *Daily Star*, April 16, 1912

"Nearly 1,300 Souls Perish..." --- *Pittsburgh Leader*, April 16, 1912

"*Titanic* Sinks; 1,300 Drowned" -- *Chicago Daily Tribune*, April 16, 1912.

"Estimates Vary from 1300 to 1800." --- (Toronto) *Globe*, April 16, 1912

"1,304 Lives Lost" --- *Indianapolis Star*, April 16, 1912

"*Titanic*...1,314 Victims" --- *Minneapolis Journal*, April 16, 1912

"1,334 Lives are Lost..." --- *Detroit Free Press*, April 16, 1912

"...Took 1,341 Persons" --- *Columbus* (OH) *Evening Dispatch*, April 16, 1912

"1,350 Are Lost" --- *Calumet* (MI) *News*, April 16, 1912

"*Titanic* Sinks--1,400 Drown" -- *Milwaukee Free Press*, April 16, 1912

"1,490 Awful Death Toll..." --- *Milwaukee Journal*, April 16, 1912

"*Titanic* Sinks; 1,492 Lost" -- *Grand Rapids* (MI) *News*, April 16, 1912

"1,500 Perish...*Titanic*...." --- *Cleveland Plain Dealer*, April 16, 1912

"Over 1,500 Lives Lost" -- *Duluth News Tribune*, April 16, 1912

"1,505 Lives Lost As *Titanic* Sinks" --- *Cleveland Leader*, April 16, 1912

"1,525 Persons Reported Drowned" -- *Sheboygan* (WI) *Press*, April 16, 1912

"1,600 Drown When...*Titanic* Founders" -- Chicago *Inter Ocean*, April 16, 1912

"Loss likely to total 1,800 souls" --- *Globe,* Toronto, Ontario, April 16, 1912

"*Titanic*..., 1,800 Go To Grave" --- *Peoria* (IL) *Herald-Transcript*, April 16, 1912

This was an era of newspaper independence, when finances and attitudes were such that each newspaper sent its own reporter(s) to cover an important event rather than share the reporting of a sole journalist (which is the basis of today's news agencies, institutions which thrived only after the print media found themselves seriously challenged and financially disadvantaged by the rapid development of electronic media). Some newspapers had begun their own wireless surveillance of the airwaves for newsworthy reports, and their sources of information varied in volume, location, intensity, accuracy and reliability.

The initial source of news about *Titanic's* accident came from a few shipboard wireless operations in the North Atlantic which had picked up *Titanic's* distress call and responded. One or two seaboard stations received the wireless messages, or scraps of messages, as weather conditions allowed. What they had, they relayed to other wireless operators, including those run by newspapers and those representing existing news agencies.

Somewhere along the line, journalists (in the loosest sense of that word) attempted to fill in the many missing pieces, often with incorrect or downright ludicrous results: *Titanic* had hit the iceberg head-on, several of them wrote. Many passengers would have been saved had they been wearing lifebelts, concluded others. Two hundred crewmembers working in the bow were instantly killed during the collision, reported a handful. Captain Smith had committed suicide with a revolver as he stood on the bridge of his sinking ship, disclosed some. A few even reported that the *Carpathia* arrived in New York harbor with the *Titanic* survivors, 75 of whom were dead and 15 of whom had gone insane. All of these stories proved false. People upon whom the public depended for the truth communicated lies and inaccuracies instead. For many newspapers, the reporting of the *Titanic* disaster became a case of bad news being reported badly.

Inevitably, newspapers bickered among themselves about which paper had made up which "facts" and how much faster one newspaper was in publicizing stories than another. This era of intense competition witnessed the publication of two or more daily newspapers in numerous cities in the Great Lakes. The Toledo *Blade* competed with the Toledo *News-Bee*. In Youngstown, Ohio, the *Vindicator* and the *Telegram* duked it out, with the latter devoting a large front page story detailing its claim of having presented much of the *Titanic* news to its readers hours ahead of its rival. Detroit saw the *Free Press* and the *News* as the main contenders there. Newspaper-rich Chicago presented a small herd of journalistic competitors, chief among them being the *Tribune*, the *Daily Journal*, and the *Inter Ocean*. In Milwaukee, the *Journal* and the *Free Press* fought each other for circulation increases. Pittsburgh saw its competition among the *Dispatch*, the *Leader,* the *Post*, and the *Press*. In Michigan, the Grand Rapids *Herald* vied with the Grand Rapids *News*. Even little Manistee, Michigan, offered its readership rival viewpoints in the *Daily News* and the *Daily Advocate*. It was the golden age of newspapers, when the number of different publications appearing daily in the U.S.A. was well over 2,000 (that number has fallen to about 1,500 today) and about 170 in Canada (under 100 today).

The competition for readership was intense, with no possible advantage going unused or unpublicized. Fact hounds at *The Globe* in Toronto denounced many American and several Canadian newspapers which had published graphic details of the *Titanic* disaster, descriptions they had attributed to the wireless operator on board the steamer, *Bruce*. When the *Bruce* arrived at St. John's, Newfoundland, its personnel claimed ignorance of details -- prompting a smug *Globe* to proclaim in large letters, "Another Falsehood Nailed."

DESECRATION

Above: The publication of incorrect *Titanic* information riled some Great Lakes newspapers to the point where the reporting of falsehoods itself became news. In the drawing above, the Toronto *Globe* of April 19, 1912, denounced as "fake" the extensive sensationalistic and outrightly wrong statements circulated among the public by some news distributors. *Below, left:* The *Detroit Free Press,* on April 19, 1912, published this statement claiming reliable news. *Below, right:* Some newspapers, such as the *Cleveland Leader* on April 19, 1912, offered themselves as public service agents for anyone seeking information about *Titanic* survivors.   ALL: AUTHOR'S COLLECTION.

RELIABLE NEWS

The Detroit Free Press

today presents its readers the latest reliable news of the

Titanic Disaster

The Free Press has the New York Sun News Service and the Associated Press service, the two most reliable news-gathering agencies in America. Their reports on the disaster at sea which has shocked the civilized world have been sane, conservative and truthful from day to day.

It has not been necessary to deny or modify their reports, which have met continuous verification.

The Free Press does not lend its columns to faking, falsifying news agencies.

It does not employ the Hearst news-manufacturing agency, to furnish fiction to bewilder, shock and deceive its readers.

The Free Press will continue to present on the Titanic disaster and on all other important happenings only

RELIABLE NEWS

LET LEADER GET NEWS OF SURVIVORS FOR YOU

DID you have a relative or a friend aboard the Titanic whose fate you wish to learn? Is some one dear to you aboard the Carpathia, which docked at New York last night?

Let the Leader help you in getting word from them or about them.

The Leader has a staff of men in New York at your disposal. They will look up your loved ones if any of them were aboard the Carpathia, and the Leader will keep you informed of their condition. Telegraphic information on their condition will be transmitted immediately through the Leader office to you.

If you live in the city, or in northern Ohio, call the city editor of the Leader at Main 4747 on the Bell telephone, or Erie 2 on the Cuyahoga. Tell him whom you wish to hear about.

The Leader will call you up at any hour up to 3 a. m. when word is received. If you do not live in the city the Leader will call you by long distance telephone. If you have no telephone any message will be mailed you, free, by special delivery.

The Leader men in New York met the Carpathia last night and their first efforts were bent towards getting Cleveland and northern Ohio bound survivors to places of shelter. They began work on ascertaining names of survivors and names of those who were lost. The Leader will furnish this information to you

And Then There Was One. The White Star Line advertised its trans-Atlantic crossings in many Great Lakes newspapers. Early in 1912, the company proudly announced the sailing schedules of "The Largest Steamers in the World," the *Olympic* and the *Titanic*. Sadly, one name had to be removed after April 15, 1912, and the word "steamers" became joylessly singular. These ads appeared in the *Cleveland Leader* on April 11, 1912 *(above)* and April 16, 1912 *(below)*.   AUTHOR'S COLLECTION.

The incredible variety of styles as well as facts in Great Lakes newspaper headlines announcing the *Titanic* tragedy provided potential for plenty of confusion. However, this was an era when most people stayed devoted to a single newspaper, reading it, and only it, faithfully. Those curious few

who craved a second opinion strayed beyond the scope of a single source of information into a wildly diversified world. AUTHOR'S COLLECTION.

Sources of *Titanic* news stories varied, but the main one remained the company which owned the ship. H. G. Thorley, the Toronto agent of the White Star Line, was relayed the following telegram received by the New York office from *Titanic's* sister ship, *Olympic*: "*Carpathia* reached *Titanic* position at daybreak. Found boats and wreckage only. *Titanic* sank about 2.30 a.m., in 41.16 N.; 50.14 W. All her boats accounted for containing about 675 souls saved, crew and passengers included. Nearly all saved women and children. Leyland liner *Californian* remained and searched exact position of disaster. Loss likely total 1800 souls." Thorley immediately shared this information with the city's newspapers.

The people of Toronto and other cities on the Great Lakes were sponges absorbing the press' saturation of *Titanic* news. On the street, in the streetcars, in the restaurants and cafés, indeed in every place where there was light, the only topic being read about and discussed was the terrible *Titanic* disaster. The *Toronto World* put an extra edition on the streets at 10:30 P.M. on Monday night, April 15th, the day *Titanic* sank; within 30 minutes, all 10,000 copies had been sold.

Since the White Star Line and the *Carpathia* had imposed a news blackout until the arrival of the rescue ship back in New York, newspapers scrambled to find three-and-a-half days' worth of copy to to keep the news of *Titanic* in the forefront.

Anything about *Titanic* found itself onto the pages of the desperate press endeavoring to feed its hungry public. Many articles postulated the dollar worth of the numerous "American Money Kings" who were aboard *Titanic*. Marine department officials were contacted to give information about how deep the ocean happened to be where *Titanic* sank. Experts gave scientific evidence suggesting that the ocean's water pressure at depth might keep *Titanic* from sinking to the bottom. Many newspapers on the Canadian side of the Great Lakes repeated the Canadian Press dispatch from April 10th, describing *Titanic's* near collision with the American Line steamer, *New York*, as the larger ship departed Southampton on her maiden voyage. Long lists of "Notable Marine Disasters" spanning the previous century found their way into print. Sidebars entitled "Facts About the Foundered Steamer, *Titanic*" gave readers dozens of ship's dimensions, tonnages, and crew and passenger numbers. In the Great Lakes, filler material tied to *Titanic* focused on the comparative safety features of passenger-carrying ships on these fresh waters. Nostalgia was printed. Captain Timothy Kelley in Manitowoc recalled the days when he captained "the biggest and finest sailing vessel on the lakes, the *Wells Burt*, 'the *Titanic* of the waters' at the time." (This was really stretching the truth; the *Wells Burt* was only 201 feet long, and sank in Lake Michigan on May 20, 1883 with all 11 hands lost). Aspiring poets in the Great Lakes, emotionally affected by this vastly dramatic marine tragedy, found publication in their local newspaper. Anyone who knew of someone with even the most remote possibility of being on board *Titanic* was interviewed. People who had seen icebergs during a North Atlantic crossing years before became interview fodder. Survivors of shipwrecks from the late 1800's found their rehashed stories and personal opinions coveted by the press.

The *Pontiac* (Michigan) *Press Gazette* blatantly let the public know that "...very little definite information has as yet been received by news agencies, the great portion of matter appearing in the metropolitan papers being written in New York by graphic newswriters who draw on their imagination...."

♦   ♦   ♦   ♦   ♦   ♦   ♦   ♦

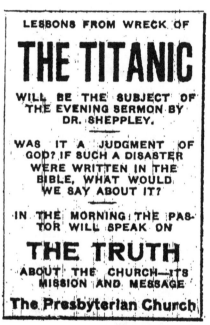

COLD COMFORT.

For the first Sunday after *Titanic's* sinking, newspapers in the Great Lakes busily took advertising for the upcoming church sermons. Their universal theme that Sabbath was inescapable. This ad appeared in the April 20, 1912, *Manitowoc* (WI) *Daily Herald.* Before long, humorous iceberg and shipwreck cartoons appeared, such as this one in the *Manistee* (MI) *Daily News* on April 22, 1912, which caused sensitive people to wince.

Passenger (nervously) — Captain, what would be the result if this boat should strike an iceberg?

Captain—It would probably shiver its timbers.

AUTHOR'S COLLECTION.

♦   ♦   ♦   ♦   ♦   ♦   ♦   ♦

Racial prejudices, stereotypes and slurs, totally politically incorrect today, but common and accepted then, appeared rampant in North American newspapers, including those in the Great Lakes region, early in the 20th century. Sample headlines include "Negroes Arrested for

Stealing Fat Chickens of Hungarian" (*Peoria, IL, Herald*, April 29, 1912), "Jap Liner Wrecked" (*Rockford, IL, Republic*, April 22, 1912), "Cuban Negroes Destroy Town" (*Joliet, IL, News*, June 3, 1912), "Murdered Girl in Love with 'Chink'" (*Detroit Free Press,* June 20, 1909) and "Jewish Women in Meat Riots" (*Joliet, IL, News*)

Some of the headlines and reporting were blatant, tough and insensitive: "Writes Suicide Note, But Is Still Here" (*Dayton, OH, Journal*, April 28, 1912), and "Baby's Hands Cut Off, But Mother Held To It" (*Columbus, OH, Evening Dispatch*, April 19, 1912), and "Drives Nail into Skull; Is Alive" (*Detroit News*, April 22, 1912).

Even 1912 advertisements are questionable by today's standards (and today's medical knowledge): "Gin Pills Stopped the [Rheumatism] Pain" (*Sarnia, ON Daily Observer*, April 30, 1912), "The Peevish Child Needs a Laxative."(*Joliet, IL, News*, June 4, 1912), and "Develop Your Bust in Fifteen Days" (*Aurora, IL, Daily Beacon-News*, April 27, 1912). Some things never change.

Some headlines are comical, at least in hindsight: "Dynamite Blasts Improve the Land" (*Joliet, IL, News*, June 3, 1912), "Chickens 'Treated' with Electricity Grow Faster Than the Ordinary Way" (*Columbus, OH, Evening Dispatch*, April 28, 1912), "Beutenmueller Denies He is Dead" (*Joliet, IL, News,* June 14, 1912), "When Is a Girl Too Old for Spanking?" (*Sarnia, ON Observer*, May 2, 1912), "Two Divorced Persons Wed" (*Aurora, IL, Beacon-News*, April 24, 1912).

With this cornucopia of offbeat topics, tactless reporting, and heady writing that had the subtlety of a blowtorch, all laced with the accepted high level of prejudice, consider these statements which appeared in a Cleveland newspaper on April 21, 1912, under the headline, "Ridicules Law of 'Save Women First'": "A man is a more valuable member of a community and of a nation than is a woman. I believe in looking at the thing in a cold, impartial light. Why should a man like Maj. Butt have to die with the *Titanic* to save an immigrant woman?... Col. Astor was a man of power. I believe that every man on that boat who died did what he thought best. They were heroes in every sense of the word. They regarded obedience to the unwritten law of the sea to be their duty. But the law is wrong." Only the fact that the speaker was a woman, Mrs. Alexander Preston, saved those utterances from total condemnation, even by 1912's standards.

One ominous headline in the *Toronto World* proclaimed "Death Toll is at Least 1312,...Only 328 of First Cabin Saved." The word "only" describing "328" was incredibly misleading. There were only 329 "First Cabin" passengers on board *Titanic* to begin with!

A bulletin originating in New York, widely published in Great Lakes newspapers, sensationally reported: "Captain Smith shot himself on the bridge; the chief engineer likewise committed suicide, and three Italians were shot to death in the struggle for the lifeboats. The passenger who first told of the captain's end said that two attempts were necessary before he succeeded in ending his life. Brother officers wrested a revolver from his hands in the library, but he broke away, rushed to the bridge, and shot himself thru [sic] the mouth." This unidentified passenger (or the reporter taking his story) imaginatively and unbelievably placed himself in the ship's library as an eyewitness, then failed to explain where Captain Smith found a second revolver which he took to the bridge where, again in front of this same witness, the captain dramatically took his life. This story is unlikely.

Emotive language was already well known as a propaganda device used by fickle journalists. The glowing superlatives originally assigned by the press to show the palatial *Titanic* in a positive light did an about-face, exemplified best by the first word in the headline appearing in the *Grand Rapids* (Michigan) *Herald*, among others, on April 16, 1912: "<u>Monster</u> *Titanic* was Regarded as...."

In a glaring example of journalistic error, one Toronto newspaper, listing "Noted Passengers on the Steamer," described Thomas Andrews, the chief designer of *Titanic*, as "a prominent sporting writer of Milwaukee [who] publishes an annual boxing review."

♦   ♦   ♦   ♦   ♦   ♦   ♦   ♦

Some of the most controversial newspaper reporting in the Great Lakes area resulted from statements made by the outspoken survivor from Toronto, Major Peuchen, who did not mince the words he reportedly spoke to the press after *Carpathia* landed.

"I do not wish to be misunderstood. The loss of the *Titanic* was due to criminal carelessness in running at full speed thru [sic] the ice with a new crew, despite the fact that he had received repeated warnings by wireless of the vast ice field and bergs that lay in his path. Capt. Smith, notwithstanding these numerous warnings, and the fact that the *Titanic* was then amidst the ice, Capt. Smith, the one man above all that should have been at his post, was quietly and leisurely partaking of a hearty dinner with a party of friends. They were in the restaurant, and were apparently having an enjoyable and social dinner.

"The hour was late and on a Sunday night. Had Capt. Smith been on the bridge, I am confident that the horrible accident would have been averted," Peuchen stated in a way reflecting his disgust.

"The captain was at dinner with Bruce Ismay and a number of millionaires for more than three hours that night....

"I was delighted with the ship and its magnificence, but disappointed to find Captain Smith in command. I didn't like his record with the *Olympic*, and said so. Then we had that accident an hour after leaving Southampton. That bothered me...."

Loyal subjects of the King back in Canada stood shocked at Peuchen's accusations leveled against Captain Smith and the crew of *Titanic*. Attempts at damage control were swift. In Lindsay, Ontario, just north of Toronto, the *Watchman-Warder* newspaper printed the recollections of one of its citizens, William Dundas, who had crossed the ocean on several vessels under the command of Captain Smith.

"Captain Smith of the *Titanic* is remembered as a great old Britisher who always wore a small silk Union Jack on the lapel of his coat when he brought his ship into New York harbor. The obligation to go down with his ship was part of his very life. So with the higher officers of the navigating crew; they were captives to the eradition [sic, probably means "tradition"] of their noble calling. The hour of danger found each man ready and each man at his station."

The same issue of the newspaper, the *Watchman-Warder* printed a letter to the editor bluntly entitled "Major Peuchen Talks Too Much." In a Toronto paper, that same letter appeared under the heading, "When Silence Would Be Golden." More criticism followed. The frowning public was having its go at Peuchen.

Peuchen failed to understand the disapproval launched at him. " I am surprised at the statements being made by people in this city [Toronto] and elsewhere regarding my conduct," he lamented. " I cannot understand them. They suggest in their remarks that I did not act as I should have done, and that I should have drowned with the other men. I do not see how they could make such statements. I did all I could do. I helped the men with the boats. What would they have done in the same circumstances?"

"I was not the first man to leave the vessel," he added more emphatically, with increased volume and agitation in his voice. "Nine boats were lowered before I left, and they all contained some men...."

Peuchen also tried to back-pedal by claiming that he had never made any harsh statements about Captain Smith, and that any newspaper that published otherwise misquoted him.

He would soon have another chance at high-profile commentary.

Major Peuchen reached his Toronto home on Saturday morning, April 20, 1912. The next day, he received a telegram from Senator William A. Smith, Chairman of the Congressional Investigation Committee which had just moved from New York to Washington:

"Are you willing to come to Washington to testify on Monday before the Congressional Committee regarding the wreck of the steamer *Titanic*?"

Major Peuchen realized that the senator, like millions of others, had undoubtedly read the damning remarks attributed to him in the newspapers. But this was a request, not a command, and Peuchen saw this as his chance to set the record straight and possibly tone down the harsh criticism he was hearing about himself in his home town.

He left Toronto on the five P.M. train for Washington, D.C., only 32 hours after he had returned home from *Titanic's* sinking.

9 The Inquiries

Bruce Ismay, president of the White Star Line which had owned *Titanic,* had stepped into a lifeboat and survived the sinking. On board the *Carpathia,* he kept himself locked up behind closed cabin doors, dazed and shocked about what had transpired. Perhaps he hid in shame for having survived when so many women and children had perished. Perhaps he felt self-preservation, concerned that harm might come to him if he mingled with the other survivors. He probably felt all of these things, and more. Physical survival was also on his mind when, through telegrams sent from the *Carpathia's* wireless room, he unsuccessfully attempted to arrange the stealthy and quick return to England of himself and *Titanic's* surviving crewmembers on board another White Star Line ship departing New York before they even set foot on United States soil. Frontier justice was not his cup of tea.

Bruce Ismay almost certainly believed that the United States was a nation of mob rule compared to civilized and dignified Great Britain. Formerly separate colonies belonging to Great Britain, the states had united in defying the Mother Country with open, armed rebellion. Ismay's escape plan having been thwarted, he felt like a captured soldier of the king in the hands of the wild and wicked colonials.

Bruce Ismay was cognizant of the American psyche which appeared tolerant of small bands of citizens taking the law into their own hands and publicly executing prisoners without due process of law. Perhaps he later read the newspaper account, published the day after his arrival in New York, of the man who was lynched by a mob in Montana. Bruce Ismay, conscious of the public's need for a scapegoat in the many *Titanic* deaths, squirmed uncomfortably.

Personally, Ismay felt that he was a mere bureaucrat, far enough removed from controlling *Titanic's* physical operation that he would be excluded from the merciless maxim of the sea which states that the captain who loses his ship must not himself survive. Publicly, Ismay was the manager of the foreign company which owned *Titanic,* and he had survived the sinking in which so many U.S. citizens had perished. Now here he was, a virtual prisoner in the United States, about to be grilled mercilessly in an inquiry seeking to establish cause and guilt. He was understandably nervous about the American sense of justice.

DISOBEYING ORDERS!

This political cartoon, from the *Chicago Inter-Ocean* of April 22, 1912, took aim at the fact that Ismay kept to himself in a stateroom on board the rescue ship, *Carpathia*. However, Ismay was never guilty of "Disobeying Orders" (as captioned) when summoned to testify before the Senate members. But powerful images and captions such as this one inflamed the enraged public with the wrong impression that Ismay was antagonistic and hostile.   AUTHOR'S COLLECTION.

The first day of the inquiry was Friday, April 19, 1912, the day after the *Carpathia* had landed. Like a man walking on thin ice, Bruce Ismay worded his answers carefully, much to the frustration of Senator Smith and the media. One Toronto newspaper, abandoning traditional support of all things British, made a mockery of Ismay's responses with an article entitled "Things That Ismay Did Not Observe":

"'I saw no passengers in sight when I entered the lifeboat.'
'I did not see what happened to the lifeboats.'
'I did not look to see after leaving the *Titanic* whether she broke in two.'
'I did not look to see if there was a panic.'
'After I left the bridge, I did not see the captain.'
'I saw nothing of any explosion.'
'I saw no struggle, no confusion.'
'I did not recognize any passengers on the *Titanic* as she sank.'
'I saw no women waiting as I entered the lifeboat.'"

Ismay's answers were understandably guarded, for he was aware of the human ability to translate virtually any word or action in two ways, one positive and one negative, dependent upon the interpreter's desired outcome, with decidedly opposite consequences. His responses foiled and frustrated the senator from Michigan.

◆　　◆　　◆　　◆　　◆　　◆　　◆　　◆

Senator William Smith of Michigan was one politician who clearly feared the power of big business. He strongly opposed the J.P. Morgan trusts, including the International Mercantile Marine (I.M.M.) which owned the White Star Line, the British company that built and operated *Titanic*. One way to diminish Morgan's power, Smith calculated, was to open the owner of *Titanic* to lawsuits from U.S. citizens by proving negligence on the part of owners or crew. Ismay had not proven vulnerable, but Smith would force him to stay in the United States "for further possible testimony" as long as possible.

Although Smith came from Michigan, which later became known as "the Great Lakes state," he was a farmboy from the interior. His limited knowledge of maritime matters may have included the fact that the object of his destruction actually had a ship named after him, the steamer, *J. Pierpont Morgan,** launched at South Chicago on the shores of Lake Michigan on April 21, 1906, for Morgan's United States Steel Corporation, and lauded at that time as "the largest craft in fresh water." Such a visible showcase of Morgan's success and financial strength would surely have irked the populist senator.

◆　　◆　　◆　　◆　　◆　　◆　　◆　　◆

Maryland Senator Rayner, who was not part of the *Titanic* inquiry, delivered a vigorous indictment in the Senate on April 19, 1912, of J.

---

* Built by the Chicago Shipbuilding Company as hull number 68, this huge steel freighter measured 601' x 58' x 32' and hauled immense cargoes of iron ore to the hungry steel mills of Cleveland and other southern Great Lakes cities for many years. The aging vessel was sold to Canadian interests in 1966, who changed her name to *Heron Bay*. This bulk freighter was finally scrapped in November, 1978.

Bruce Ismay and the entire White Star Line board of directors. But it was Ismay, "the officer primarily responsible for the whole disaster, who had reached his destination in safety and unharmed," who stood trapped in the clutches of this Senate investigation.

AMERICA'S KING OF FINANCE
WHO IS 75 YEARS OF AGE TODAY

J. Pierpont Morgan, sketched from a recent photograph.

HON. WILLIAM A. SMITH,

J.P. Morgan, the richest man in the world, had organized the re-supplying of the U.S. government's depleted gold reserve in 1895, thereby relieving a Treasury crisis. But by 1912, politicians feared his power, and federal agencies investigated his operations. Morgan, the Ultimate Achiever of the American Dream, now watched the American government trying to separate him from his success. One of the companies in Morgan's trusts was the White Star Line which owned *Titanic*. Morgan was scheduled to sail on her maiden voyage, but ill health forced him to cancel. Morgan turned 75 on April 17, 1912, two days after *Titanic* sank. It was the final birthday for the aging industrialist; he died in Rome on March 31, 1913. Michigan Senator William Smith hoped to weaken Morgan's power by trapping Ismay or *Titanic's* officers or crew into admitting negligence, thereby opening the door for lawsuits against Morgan's interests.   AUTHOR'S COLLECTION.

"While there are no civil or criminal remedies available in the American courts," Senator Rayner loudly pointed out, "criminal and civil suits could be brought in the British courts." Then, realizing that he sounded as if he were surrendering control, he lashed out, "But a Congressional committee has absolute authority to subpoena everyone connected with the disaster, and if anyone should refuse to answer questions, he could be indicted and imprisoned for contempt." One way or another, Rayner was determined to demonstrate the politicians' power over the captive Ismay.

HEAD OF WHITE STAR LINE AND SENATORS
INVESTIGATING LOSS OF LIFE ON THE TITANIC

The U.S. Senate *"Titanic* Subcommittee" of the Committee on Commerce consisted of, clockwise from upper left, Michigan Senator Smith (Chairman), Ohio Senator Theodore Burton, California Senator George Perkins, Nevada Senator Francis Newlands, Oregon Senator Jonathon Bourne, Jr., and Florida Senator Duncan Fletcher. Missing is North Carolina Senator Furnifold Simmons. None of these men was known for his maritime expertise. Target Bruce Ismay is in the center.   AUTHOR'S COLLECTION.

"If this had happened on an American vessel," Rayner continued with increased agitation, "there would be no question that an indictment would be found and if the facts were sustained, the officers of the company could be convicted of manslaughter if not of murder because the evidence is clear that the vessel was not properly equipped with efficient life saving apparatus."

Then suddenly, Rayner exploded, "I care not what the rules of the English admiralty are!... All civilized nations will applaud the criminal prosecution of the management of this [White Star] line. If they can be made to suffer, no sympathy will go out to them...."

The actual participants in the *Titanic* tragedy were not as volatile.

A total of 82 witnesses provided evidence at the hearings, which ran from April 19 to May 25, 1912; 53 were British subjects (mostly officers and crew of *Titanic*), and the remaining 29 were citizens of

THIS LOOKOUT USES GLASSES

Uncle Sam keeps careful watch using binoculars to ensure public safety in this art from the *Chicago Daily News*, April 30, 1912. "This Lookout Uses Glasses," besides being a jab at the fact that the *Titanic* lookouts had not been equipped with binoculars (which, by error, had been locked up and the key was with an officer on another ship), depicted the idealistically protective work of the Senate investigation committee.   AUTHOR'S COLLECTION.

the United States. Nine witnesses were passengers residing in, or heading for, the Great Lakes region.

Major Arthur Peuchen of Toronto was a British subject who had been travelling in First Class, and not only was he the first Great Lakes area witness, but also the first *Titanic* passenger to appear before the Senate committee. On Tuesday, April 23, 1912, the fourth day of the hearings, Peuchen told his story, but now with emotional control, which had been lacking five days earlier when he first spoke to the press. Peuchen did an about-face; he had only praise for the late Captain Edward Smith. This time, he vented against quartermaster Robert Hichens for refusing to pick up any survivors in their lifeboat.

The Bishops postponed their drive back home to Dowagiac, Michigan, so they could testify. Senator Smith undoubtedly felt a kinship to them, as he was born and raised in their town, Dowagiac. On the tenth day of the hearings, April 30, 1912, they testified separately.

Helen Bishop provided no earth-shattering information, but she did defensively state twice that her husband had been pushed into the lifeboat with her. She pointed out that the conduct of the crew was "beyond criticism. It was perfect," and she praised one of the crew who, even though he had lost a brother on *Titanic,* "did the best he could to keep the women feeling cheerful all the rest of the time."

Dickinson Bishop confessed that he didn't think he could add anything to his wife's brief statement. Prodded by Senator Smith, Dickinson related information which he had "heard from some other people," but which he himself had not witnessed, about *Titanic's* crew experiencing trouble closing a watertight door on E deck. Smith expressed satisfaction at having received this hearsay information.

What tidbits of information they added to the inquiry's pot were hardly worth the Bishops' drive to Washington. In the end, their testimonies amounted to about three typewritten pages each, but their trifling statements did not assist Senator Smith in attaining his goal.

On the twelfth day of hearings, 25-year-old Olaus Abelseth, a steerage passenger heading for Minneapolis, related his harrowing account of jumping off *Titanic's* stern right when it sank, and swimming to a lifeboat. He testified that steerage passengers had ample opportunity to reach the decks without being held back.

On, the fourteenth day of the hearings, Senator Smith read an affidavit from Mahala Douglas of Minneapolis. She related her experiences the night *Titanic* sank, stating that the officers were "kind," but "inefficient" and "unseamanlike" were words used to describe the crew. But her most damning disclosure was the claim that Emily Ryerson had told her that Bruce Ismay had directly said to her that they would speed up, not slow down, when they reached the ice field.

But Emily Ryerson, of Cooperstown, New York, in her affidavit read on the fifteenth day of the hearings, May 10, 1912, made absolutely no mention of Bruce Ismay's dismissal of ice warnings.

Daisy Minahan of Green Bay, Wisconsin, provided an affidavit which Smith also read aloud on the fifteenth day of the hearings. She criticized both Captain Smith for spending hours at dinner instead of being on the bridge, and "blasphemous" Officer Lowe in her lifeboat for, among other things, not picking up survivors immediately.

First Class passenger Norman Chamber, 27, of Ithaca, New York, also testified, mainly telling how he and his wife boarded a lifeboat.

Catherine Crosby of Milwaukee provided an affidavit describing her experiences, berating mainly the poorly-equipped lifeboats.

◆　　◆　　◆　　◆　　◆　　◆　　◆　　◆

Cleveland, Ohio, largest city on the shores of Lake Erie, was the scene of a bombshell which dropped onto the Senate committee investigating the loss of *Titanic*. A German named Luis Klein, claiming to have been a sailor on board the doomed ship, told an incredible story to the press. He vividly described diving overboard just as the ship and the iceberg crashed. He swam a short distance and managed to climb upon a cake of floating ice, where he lay half frozen until picked up by a lifeboat the next morning. As implausible as this story is, the press and the authorities in Cleveland fell for it. But the part that really raised eyebrows was Klein's description of the moments before *Titanic* hit the iceberg. According to his disclosure, stewards gave the sailors on deck champagne from partly emptied bottles, leftovers from a party, and Klein insisted that many of them felt the effects. He clearly stated that the sole lookout in the crowsnest was asleep for some time before *Titanic* collided with the iceberg.

Many newspapers picked up this news story from the wires, and shocked senators in Washington took action. A summons for Klein reached the office of the U.S. Attorney in Cleveland early Sunday afternoon, with the order, "Please serve process on Luis Klein, Cleveland, O., to appear before subcommittee on commerce, United States senate...forthwith...." Another telegram followed quickly, directing that a U.S. marshall be in charge of bringing Klein to Washington.

Then, just as mysteriously as he had appeared, Luis Klein disappeared. His imaginative story and his picture were printed in the newspaper, but it turned out that he had never been on board *Titanic*.

◆　　◆　　◆　　◆　　◆　　◆　　◆　　◆

Some of Senator Smith's methods and statements were questionable, to say the least. At one point, he openly charged that an attempt to shape the course of the inquiry had been made and would not be tolerated by the committee. He exonerated the officers and crew of *Titanic,* but gave a veiled hint that his shaft was aimed at Bruce Ismay.

"HERE'S TO THE RECORD."

When a man in Cleveland, Ohio, claiming to have been a *Titanic* sailor, strongly accused the *Titanic* lookout, as well as other crewmembers, of being intoxicated at the time of the collision, outrage flared, particularly with a *Detroit News* artist whose resulting work appeared in print on April 23, 1912. The "record" refers to the speed record some claim *Titanic* was trying to set on her maiden voyage. A competing newspaper published a deploring letter to the editor which stated, in part, "Even after this story [of Klein claiming drunkenness on the part of *Titanic's* crew] had been denied and discredited, a cartoon with the story as its theme appeared on the first page of the evening edition of the *Detroit News*....Of all the yellow journal impositions that have been foisted on a long suffering public in the past year, this is the most abominable...." AUTHOR'S COLLECTION.

When Ismay demanded to be put back on the stand to respond to this new allegation, Smith refused, offering no explanation, although he was further agitated by the apparent female fascination with the dashing, sophisticated Ismay, and the presence of "scores of beautifully dressed women [who] stood for more than two hours in front of the committee room waiting for the doors to be opened....Women scrambled into the committee room, taking the seats that had been re-

Above: Newspapers in the Great Lakes region maintained their readers' interest in *Titanic,* which had become a hot commodity that sold thousands of newspapers, with as many banner headlines and front-page stories as possible. Attempts to make Ismay the scapegoat, although ill-aimed, continually kept the story of the tragedy in the forefront. One Pittsburgh newspaper published "Phrenological Developments of Ismay" with a photo of a dozen arrows pointing to various parts of his head, explaining what each meant; he did not fare well. A Toledo newspaper reported that the word "Ismay" had become a verb, and gave the example of a bartender warning a troublesome customer, "You jest gently 'Ismay' outen dis heah place while the 'Ismayin'' is good." Some boys in one Great Lakes city reportedly gave the name "Ismay" to a tree "because it was one of the first to leaf." *Below:* The press brutally crucified Ismay in this front-page item published in a major Great Lakes newspaper on April 20, 1912. This propaganda image of a drowning victim's hand pointing to Bruce Ismay with the accusation, "This Is The Man," had the potential to light dangerous hate fires under readers.   AUTHOR'S COLLECTION.

THIS IS THE MAN

served for the press and even occupying those around the long table where the investigators sit...." One newspaper, under the headlines, "Women Jam Room" and "Committee Disgusted with Feminine Crowd, Pushing Their Way Into Seats and Disturbing All," described the situation without even attempting an explanation: "Throughout the hearing Ismay has been the center of all eyes," reported the *Grand Rapids* (Michigan) *News* on April 24, 1912, "Whenever he enters the room the spectators jump to their feet and stare at him. Little attention is paid to witnesses, the majority of the women studying the features of the steamship company's chief..."

♦   ♦   ♦   ♦   ♦   ♦   ♦   ♦

Generally, academics absolved Ismay of any blame. The University of Michigan's Dean M.E. Cooley claimed that the *Titanic* tragedy was the result of a speed-mad America, and that although *Titanic* was a British ship, she was a British ship demanded by the American people. And the American people had to pay the price.

"Civilization is getting precisely what it demands," Cooley argued, "and civilization is paying the price. Great God, what a price! Fundamentally we as a people are responsible for that accident, and we must not attempt to put the blame on any individual. The *Titanic* is the outgrowth of the times,.... You can't hold Captain Smith responsible, nor can you hold J. Bruce Ismay responsible for that disaster, any more than you can hold managers or officers of any company responsible when contributing things the public demands.... The same thing which demanded the *Titanic,* has demanded 18-hour trains from Chicago to New York, and the trains being provided, the people must pay the fare whether it be in dollars or in human lives...."

Even U.S. politicians, such as North Dakota Senator McCumber, sympathized with Ismay. "Yesterday one man connected with the *Titanic* disaster was tried, convicted, sentenced and executed here in the senate of the United States," McCumber declared, "and as a senator and a citizen I desire to register my protest against the trial of anyone connected with the running of the boat without fair, honest and full consideration. The Lord knows that the habit of condemning public men without a hearing is bad enough, but it is not fraught with so much danger as our condemnation in a crisis when public feeling demands a victim. At such time we certainly should suspend judgment."

Great Lakes Captain Thomas G. Ellis wrote on April 22, 1912, from Windsor, Ontario, to the editor of a Detroit newspaper, that "...The cartoons and press comments putting the whole fault of the accident on J. Bruce Ismay are deplorable. The ignorance of the public as to the laws governing licensed officers and vessels licensed to carry passengers make the situation far worse. If Mr. Ismay were lynched, the press of the country would be entirely to blame, for they have done nothing but incite the public to wrath...." A pastor publicly defended Ismay in the Detroit press on April 22, 1912.

In the end, Bruce Ismay was exonerated by the inquiry of the charge that he had influenced *Titanic's* speed, or that he or any of the ship's officers or crew had been negligent in their duties. Captain Edward J. Smith, the late *Titanic* master, was held directly responsible.

Ismay returned home to England and faced the British inquiry, under Lord Mersey's Board of Trade, which, much to his relief, was more sympathetic to his position and which also ultimately held that

Bruce Ismay had several times requested to be allowed to return to England (besides his business responsbilities there, his wife was ill), but Senator Smith denied permission, stating a possible need to question Ismay further at a later date. Ismay was finally allowed to board a ship for England on May 2, 1912, and, although exonerated by the Senate committee, he left in undeserved disgrace, never to return. Ismay was unfairly pilloried in the USA right to the moment of his departure. He fared better at the British inquiry and with the British press. AUTHOR'S COLLECTION.

ISMAY STARTS HOME FEELING VERY TIRED.—*Newspaper Headline.*

Captain Smith could not divest himself of the responsibilities entailed by his position as captain. The British strongly denounced the American, Captain Stanley Lord, of the steamer, *Californian,* which was stopped for the night at the ice field's edge only about ten miles (about a 40-minute run) from *Titanic,* for being alerted to the distress signals yet failing to respond; they could have saved all on board.

Bruce Ismay went into semi-retirement in 1912 and lived the rest of his life in quiet isolation, alternating between his homes in London and Ireland, until his death at the age of 74 on October 17, 1937.

10 The Great Lakes White Star Line

While Britain's White Star Line produced immense ships for trans-Atlantic service, another shipping company named the White Star Line specialized in passenger service in the middle of the Great Lakes.

With its head office in Detroit, Michigan, the smaller White Star Line was totally unrelated to the famous one across the saltwater sea. Their company burgees, depicting a five-pointed white star on a red background, were quite similar, but the Great Lakes version placed its star within a blue circle. Also similar was the color scheme of the companies' smokestacks: black on top and buff below.

Like its counterparts in the saltwater seas, the White Star Line's excursion ships were among the most famous and the most beloved of all those in the inland seas.

◆　◆　◆　◆　◆　◆　◆　◆

In the 1850's, the shipping of passengers and freight on the St. Clair River was the domain of Detroit's Ward family. Their steamboat empire was challenged in the 1880's by a modest company named the Star Line. In 1888, Captain Darius Cole of Bay City, Michigan, took over the fledgling company and renamed it the Star-Cole Line. That same year, a firm called the Red Star Line virtually took over the Detroit-to-Toledo (Ohio) shipping route. In the mid-1890's, the Star-Cole and the Red Star Lines reached an agreement to form a new company.

An excursion steamer on the Detroit River.

The White Star Line formally came into existence on April 4, 1896, with capital of $85,000 (more than $2,000,000 in today's dollars). Aaron Adolph Parker (1843-1914) was the company's first President, with John Pridgeon, Jr. (1852-1929, and a past mayor of Detroit) as Vice-President, and Charles F. Bielman (1859-1920) as Secretary and Traffic Manager.

These men were so well-known in Great Lakes maritime circles that they already had freighters named after them at the time they started the White Star Line.

The new company's first steamer was the *City of Toledo*.

The line operated under a pooling agreement with the Star-Cole Line and the Red Star Line during the seasons of 1896, 1897 and 1898. But in January, 1899, the White Star Line purchased Tashmoo Park, with its large picnic area and dock at the south end of beautiful Harsen's Island in the St. Clair River. So large were the shipboard throngs of excursionists heading to this new park in the St. Clair River that the company's stock more than doubled in value by year's end.

On December 30, 1899, the White Star Line was responsible for launching the last Great Lakes ship of the 1800's, a sidewheel passenger steamer destined to become their company flagship. This vessel was designed by noted naval architect Frank E. Kirby, who later designed the *City of Detroit III*. The White Star Line decided to name this 320-foot steel steamer with the 72-foot beam the *Tashmoo*, after their island resort in the St. Clair River. The original Tashmoo was the son of a Chippewa Indian chief, and the name meant "tall and noble," and the graceful, sturdy ship was certainly that. But the *Tashmoo* was not just another pretty hull; the ship's inclined expansion engines, capable of producing 3,150 horsepower, propelled the steamer at over 20 miles an hour when fully loaded at her 3,500-passenger day-excursion capacity. This was quite a Great Lakes feat!

The new steel steamer, *Greyhound*, with its capacity for 3,368 day excursionists, was added to the White Star Line fleet in early 1902. By the end of the 1902 season, the company was worth more than six times its 1896 value.

With funds to increase the fleet size, the White Star Line purchased the steel steamer, *Pennsylvania*, on October 11, 1902, and renamed it the *Owana*. The company purchased Sugar Island, at the lower end of the Detroit River, on September 15, 1905, and spent vast sums of money on improving it for use as a picnic and excursion park for the company's downriver (from Detroit) and Toledo, Ohio, patrons.

After the company purchased docks, warehouses and office buildings in December, 1906, at the foot of Griswold Street in Detroit and Butler Street in Port Huron, for their ships' use, the company's stock swelled to nine times its 1896 value.

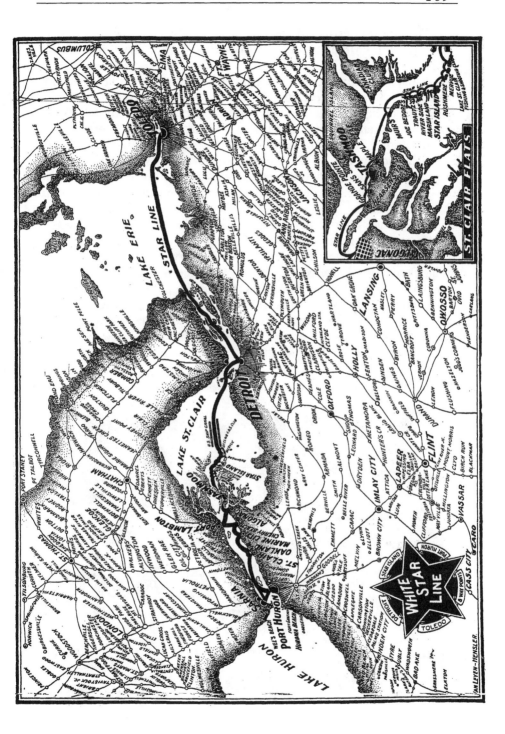

The newly-constructed steel passenger steamer, *Wauketa,* with its capacity of 1,800 day passengers, joined the White Star Line fleet in 1909.

In the 1896 season, the company's sole ship carried about 80,000 passengers. In contrast, during the 1910 season, the White Star Line owned five ships and two island parks, and transported over 750,000 excursionists and a large amount of package freight. Three of its steamers cruised between Detroit and Port Huron (that is, across Lake St. Clair and up the St. Clair River to the point where Lake Huron begins, and return), while the other two vessels followed the current down the Detroit River and traversed a portion of western Lake Erie to Toledo and back.

The White Star Line was the Great Lakes' most successful passenger ship company when the foreign White Star Line passenger ship, *Titanic,* hit the iceberg and sank. The five ships owned by the White Star Line of Detroit in 1912 at the time of the *Titanic* tragedy were the *City of Toledo* (1891-1948), captained by J. J. Stover; the *Tashmoo* (1899-1936), captained by B. S. Baker; the *Greyhound* (1902-1936), captained by Thomas Meiklehan; the *Owana* (1894-1975), captained by Charles G. Merkel; and the *Wauketa* (1908-1952), captained by W. G. Adams.

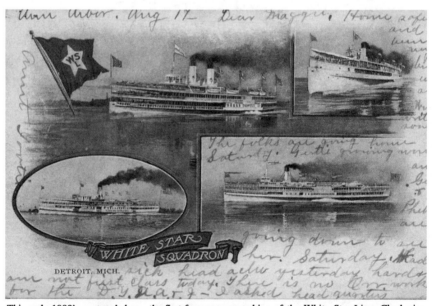

This early 1900's postcard shows the first four passenger ships of the White Star Line. Clockwise from upper left, the White Star Line's company burgee, followed by the flagship *Tashmoo, Owana, Greyhound*, and *City of Toledo*. Postmarked August 17, 1905.   AUTHOR'S COLLECTION.

Of all of Detroit's famous passenger ships, none is better remembered than the *Tashmoo*. During the first third of the twentieth century, she became a lasting part of the Motor City's waterfront tradition. From May to October every year, she cruised between Detroit and Port Huron, with occasional scheduling to Toledo, Ohio. So frequent and reliable was the *Tashmoo* that local inhabitants checked their watches by the sound of her whistles.

The steel-hulled sidewheel passenger steamer, *Tashmoo*, arrives at the White Star Line dock in Port Huron, Michigan, on the St. Clair River, in this postcard published in 1906 by the Detroit Publishing Company. No postmark.   AUTHOR'S COLLECTION.

The *Tashmoo* ended her cherished runs on June 18, 1936, after striking an obstruction in the Detroit River. Apparently some recently-added structural support to the keel area gave way during this collision, and the ship took on water swiftly. Captain Donald McAlpine calmly guided his ship to the dock at Amherstburg, Ontario, and evacuated the 1,400 passengers before his vessel sank in 14 feet of water. The aging 36-year-old *Tashmoo* was scrapped instead of returned to service. Her pilot house became a summer cottage near Wallaceburg, Ontario, for some years afterwards, her bell is on exhibit in Greenfield Village Museum in Dearborn, and her wheel is featured in marine artist Jim Clary's studio in St. Clair, Michigan. Many people lost an old friend the day the *Tashmoo* sank.

◆   ◆   ◆   ◆   ◆   ◆   ◆   ◆

Needless to say, during the last half of April, 1912, many telephone calls and telegrams arrived at the Detroit office of the White Star Line (the Great Lakes one) from desperate people urgently requesting information about relatives who had sailed on board *Titanic*. The best that could be done was to direct the inquiries over to the Detroit office of the *other* White Star Line (the ocean traffic one).

But the 1912 President of the White Star Line in the Great Lakes, B. W. Parker, felt concern over the decline in passenger attendance experienced by his company that season.

"It may be owing to one or several causes," Parker reasoned. "It may be that the passenger traffic has been affected by the loss of the *Titanic* or it may have been the continued cold weather, which we had up to the first of this month or perhaps because of the great noise made over the installation of additional equipment on passenger boats for the protection of passengers.

Earlier in the season (May 22, 1912, not long after *Titanic* sank), Parker had told a reporter, "We are making arrangements to take better care of our patrons than ever before. During the present season, we will have a porter on our dock to assist women and children from the ticket window to the steamers."

It was the best the White Star Line company in the Great Lakes could offer, since their impressive safety record precluded them from hiring porters to assist women and children from a sinking ship into a lifeboat.

"We propose," Parker continued, "to make our boats just as attractive as possible and in doing this, we will try to remove all possibility of accident or inconvenience to those who visit our docks and prevent all disorderliness on the boats. For the same reason, we have barred the sale of liquor on White Star Line boats. The space formerly occupied by the bars has been rearranged as an attractive place where soft drinks and ice cream may be secured...."

Prosperity was another reason given for the decline in passenger steamboat commerce. In Detroit, the factories were running at full capacity and all other lines of business showed great activity. Everyone was too busy working to have time for boat trips. Or were they?

Perhaps prosperous people sailed on ships with bars.

Several years later, the 1920's saw an enormous increase in automobile ownership, and more people began transporting themselves to picnic areas of their own personal choice. Passenger numbers declined on the river steamers and the White Star Line fell upon hard times. Finally, the company was liquidated in early 1925, and its fleet of passenger ships was split up and sold to different owners.

By then, the Great Lakes excursion steamship era was almost over.

11 Great Lakes Leviathan: The *City of Detroit III*

"Palatial Steamer"
"...the mammoth sidewheeler, the largest in the world...."
"Newest Leviathan of the Great Lakes"
"Mammoth Floating Hotel of Palatial Equipment"

These and other such superlatives soared in Detroit newspapers and Great Lakes marine publications when the Detroit and Cleveland Navigation Company (the "D&C," as the company was affectionately known to Great Lakes locals) launched their new steel-hulled *City of Detroit III* on October 7, 1911.

The applause and acclaim only grew louder in the spring of 1912 when her fitting out neared completion and her engines pounded in test runs. Generous journalists spread their praise for the ship:

The magnificent new leviathan, the steamer *City of Detroit III*, will make her maiden voyage to Buffalo Monday, to commence her first season in the service of the Detroit & Cleveland Navigation Company.

The appointments of the new steamer for the safety and convenience of passengers is approached in splendor and magnificence nowhere on fresh water.... She is 500 feet long with 100 feet beam and is the last word in marine construction.

The recent tragedy of *Titanic* had made the public cautious. The ship's owners knew what their potential excursionists wanted to hear:

The new boat is equipped with Marconi wireless service and will be in constant touch with shore and other lake steamers, similarly equipped, throughout the season.

The safety of patrons has been made paramount in the building of the new boat. Among the appliances installed to achieve that end are life boats and life rafts sufficient to carry all the regular passengers, 4,200 life preservers, an automatic sprinkling system, a thermostat fire alarm system which gives the alarm simultaneously to the captain, chief engineer and purser, and indicates the exact location. There are two fire walls aboard the boat, an overhead freight deck, asbestos and galvanized lining in the linen rooms and other places where there might be at any time a possible danger of fire, eleven watertight bulkhead compartments, a powerful searchlight and rockets and modern equipment for use in cases of emergency.

The men are thoroughly disciplined, and boat and fire drill will be held twice a week throughout the entire season, while patrolmen will be on duty on all decks at all times.

All of the machinery on the boat is examined daily and fifty per cent more life saving apparatus is carried than is required in the government regulations.

Only after these safety assurances were clearly laid out could the ship's power and luxury features be detailed:

To give the great ship life and power there is a set of double expansion engines of the inclined cylinder type with the cranks connected direct [sic] to the main shaft. This shaft is the largest that has ever been cast for use in a steamer on fresh water and weighs one hundred tons. The low pressure cylinders are eight feet in diameter, large enough for a horse and wagon to be driven through them; the paddle wheels of the feathering type are thirty-one feet six inches in diameter and each have [sic] eleven paddles fourteen feet six inches long and five wide; the buckets weigh two tons each; the engines will develop twelve thousand horsepower capable of giving the ship at least twenty-three miles an hour. Although the great engines are of the utmost importance, they do not constitute the entire mechanical equipment; there are compound feed pumps to supply water to the huge boilers, powerful fire pumps, a sanitary pump; also hot draft and ventilating fans, double steam steering gears and engines, two gypsy capstans, one deck capstan and a compound steam windlass and capstan; there is also an electric light plant. To furnish steam or the engines and auxiliaries there are six boilers having a working pressure of one hundred and sixty pounds to the square inch.

The general arrangements of cabins, passageways and staterooms is such that a very large portion of the ship has the best of natural ventilation; in some places where artificial circulation is desirable, a new system is installed whereby inside rooms are continually supplied with washed fresh air, making them as comfortable and desirable as outside rooms.

The main dining room is located aft of the lobby on the main deck, is 90 feet long and 65 feet wide, furnishing accommodations for 350 people; the broad bay windows on either side afford a superb outlook over the water as the steamer speeds on her way. Those desiring seclusion will find private dining rooms having all the conveniences of the main dining room. The ceiling which is supported by richly carved pilasters and columns, is paneled and decorated in harmonious colors, while the furniture is executed in solid old mahogany of colonial design.

Located directly below the main dining room is a lounge to which one descends as to the vaults of famous cloister cellars of the Rhine; the ceiling is supported by massive columns, while the chief decorative feature is the wine casks of German manufacture beautifully carved, the heads of which are picked out in burnt wood beautifully colored. The furniture consists of heavy oak tables and chairs with settees built in walls, upholstered with soft leather cushions. The lighting fixtures are of old hammered brass design and add to the glamor that age lends to a place of this kind.

The Grand Salon on the promenade deck is a place of exquisite beauty and splendor that affords the traveler a glimpse into fairy land; beautiful mural paintings which the soft light properly illuminates, adorn the ceilings; directly above the grand stairway leading to the gallery and upper decks is a spacious dome supported by massive Corinthian columns and carved pilasters; in the dome are exquisite panels surrounded by richly carved frames; the color scheme of the grand salon is blended in gray ivory, pearl gray and white, lightly embellished with Roman gold; the carpets are in shades of green to harmonize with the mahogany wood work and furnishings; on the gallery deck the carpets are in shades of old rose in harmony with the gray tones of the decorations; on the promenade deck is located an imported orchestrion costing $10,000; all the latest popular, classic and operatic selections being played while the boat is under way.

The *City of Detroit III*, 456 feet long at the keel (500 feet over-all), was the largest sidewheel steamer in the world. This postcard, postmarked at Detroit on November 18, 1912, shows the dramatic, if fanciful and exaggerated, perspective which grew to be called "the mile-long style" of marine art. It made the company's ships appear longer than they really were, even though the *City of Detroit III* needed no illusory augmentation to impress the public.   AUTHOR'S COLLECTION.

Aft of the main salon on the gallery deck is a sumptuous drawing room designed in the Marie Antoinette style; the walls and ceilings are paneled and finished in gray ivory enamel; the color scheme is gray and cerulean blue with which the carpets and draperies are in perfect harmony; the furniture is carved in Italian walnut with Roman gold mounts, the upholstering is in velvet, while the lighting fixtures consist of carved standards of Roman gold with silk shades.

The Palm Court is a new feature located on the upper deck directly above the drawing room; it is finished in pure white, decorated with trellis panels and pilasters; there are beautifully carved flower stands filled with natural vines and flowers, a charming fountain with running water; in the center of the room is a pergola decorated with trellis and natural vines and supported by beautifully carved fauns and columns. The lighting is from concealed lamps in the cornice and illuminates the bright Mediterranean sky partly concealed by natural vines. The furnishings of the room will be in keeping with the general decorative scheme.

The Gothic Room, located forward on the upper deck, is finished in old English Gothic, displaying the quiet grandeur of the interior of an old chapel or European mansion. The woodwork is of elaborately carved English oak, embellished in strong colors and gold, finished in antique style. Large columns support richly carved arches and spandrels separate and divide the room into cozy recesses; soft upholstered settees are built into these spaces and so arranged with chairs as to form convenient groups for partners; in the center of the room is a cheerful fireplace and at the forward end is a large pipe organ built in place, which fills the room with melodious music; at the after end is a beautiful imported stained glass window representing landscapes of the early days of Detroit.

The steamer *City of Detroit III* will have six hundred staterooms, private verandas, 25 parlors with bath, hot and cold running water, Thermos bottles, electric fans, electric heaters, chiffoniers and other conveniences built in place, 50 semi-parlors with private toilets, running water in every stateroom, also telephone with shore connections while boat is at the dock....

In short, the new steamer was the largest, most luxurious passenger ship on the Great Lakes.

◆   ◆   ◆   ◆   ◆   ◆   ◆   ◆

The *City of Detroit III* had to share her eminence with another record setter when it came to size. *Titanic* received similarly extensive and positive newspaper coverage in the Great Lakes region, both before and after the collision. Superlatives and styles flew fast and furious in a *Toronto World* article titled "*Titanic* The Last Word World's [sic] Greatest Ship" which appeared on April 16, 1912:

The *Titanic* was the largest ship ever built.... The *Titanic* measured 882 1-2 feet in length, while the Woolworth building in New York City is only 750 feet high....

It is almost impossible for the average mind to comprehend the colossal magnificence, the wealth, the luxurious fitting of this boat.

The entrance hall and grand staircase in the forward section were among the show features of the *Titanic*. Seven decks were served by the staircase, five of which were reached by the three electric elevators. The model of the staircase was somewhat after the style followed during the reign of William and Mary.

Designed after the style of the Georgian era between 1770 and 1780 the reading and writing rooms were masterpieces of all that money could do, while the a la carte restaurant was decorated after the manner of the Louis Seize period.

A panel of fine French tapestry adorned the reception room, which extended the whole width of the ship. This tapestry was selected from a series entitled "Chasse de Guise," at the National Garde Meuble.

With a seating accommodation for 550 passengers the grand dining saloon on the *Titanic* was the largest apartment on any steamer afloat. It extended the full length [sic; perhaps "width"] of the ship, and the decorations, which were after the style of the Seventeenth Century, had been adopted from noted Jacobean houses. Numerous alcoves were at the side of the saloon, and the chairs were movable.

Two verandah and palm courts were situated just aft of the smoke room on the upper promenade deck, and the embellishment was after the lines of Louis XI time.

Great bookcases containing the works of all the renowned authors were to be found in the "lounge" and the furnishings of this room were most luxurious, while the decorative details had been taken from the Palace of Versailles. Cards and conversation could be indulged in and lunches and refreshments served from a special pantry adjoining. A delicately-shaded carpet and richly upholstered furniture lent a home-like touch to this room.

The magnificent 882-foot-long *Titanic* was the largest and the most luxurious passenger steamer in the world in early 1912.   COURTESY OF THE MARINERS' MUSEUM, NEWPORT NEWS, VIRGINIA.

No other ship had a smoke room which could rival that of the Titanic. This apartment was furnished and decorated after the style of the early Georges about 1720. The heavy carvings had been omitted and inlaid work in mother-of-pearl substituted, the windows were of stained glass and the deep-seated chairs were upholstered with embossed leather of a delicate green.

Probably the most interesting feature of the great boat was the cooling room of the Turkish and electrical bath establishment. The floors were laid with superb tiles from the Tekyet des Dervictes. That mysterious spirit of the east seemed to predominate, but the Arabian style of the seventeenth century had also a powerful sway.

A salt-water swimming pool 32 x 13 feet of varying depths was constructed of white tiles and decorated in blue with a marine design.

The installation of a squash racquet court was made possible by the steadiness of the vessel even in a storm, and a special gallery was provided for the spectators.

Located on the sun-deck the gymnasium got the full benefit of the sea breezes. Dumb bells, Indian clubs, bar bells, rowing, weight machines, punching bags were all included in this section of the ship.

Above: The overwhelming bow of the *City of Detroit III* impressed its audience on October 7, 1911, just hours before the majestic hull slid down the ramp into the Detroit River. The launching party grandstand is in the foreground. AUTHOR'S COLLECTION.

Below: The even more impressive bow of *Titanic*, the world's largest passenger ship, seemed mountain-like as it neared launch time in Belfast, Ireland. AUTHOR'S COLLECTION.

Above: The *City of Detroit III* hull neared completion along the shores of the Detroit River by late summer, 1911. The steel hull of this huge passenger sidewheeler slid into Great Lakes waters on October 7, 1911, after being christened by Miss Doris McMillan, the daughter of a Michigan Senator.   AUTHOR'S COLLECTION.

Below: With almost 24 tons of tallow, oil and grease lubricating her route, *Titanic's* bare hull slid down the ways stern-first into Belfast Harbor. Thousands of spectators cheered and waved caps during the one-minute launch. *Titanic* was not formally christened, a Harland & Wolff custom viewed by the public as a punishable oversight after the ship sank.   COURTESY OF THE MARINERS' MUSEUM, NEWPORT NEWS, VIRGINIA.

Above: This undated postcard from the Detroit Publishing Company depicts the *City of Detroit III's* grand stairway to the forward gallery deck. At the top of the stair, a large mural represents a peaceful pastoral scene from ancient Greece.   AUTHOR'S COLLECTION.

Below: The First Class grand staircase was *Titanic's* crowning and most memorable interior feature, a breathtaking combination of wrought iron work, polished oak carving, and gilted balustrades, with the sculpted woodwork panel surrounding the clock at the top of the stairs symbolizing Honor and Glory crowning Time. Bronze cherubs bearing electric torches augmented the light streaming in from the overhead glass dome. COURTESY OF THE MARINERS' MUSEUM, NEWPORT NEWS, VIRGINIA.

Above: Coincidentally, each magificent ship featured a garden-like lounge named the "Palm
Court." On the *City of Detroit III,* ivy grew along trellis-covered upper walls, arched
windows allowed views of the passing scenery, and white wicker furniture offered
an untroubled, restful setting for passengers.   AUTHOR'S COLLECTION.

Below: On *Titanic,* the Palm Court displayed many of the same characteristics as those on the
City of Detroit III, all of which combined to provide a refreshing outdoor atmosphere
for the traveller.   COURTESY OF THE MARINERS' MUSEUM, NEWPORT NEWS, VIRGINIA.

NEW BOAT IS AS HIGH AS FORD
AND MAJESTIC BUILDINGS COMBINED

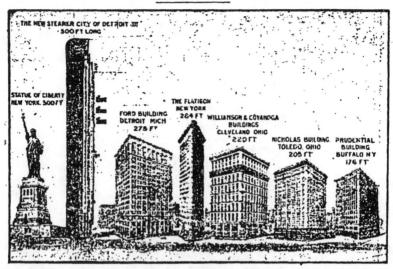

Above: Standing their steamers on end and showing their respective size in relation to well-known buildings or famous structures was popular on both sides of the Atlantic. In this figurative position, the *City of Detroit III* towered high over easily recognized edifices in the Great Lakes, as well as the Statue of Liberty.   AUTHOR'S COLLECTION.

Below: *Titanic* towered high above anything previously built by man, including New York landmarks, St. Peter's in Rome, and the Pyramids of Egypt.   AUTHOR'S COLLECTION.

Surpassing the Greatest Buildings and Memorials of Earth
The Largest and Finest Steamers in the World ☆ **"OLYMPIC" AND "TITANIC"**
White Star Line's New Leviathans ☆ 882½ Feet Long   92½ Feet Broad   45,000 Tons

1 Bunker Hill Monument, Boston	221 Feet High	6 White Star Line's Triple Screw Steamers
2 Public Buildings, Philadelphia	534 Feet High	"OLYMPIC" and "TITANIC" 882½ Feet Long
3 Washington Monument, Washington	555 Feet High	7 Cologne Cathedral, Cologne, Germany 516 Feet High
4 Metropolitan Tower, New York	700 Feet High	8 Grand Pyramid, Gizeh, Africa 451 Feet High
5 New Woolworth Building, New York	750 Feet High	9 St. Peter's Church, Rome, Italy 448 Feet High

The word "Titanic" is derived from the old race of Titans, who were noted for their strength and superiority over other races. The name has also a touch of the superhuman about it. No other name would have suited the boat so well. "Titanic" takes in "huge," "vast," "enormous," "gigantic," and the liner was truly all of these until swallowed by the Atlantic.

This writer did not mention anything about safety and survival features, or lack thereof, which was to make headlines at a later date.

◆   ◆   ◆   ◆   ◆   ◆   ◆   ◆

The *City of Detroit III* almost failed to begin her first trial run. On May 30, 1912, the new ship was being brought about from her slip in the Detroit River at the foot of the Orleans Street yard of the Detroit Shipbuilding Company preparatory to starting for Lake Erie on a test run. The huge vessel swung away from the dock against which she had been tied, her bow pointing upstream. As she came around, an unfortunate misunderstanding of signals delayed the backing of the engine. The gigantic bow bumped into the side of the small, wooden river steamer, *Joseph C. Suit,* docked at the foot of DuBois Street.

All nine people on board the *Joseph C. Suit,* Captain J. A. Schaffer, his wife and seven crewmembers, were alerted to the danger by the shouts of those on board the *City of Detroit III.* They simultaneously escaped onto the dock and remained safely on shore. The *Suit* was torn from her moorings, became wedged between the *City of Detroit III's* anchor and bow, and began heading downstream out of control.

The moderate current carried the two ships tightly jammed together, a marine mouse trapped in the shadow of a nautical elephant that had temporarily lost its balance. The crew of the tug, *C. A. Lorman,* responding to a signal for assistance from the desperate *City of Detroit III,* rushed to the rescue, but broke the cable which they at first attached to the *Suit.* Their second attempt succeeded in dragging the small, crewless steamer free from the towering giant.

The *Joseph C. Suit,* perhaps best known for having taken dynamite, a hardhat diver and a steam crane to Isle Royale in Lake Superior in the spring of 1903 to recover 80 tons of railroad iron from the 1885 wreck of the steamer, *Algoma,* sank almost immediately in 25 feet to the gravel and mud river bottom, having been nearly cut in two by the brand new *City of Detroit III.* The wrecked vessel's spar, smokestack and deckhouse remained above water, with her bow pointing out from shore and her hull tilted to starboard.

Detroiters R. E. Hall and Harry E. L'Hote, had bought the *Joseph C. Suit* two months earlier from Dell McMann in Harbor Beach, Michigan. They spent considerable money rebuilding the vessel as a package freight carrier for use along the Detroit River. Their 28-year-old boat was not insured, but the passenger boat's underwriters settled by giving them $5,000 and new clothes. The wreck was later removed

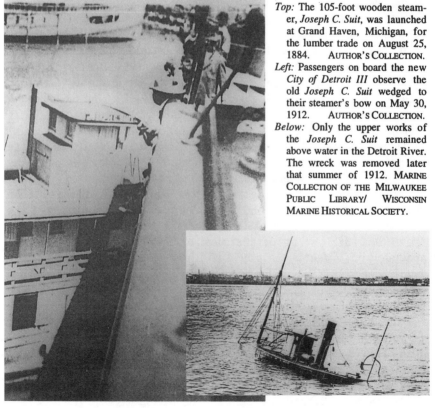

Top: The 105-foot wooden steamer, *Joseph C. Suit*, was launched at Grand Haven, Michigan, for the lumber trade on August 25, 1884. AUTHOR'S COLLECTION.

Left: Passengers on board the new *City of Detroit III* observe the old *Joseph C. Suit* wedged to their steamer's bow on May 30, 1912. AUTHOR'S COLLECTION.

Below: Only the upper works of the *Joseph C. Suit* remained above water in the Detroit River. The wreck was removed later that summer of 1912. MARINE COLLECTION OF THE MILWAUKEE PUBLIC LIBRARY/ WISCONSIN MARINE HISTORICAL SOCIETY.

The *City of Detroit III,* sustaining only a few scratches in the mishap, proceeded as planned into Lake Erie. She was delayed only by an hour. As far as the new steamer's trial run went, "Successful in every way" was the verdict of the vessel's designer, Frank E. Kirby.

But the accident had marred the *City of Detroit III's* departure. Bids on the removal of the mammoth new steamer's victim, the *Joseph C. Suit,* were taken in the United State's engineer's office in Detroit until August 6, 1912, and by summer's end, the shipwreck was successfully removed from the Detroit River and scrapped.

◆   ◆   ◆   ◆   ◆   ◆   ◆   ◆

Titanic almost failed to begin her maiden voyage. An eyewitness reporter described her near-collision with a docked ocean liner at Southampton:

"...It is not very long since the *Majestic* was regarded as one of the world's wonders. This morning we looked down and laughed a kindly laugh at her and the two American Line boats moored beside her. They seemed such small affairs, with 10,000 or 11,000 tons, compared with the *Titanic's* 46,000....

"It was just noon when the vast steel wall in front of us began to move. For the first yard a caterpillar could have raced the *Titanic*....

"She had to go round a bend to the left -- not at all a sharp bend -- about half a mile further on, in order to clear the end of a long quay which juts out slantwise into Southampton Water. It was while trying to round this bit of a bend that the *Titanic* pulled the 10,798-ton *New York* from her berth....

"The *Oceanic* lay moored along the quayside. A few minutes before the *New York* was moored close beside her. Now the *New York* was adrift and sweeping towards the *Titanic.* What was said to have happened seemed a fantastic absurdity until I saw the frayed end of a steel wire hawser, about as thick as a man's wrist, lying on the quay. 'It snapped like the crack of a gun,' a man told me who saw it break. Broken hemp cables hung down the *New York's* side.

"The crowd was breathless with excitement.... As soon as the *New York* broke loose the *Titanic* reversed her engines, and in a brief space of time stopped dead and began to back. Then the tugs *Neptune* and *Vulcan* raced at the *New York*, caught her with ropes by the bows and the stern, and tried to lug her back to her place.

"...There was not much room to spare between the *New York's* stern and the *Titanic's* side, or between her bows and the side of the *Oceanic.*

"...A master of port navigation, with a megaphone, stood stolidly on the quay, issuing orders across the water as calmly as if he were having his tea. He had the *New York* pulled back across the *Oceanic's* bow, and round the bend to the quay, and there moored securely, and then he let the *Titanic* come on again towards the open water. She had backed right away towards the deep end dock while the *New York* was being tugged about like a naughty child.

"It was a relief to everyone when the *Titanic* at last passed the bend and glided slowly away to sea, with the Royal Mail liner *Tagus* following her, like a maid of honor holding the train of a queen.

"It was a thrilling start for the maiden voyage of the largest steamer in the world."

As *Titanic* left Southampton harbor in England on her maiden voyage to New York on April 10, 1912, the suction created by her passing mass caused a docked ocean liner, the *New York* (above left), to pop her docklines and swing into *Titanic's* path. A collision was narrowly averted.   COURTESY OF THE MARINERS' MUSEUM, NEWPORT NEWS, VIRGINIA.

Several people viewed the one-hour delay caused by this near-accident as an ill omen, among them Major Peuchen, a surviving passenger on *Titanic*.

In light of *Titanic's* fate, the misfortune of colliding with the steamer, *New York*, in Southampton harbor would have forced a welcomed delay to her maiden voyage.

In an interesting aside, two ships left England on April 10, 1912, both captained by men named Smith: *Titanic,* the newest ship in the world, and *Success,* touted as the oldest vessel in the world. The *Success,* a 135-foot teak barquentine, was built in India in 1840 (not in 1790 as claimed by promoters). It took 96 days to sail from Liverpool to Boston, but, unlike *Titanic,* the small sailing ship arrived in North America. For over two decades, it toured the East and West Coasts (transiting the Panama Canal in the process) as "The Convict Ship," a role it had played in Australia in the mid-1800's, and ended up in the Great Lakes, where, on the Fourth of July, 1946, an accidental fire destroyed her at Port Clinton, Ohio, on Lake Erie. The bones of *Success* found a permanent home in the Great Lakes.

◆   ◆   ◆   ◆   ◆   ◆   ◆   ◆

The fortuitous *City of Detroit III* fared much better than the ill-fated *Titanic*. She served the central Great Lakes region free of major accidents or disaster for several decades, transporting and impressing hundreds of thousands of appreciative passengers before being dismantled and forced to bow to the scrapper's blowtorch at the Steel

Above: The central panel of the large stained glass window from the original Gothic Room on board the steamer, *City of Detroit III*, depicts a scene of the early Great Lakes explorer, LaSalle.   PHOTO BY CRIS KOHL.

Below: Under the nostalgic housing of the *City of Detroit III's* beautifully restored Gothic Room at the Dossin Marine Museum on Belle Isle at Detroit, the ship's heavy bell radiates the vessel's name and year of her maiden voyage.   PHOTO BY CRIS KOHL.

Company of Canada in Hamilton, Ontario, in 1957. Several of the passenger steamer's ornate wooden rooms had been acquired by a wealthy Clevelander. The Great Lakes Maritime Institute successfully raised enough money to purchase, restore and exhibit the fine carved wood and stained glass of the *City of Detroit III's* Gothic Room at its Dossin Marine Museum on Belle Isle in the Detroit River at Detroit, ensuring that part, at least, of this historic ship would remain with us.

The ship's wheel, symbol of stability and direction, stands mounted amidst the restored carved oak splendors of the *City of Detroit III's* past in the entranceway to the Dossin Marine Museum on Belle Isle in the Detroit River.   PHOTO BY CRIS KOHL.

12 Wireless on the Inland Seas

"The wireless business on a yacht is not fast enough for me," proclaimed the young Englishman who was working as a Marconi wireless operator in the summer of 1910 on board Gordon Bennett's private yacht, *Lysistrata,* while on Lake St. Clair in the middle of the Great Lakes near Detroit.

Twenty-three-year-old John "Jack" G. Phillips soon found work in the wireless room on board the White Star Line's passenger steamer, *Oceanic.* In 1912, he was honored with one of the highest posts in the business when he was given the position of senior wireless operator on the new luxury liner *Titanic.*

John "Jack" Phillips was employed as a wireless operator on a private yacht in the Great Lakes before working on *Titanic.* COURTESY OF THE MARINERS' MUSEUM, NEWPORT NEWS, VIRGINIA.

Jack Phillips had found the fast business he sought.

The day after *Titanic* left Southampton on her maiden voyage, he celebrated his 25th birthday on board. It was his last.

When the great ship sank four days later, Jack Phillips zealously transmitted both distress signals, the old CQD and the new SOS, to all nearby ships until the electrical power failed, 15 minutes after Captain Smith formally released him from his duties. This was the last distress call in which CQD was used.

Phillips remained at his post above and beyond the call of duty, and he was not one of the survivors. His workmate, *Titanic's* junior wireless operator, Harold Bride, who himself barely survived the sinking, related the story of Phillips' heroism in detail to the New York City press upon his arrival on board the *Carpathia*.

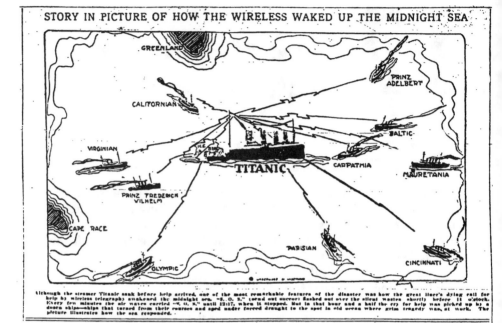

STORY IN PICTURE OF HOW THE WIRELESS WAKED UP THE MIDNIGHT SEA

Although the steamer Titanic sank before help arrived, one of the most remarkable features of the disaster was how the great liner's dying call for help by wireless telegraphy awakened the midnight sea. "S. O. S." (send out succor) flashed out over the silent wastes shortly before 11 o'clock. Every few minutes the air waves carried "S. O. S." until 12:17, when it stopped. But in that hour and a half the cry for help was picked up by a dozen ships—ships that turned from their courses and sped under forced draught to the spot in old ocean where grim tragedy was at work. The picture illustrates how the sea responded.

Above: This art, from the April 18, 1912, *Detroit Times*, shows the use of wireless the night *Titanic* sank. The caption reads, "Although the steamer *Titanic* sank before help arrived, one of the most remarkable features of the disaster was how the liner's dying call for help by wireless telegraphy awakened the midnight sea. 'S.O.S.' (Send Out Succor) flashed out over the silent wastes.... in that hour and a half, the cry for help was picked up by a dozen ships --- ships that turned from their courses and sped under forced draught to the spot in old ocean where grim tragedy was at work...." But the steamer, *Lena,* 30 miles from *Titanic,* carried no wireless. AUTHOR'S COLLECTION.

Below: On April 15, 1912, some newspapers such as the *Hamilton* (ON) *Spectator* published an early front page story about *Titanic,* but the news they themselves had received at that early time was fragmentary and incorrect. While many people ended up dying on *Titanic,* the tragedy would have been compounded without Marconi's "noble" wireless. AUTHOR'S COLLECTION.

◆　　◆　　◆　　◆　　◆　　◆　　◆　　◆

The story of how the role of wireless in the sinking of *Titanic* in the Atlantic Ocean affected shipping on the Great Lakes actually began years earlier.

Guglielmo Marconi (1874-1937)
AUTHOR'S COLLECTION.

An Italian physicist named Guglielmo Marconi is generally credited with the invention of wireless telegraphy. Until Marconi's experiments in the 1890's, a message could be sent almost instantly over great distances only by telegraph, an 1840's invention utilizing a code of dots and dashes representing each letter of the alphabet and sent through great lengths of wires, or by telephone, an 1860's invention whereby the human voice could actually be sent through the wires to the ear of another human. But telegraph and telephone required miles and miles of wires suspended from long series of telegraph poles. Until these cumbersome wires could be eliminated, this was an impossible medium of communication for ships at sea.

Marconi's "wireless" invention of sending dots-and-dashes code signals using electromagnetic airwaves instead of wires took shape slowly. In 1895, he succeeded in transmitting signals through the air a distance of one-and-a-half miles. In 1896, this was increased to four miles. In 1897, Marconi arranged for two Italian warships to communicate with each other across a distance of 12 miles. By 1899, British battleships 75 miles apart exchanged messages. Just months before the turn of the century, Marconi set up two ships with his wireless invention, and when they quickly reported the details of the America's Cup sailing race to New York City newspapers, wireless aroused worldwide excitement resulting in the birth of both the British and the American Marconi Companies. In 1900, the German *Kaiser Wilhelm der Grosser* became the first commercial ship to be equipped with wireless. On December 12, 1901, Marconi successfully sent a wireless signal across the Atlantic Ocean. His experiments continued ceaselessly, even after he received the Nobel Prize for Physics in 1909.

In 1910, he transmitted a message 6,000 miles from Ireland to Argentina, and in 1918, he electromagnetically bridged the 11,000 miles between England and Australia. Not long after that, other scientists developed human voice transmission to replace the time-consuming code signals which had to be sent out one letter at a time.

♦　　♦　　♦　　♦　　♦　　♦　　♦　　♦

Titanic was not the first ship to send out a wireless distress signal.

Twelve years and five months before the *Titanic* tragedy, wireless was used for the first time to aid a ship at sea. It was November 15, 1899, on the eve of a new century, and the American ocean liner, *St. Paul,* was completing her 52nd voyage across the Atlantic. As she approached the Needles in the British Isles, a heavy fog shrouded the area. A land station on the Isle of Wight guided the ship, which was still 66 nautical miles away, through the fog.

Another early ocean use of wireless occurred on October 9, 1905. The whaleback freighter, *City of Everett,* traveling between Port Arthur, Texas and New York City with an oil cargo, developed a major leak during an Atlantic Ocean storm. By means of wireless, the ship contacted another steamer to stand alongside, creating a lee for the disabled craft for 29 hours while emergency repairs were made and her flooded compartment was pumped out.

Wireless had to be tested in the crucible of disaster before being recognized as a reliable safety device. The first highly publicized rescue of many lives aboard a large ship using wireless occurred on the foggy early morning of January 23, 1909. When the steamer, *Florida,* rammed the White Star Liner, *Republic,* under the command of Captain Inman Sealby, off Nantucket Lightship in the Atlantic Ocean, hundreds of lives were saved through quick work on the part of a 26-year-old wireless telegraph operator named Jack Binns in summoning assistance. Even though wireless had been in use for several years, only 180 ships carried the invention at that time, and only the trying drama of a near-tragedy on the high seas yielded a performance hailed as heralding a new era in shipping safety.

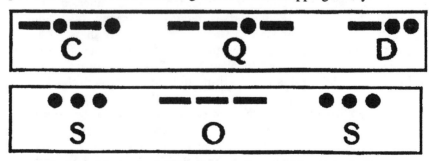

The Marconi danger signal, SOS, which gradually replaced the old signal, CQD.

Binns tapped out the emergency distress call established in 1904: the letters CQD (CQ: "All Stations Attention," D: "Distress"). In 1908, by international agreement, SOS replaced CQD. People in search of meaning soon spread the stories that SOS stood for "Save Our Ship" or "Save Our Souls," but in reality, the change was for more pragmatic reasons: the letters SOS were simply quicker to send and more easily recognized by the ear. But by early 1909, not all nations had agreed to the new signal, and many of the established wireless operators continued to use the old CQD.

Five ships responded to the *Republic's* emergency call: the *Baltic,* the French ocean liner *La Lorraine,* the *Furnessia* of Glasgow, the whaleback steamer *City of Everett,* and the *Lucania* from Liverpool.

Meanwhile, the passengers from the sinking *Republic* were transferred to the damaged *Florida* (which carried no wireless). Once the *Baltic* arrived at the scene, all 1,650 passengers, the combined total of both ships in the collision, were transferred to her secure decks.

While the *Republic* was being towed towards New York, she sank in 45 fathoms, and Captain Sealby, who had remained on his ship, was rescued. The *Florida* limped into safe harbor two days later. Two *Republic* passengers and four *Florida* crewmen had died, but the death toll could have reached the hundreds had it not been for wireless.

The world hailed Guglielmo Marconi as a benefactor of mankind.

"I am exceedingly gratified and very grateful that wireless telegraphy has been the means of saving so many lives," he proclaimed in London. "I am confident its usefulness will go on increasing with the extension of the system...."

The loss of the ocean liner, *Republic,* quickened interest in the safety aspects of wireless on the Great Lakes. In 1908, only three Great Lakes merchant vessels carried wireless equipment. In March, 1909, shortly after the *Republic* incident, five of the ships from Detroit's D&C and D&B Lines had wireless equipment installed.*

---

* These five Detroit & Cleveland and Detroit & Buffalo ships were:

1. The *Western States,* a paddle wheel steamer built by the Detroit Shipbuilding Company in 1902, measured 360 feet in length and was one of the first modern palatial passenger ships on the Great Lakes carrying people and freight between Detroit and Cleveland. But in 1955, the ship was docked at Tawas City, Michigan, and used as a floating hotel before finally being scrapped in 1959.

2. The *Eastern States,* sister ship to the *Western States* and also built in 1902 by the Detroit Shipbuilding Company for the Detroit & Cleveland Navigation Company, carried uncountable passengers during her more than a half century plying Great Lakes waters before finally being scrapped at Hamilton, ON, in 1957.

3. The paddle wheel steamer, *City of Cleveland,* launched in 1908 by her builder, the Detroit Shipbuilding Company, at Wyandotte, Michigan (near Detroit), measured 402 feet in length and was later renamed the *City of Cleveland III.* Retired from service in 1950, the once-popular ship was finally scrapped in 1956.

A.A. Schantz, manager of both lines, stated that "It will not be long before every large boat on the lakes will be provided with the system and [wireless] stations established at all important points along the shores from Duluth to Buffalo." Vesselmen at Duluth on Lake Superior petitioned in November, 1909, for the lifesaving station there to be equipped with wireless because the telephone's party line system often rendered it useless for as long as half an hour at a time.

By 1913, the number of Great Lakes merchant ships equipped with wireless had increased to 40, still only a fraction of the total.

◆   ◆   ◆   ◆   ◆   ◆   ◆   ◆

Ships on the Great Lakes, too, had their share of dramatic rescues facilitated by wireless before *Titanic's* loss.

In June, 1909, the Goodrich Liner, *City of Racine,* was disabled off Waukegan, Illinois, in Lake Michigan. The steamer, *Chicago,* and the whaleback passenger steamer, *Christopher Columbus,* responded to the emergency wireless signal and removed all 260 passengers as a safety precaution. The *City of Racine* limped into harbor for repairs.

On June 15, 1911, the passenger steamer, *City of Cleveland,* responding to an emergency wireless message, rushed to the aid of the *Western States* in Lake Erie after the latter blew a cylinder head and became disabled. All 225 passengers were transferred to the *City of Cleveland.* The damaged vessel hobbled slowly back to Detroit.

Three men in two inoperative motorboats which they had lashed together faced death in Lake Erie's heavy seas on June 20, 1911. The passing steamer, *Eastland,* spotted them and transmitted a wireless to the local lifesaving crew, which quickly rescued all three of the men.

By the time of *Titanic's* sinking in 1912, wireless had been utilized as a lifesaving measure on the Great Lakes for over a decade.

In 1901, Detroiter Thomas E. Clark commenced the installation of the wireless telegraphy system on the Great Lakes. He started with stations in the Detroit area to communicate with ships passing on the Detroit River. He arranged with Senator James McMillan, owner of the D&C Line of ships, to equip those passenger boats with wireless. Soon Clark opened stations at Buffalo, Cleveland, Toledo, Port Huron, Sault

---

4. The *City of Detroit,* constructed by the Detroit Dry Dock Company of Wyandotte, Michigan, in 1889 and measuring just over 297 feet in length, was renamed the *City of Detroit II* in 1912, and *Goodtime* in 1925. Thousands of passengers journeyed between Detroit and Buffalo on board this vessel. The ship was scrapped in 1941 after sitting idle at Erie, PA, for a year.

5. The 283-foot-long *City of St. Ignace,* launched as the *City of Cleveland* in 1886 at the Detroit Dry Dock Company's Wyandotte Yard, was renamed in 1906 (and given its final name, *Keystone,* in 1929). A fire at Ecorse, Michigan, on June 23, 1932, sent this old passenger steamer to the scrappers.

Ste. Marie, Marquette and Duluth as the first string of what he planned would become an unbroken line of wireless communication from one end of the upper Great Lakes to the other.

On April 30, 1906, the International Clark Wireless Telegraph Company formally came into existence.

To the hundreds of thousands of passengers traveling each summer on Great Lakes ships, the novel sound of static produced by sending dots and dashes in the transmission of messages without wires was soon commonplace, although the mystery of wireless never ceased to amaze. The Great Lakes ship without wireless equipment quickly found itself in the minority. Vesselmen saw wireless as an incredible safety device immediately able to call for assistance in time of danger; passengers viewed it as a popular gimmick by which to send"having-a-great-time" telegrams from the inland seas to family and friends. During the 1908 season, the Clark system handled over 300,000 messages, evidence of the rapidity and foothold that the company gained in this special field.

Illustrating Electric Waves in Clark's Wireless Telegraph Transmission.

Thos. E. Clark Wireless Telegraph-Telephone Company.
FACTORY, LABORATORY AND TESTING STATIONS,
DETROIT, MICH., U. S. A.

An early advertisement for Clark's wireless company depicted one of its stations in the busy Detroit River.   BEESON'S MARINE DIRECTORY, 1902.

But by 1908, the Clark Company was experimenting with wireless telephone conversations, successfully sending vocal communications a distance of 70 miles between a land station and a ship on the inland waters. In early 1909, Thomas Clark himself was predicting the feat of talking 1,000 miles without the use of wires becoming a reality, "outdistancing the wildest flights of fancy of a few years since."

Clark Wireless Telegraph Service

Marine interests will find it to their advantage to use this service in reporting their vessel passages. Clark Wireless Stations in operation at all important points on the Great Lakes.

We are prepared to equip passenger steamers, freighters, yachts, tugs, with our Wireless Telegraph and Telephone Service.

CLARK WIRELESS TELEGRAPH-TELEPHONE CO., Inc.
Main Office, Detroit Michigan. See page 149.

A Great Lakes wireless advertisement.　　　BEESON'S MARINE DIRECTORY, 1909.

Other companies jumped onto the wireless telephone experimental bandwagon, but, one by one, they all admitted to having too many "bugs" in their systems; they could not guarantee that their method would work when it was needed the most. The Great Lakes Radio Telephone Company, which had set up offices in various Great Lakes ports, closed them all by the summer of 1910. In late July, a Duluth

For an invention in its infancy at a time before women had the right to vote, it is surprising that there were actually two females employed in the wireless profession in North America in 1911. One of them was 26-year-old Mae Redfern, who helped operate the wireless station at Duluth on Lake Superior. Other women beseiged her with requests for wireless instruction after a newspaper article about Mae and her profession appeared in the summer of 1911.　　AUTHOR'S COLLECTION.

newspaper reported that "...the telephone system did not work....the company which established the telegraph system here...is still operating, and the mariners must be content to receive their news of the world, while on sea, through the telegraphic system, until some more successful company can give them telephones on board." Six weeks later, wireless telegraphy on the Great Lakes proved itself in its first dramatic use during a major emergency.

On September 9, 1910, on Lake Michigan 20 miles off Port Washington, Wisconsin, the railroad car ferry *Pere Marquette No. 18,* flagship of a fleet of six steel car ferries owned and operated by the Pere Marquette Railroad Company, sank in an incident which cost 29 lives.

"Car ferry *No. 18* sinking --- Help!" was the wireless message repeated again and again between five and six o'clock that morning. At 4:00 A.M., the wheelsman had felt the ship responding sluggishly. Subsequent investigation of the compartment aft of the engine room found it almost half full of water, though not enough to disturb the firemen and deck hands who slept soundly there just above the water.

The *Pere Marquette No. 18's* sister ship, *No. 17,* picked up the wireless distress call and raced to her rescue.

The first major Great Lakes emergency to utilize wireless in a lifesaving capacity occurred on Lake Michigan on September 9, 1910, when the steamer, *Pere Marquette No. 18*, called her sister ship, *Pere Marquette No. 17,* for assistance. This postcard, postmarked at Manitowoc, Wisconsin, November 12, 1911, depicts the crucial moment of sinking.   AUTHOR'S COLLECTION.

Arriving at the scene of the sinking ship, it was clear that Captain Peter Kilty of the *No. 18* did not believe that his vessel was in any immediate danger, as he asked *No. 17* simply to stand by once she arrived while he continued to direct his ailing ship towards the western shore of the lake. In an effort to lighten his vessel, Kilty had even ordered nine of the 29 railroad cars on board to be dropped off the stern. This extended the ship's life only somewhat. Captain Russell on board *No. 17*, disagreeing with Kilty, lowered his lifeboats at 7:00 A.M. in anticipation of a rescue. Just then, *No. 18* lurched and went to the bottom stern-first in about 380 feet of water.

All of the survivors jumped or were thrown from the ship when she sank. *No 17's* lifeboats picked up 28 of the 62 people on board the *No. 18*. Four other boats arrived just after the sinking and picked up another seven survivors and eight bodies bobbing in the mounting seas. Two of the *No. 17's* crew died while launching their lifeboat.

The ten-year-old, 358-foot-long, steel *Pere Marquette No. 18* was valued at an astounding (for 1910) $400,000.00, while her cargo of railroad cars was appraised at $150,000.00. The property loss was fully covered by Lloyd's of London, but the lost lives could never be replaced. The dead included all the officers, including Captain Kilty.

There was no storm at the time, the vessel was not overloaded, and there was no mechanical failure, so lakemen were stymied as to why the ship sank. Later investigation revealed that a design oversight had left off a stern sea-gate, resulting in waves washing over the stern and flooding the aft hold. The wreck remains in her unsalvageable depth.

But wireless had definitely saved 33 of the 60 people on board. Stephan F. Sczepanek became the first wireless operator to die in active service on the Great Lakes. He is one of several wireless operators who gave their lives in the line of duty commemorated in a monument in Battery Park, New York City. His body was recovered.

Titanic's loss had a sobering effect upon the Great Lakes shipowners who had not yet installed wireless on board their vessels. The Canadian Pacific Railroad announced on April 22, 1912, that all five of its large, steel-hulled passengers steamers comprising its upper Great Lakes fleet,* were in harbor at Owen Sound, Ontario, being

---

* The vessels of the Canadian Pacific Railroad's upper lakes fleet were:

1. The *Alberta*, built in Glasgow, Scotland in 1883 and measuring just over 262 feet in length, the ship had to be cut in half for transit through the Welland Canal into the upper Great Lakes, where it was later re-welded; 42 feet of length were added in 1911. The *Alberta* was scrapped after a long career at Indiana Harbor, IN, on Lake Michigan in 1947.

2. The *Athabasca*, *Alberta's* sister ship, was also built in Glasgow, Scotland in 1883 and entered the upper lakes the same way as the *Alberta*; she initially measured 262 feet in length, but had 36 feet added at Collingwood, ON, in 1910. She was scrapped in 1947 at Hamilton, ON, on Lake Ontario.

3. The *Manitoba*, measuring 320 feet in length, was constructed at Owen Sound, ON, on Georgian Bay, Lake Huron, in 1889; she was scrapped in 1950 at Hamilton.

equipped with Marconi wireless installations. Only a week after the ocean tragedy, transmitter and reception houses had been constructed

ALL CREDIT TO THE QUEEN OF THE SEAS

The *Titanic* drama finally opened the world's (and the Great Lakes') eyes to the potential of wireless as a lifesaving device on board ships, as this drawing from the *Duluth News Tribune*, April 20, 1912, shows.   AUTHOR'S COLLECTION.

4. Two more sister ships were built in Scotland for the C.P.R. in 1907, each 346 feet long and again requiring bi-section and re-assembly to get them to the upper Great Lakes above Niagara Falls. The *Assiniboia* was sold in 1968 and taken to the east coast, where she burned to a total loss at her pier in Philadelphia, PA, in 1969.

5. The *Keewatin,* after nearly 60 years of active duty on the Great Lakes, was sold in 1966 and converted to a museum ship at Saugatuck, MI, on Lake Michigan in 1967.

on the hurricane decks of all five of these Great Lakes vessels. The accumulator apparatus was due to be placed on each ship within days, while the company announced that all the installations were of "the most approved pattern," and when complete, the C.P.R. ships would be "as well equipped in this respect as any of the modern ocean liners." The company also advertised that there would be wireless shore stations near Midland (on Georgian Bay), at the Soo (Sault Ste. Marie), at Port Arthur (present-day Thunder Bay, Ontario, on Lake Superior), and "in all probability" at Tobermory, at the northern tip of the Bruce Peninsula in Lake Huron.

Titanic's loss made some Great Lakes passengers jumpy. On June 20, 1912, aboard the steamer, *City of Holland*, bound for Chicago, the engines broke down and the vessel stopped dead in the middle of the lake. A wireless call of distress was transmitted, and when some of the passengers heard the clicking of the instrument, their fears were aggravated. A panic and a near-riot occurred. Many passengers cried for the lifeboats to be lowered, and two male travelers even went so far as to lower one without the consent of the officers on board. When the steamer, *Puritan,* took the *City of Holland* in tow, many passengers clamored for transfer to the towing vessel, persistent in the belief that their ship was doomed to sink. They reached Chicago safely.

The only commercial wireless in Toronto in the spring of 1912 operated from the rooftop of the Goodyear Rubber Works office on East Queen Street, connected by the Clark system of wireless with their factory at Bowmanville (the Eaton's station had not yet opened for the season). Fred Barton and Hunter MacLaren, Goodyear wireless operators, picked up some of the wireless transmissions being sent to the *Carpathia* from east coast cities after the *Titanic* survivors had been picked up, but they were out of range for the replies.

By the time *Carpathia* landed at New York with the *Titanic* survivors, authorities in England were condemning the "Wireless Chaos Possible Only in America." Major Flood Page addressed the London Chamber of Commerce with bitter denunciations:

"As the first representative who ever sat upon the council in connection with wireless telegraphy, I would like to say that we are all pre-eminently dissatisfied with what has taken place on the other side of the Atlantic in reference to communications concerning that great disaster. Such a thing could not happen in England. The United States is the only country in the world where the telegraphs do not belong to the government, and, unfortunately, it has become the fashion in that country to permit amateur wireless operators. When we read that marconigrams can be tapped, we must remember that the United States is the only country in which that can be done."

President Taft, however, was ahead of the critics on that matter. On April 16, 1912, he consulted with Secretary of War Stimson on the state of wireless communication in the United States, and on the details of a new bill prepared by the Navy to give effect to the requirements of the general wireless telegraphic convention to which the United States had just recently agreed to adhere.

Amateur wireless operators were causing so much confusion with the transmitted signals that, on April 17th, the Marconi Company formally requested assistance from the United States government in an attempt to clear the Atlantic wireless zones from interruptions. In fact, Marconi blamed the many interfering amateur wireless operators, as well as irresponsible journalists, for the erroneous newspaper reports which initially claimed that *Titanic* was being towed to Halifax.

In July, 1912, the Senate Subcommittee considering legislation to promote general safety of travelers on water heard testimony in Washington, D.C. from concerned parties. Among those representing the Great Lakes were William Livingstone and Harvey D. Goulder, both of Detroit, President and attorney respectively of the Lake Carriers Association. They opposed any legislation making wireless mandatory on ships of the inland seas.

"Wireless apparatus on freight-carrying boats on the Great Lakes is absolutely unnecessary," they both argued. "The installation of wireless on these non-passenger boats would cost $1,000,000 without any means of compensation. Our freight boats pass each other frequently and have ample lifesaving equipment."

They were surprised when another Detroiter opposed their stance. A.A. Schantz, general manager of Detroit's D&C Line of passenger ships, testified the very next day.

"No friction exists between the passenger steamboat lines and the freight lines," Schantz claimed. "The suggestion that wireless apparatus be required on freight vessels which was made by passenger boat men at the hearing in Washington a few weeks ago, was not made for the purpose of getting the owners of freight vessels in bad, but was offered as indicating a way of increasing the efficiency of wireless apparatus as a safeguard.

"Wireless stations on the lakes are not numerous and the passenger boat men took the view that were freighters equipped with wireless apparatus, assistance would more speedily be brought to any passenger steamer in case of accident....

"I suggested that every lighthouse be made a wireless station. The D&C voluntarily equipped its steamers with wireless apparatus, before the law was proposed, because we believe the system affords a protection and increases the assurance of safety of our passengers...."

Livingstone agreed, at least in part, with Schantz.

"I urge the advisability of equipping all lifesaving stations on the lakes with wireless apparatus," Livingstone echoed, adding that there were about 60 lifesaving stations on the U.S. side of the Great Lakes

(31 on Lake Michigan, nine on Lake Superior, ten on Lake Huron, six on Lake Erie and four on Lake Ontario).

In late July, 1912, Washington announced that, after October 1, 1912, all vessels of the United States or of any foreign country or the Great Lakes and licensed to carry 50 or more persons, including passengers or crew, or both, on trips exceeding 200 miles had to be equipped with wireless telegraphy. The radio, or wireless, had to be capable of transmitting and receiving messages over a distance of at least 100 miles, day or night (transmission distance is usually considerably greater at night, a characteristic of electromagnetic waves).

The 1912 regulations included a requirement that "an auxiliary power plant, independent of the vessel's main electric power plant, must be maintained. This plant must be of sufficient capacity to enable the sending of messages at least four hours, and the radio equipment must be in charge of two or more persons skilled in the use of such apparatus."

The call for an independent power plant for radio transmissions fell by the wayside with future changes in radio legislation, with devastating effect on the Great Lakes in modern times.

In late November, 1966, the aging steel steamer, *Daniel J. Morrell*, built in 1906, broke in half during a violent storm on Lake Huron. Of the 28 men on board, there was only a sole survivor, who drifted on a liferaft for 36 hours before being rescued. No radio distress call had been sent, and the question on everyone's lips was, "Why not?"

Dennis Hale, the *Morrell's* survivor, answered that question recently when the author visited him in Ashtabula, Ohio.

"I was probably just as surprised as the next person that they didn't send a radio distress call out," explained Dennis. "When I first woke up in my berth in the bow section, there were no lights working on the ship, no electricity. I went out and when I got to the raft, the skipper had come down with the First Mate, and everybody was standing there, and I wasn't too concerned because I figured that somebody would come and get us pretty quick, you know? And then they said that they got no SOS off. The first loud noise that I had heard sounded like an explosion, and it was the bottom of the ship fracturing. The second was the starboard side of the hull breaking. It was one of those two explosions that broke the cable right there, and that's why we lost all of our power forward.

"It was really strange. We were sitting on the bow of the ship, watching this thing sink, looking at the after end with its lights still on! Even the cargo hold had lights in it. But nothing in the bow. After this [the sinking of the *Morrell*], ships were modified to have their own independent power source forward for the radio. A lot of changes were made because of the *Morrell*, like your safety suits and your covered rafts. The liferafts are all enclosed now...."

The problem with the radio's power source could have been eliminated in this tragic 1966 sinking had the initial 1912 legislation been extended into modern radio laws.

As it was in 1912, the Radio-Communication Act affecting the 400 American ships equipped with wireless and the nearly 100 commercial wireless stations in the U.S.A. went into effect on December 13, 1912. The act established a complete federal control system over radio communication and required licensing of all wireless operators working across state lines or in communication with ships at sea. The licensing of Great Lakes vessels meeting the act's requirements would not begin until the spring of 1913.

The *Duluth Herald* reported in December, 1912, that "The new law was framed shortly after the *Titanic* disaster, and one of its provisions gives a right-of-way for [ships'] distress signals."

The *Toledo Blade* stated that "Uncle Sam, on Friday, the 13th day of December [1912], for the first time in the history of the American government, assumed jurisdiction over the air. He has laid his powerful hands on every wireless telegraph station the country, including two or three amateur outfits in Toledo. For the time being, thousands of wireless apparatus [sic] located in every state in the union will be out of commission until the owners pass examination and obtain licenses from the department of commerce and labor...."

Marconi was as ruthless a businessman as he was an imaginative inventor. By mid-1912, the powerful Marconi Wireless Company obtained control of all the independent wireless companies and most of the stations on the U.S. side of the Great Lakes, including those in Detroit, Buffalo, Cleveland, Duluth, Chicago and other big lake ports. *Beeson's Marine Directory* of 1912 reported that "This development is of particular interest at this time in connection with the triumph of the Marconi wireless in the wreck of the *Titanic,* hundreds of persons aboard the doomed boat being saved by the Marconi operator, who stuck by his powerful instrument and summoned help....

"There have been quite a number of small wireless companies on the Great Lakes and but one or two of them have been at all success-ful. Many of them have been in financial difficulties constantly and some of them, have gone into bankruptcy courts. Wireless stations dot the Great Lakes from end to end and the acquisition of this chain of stations is an important step forward for the Marconi company. It now controls the ocean wireless systems as well as the larger share of the land stations on this side of the Atlantic as well as many in Europe."

Even the Clark Wireless Telegraph Company had encountered a power struggle in 1911 with the United Wireless Company. Clark lost, and his wireless equipment was removed from the D&C boats and replaced by United Wireless furnishings. The original Clark wireless equipment reportedly ended up in Detroit's Dossin Marine Museum.

The Marconi Wireless Telegraph Company of Canada had established a station at Port Arthur, Ontario, in December, 1910, and within two years had expanded under arrangements made with the Dominion government to include stations at Midland, Tobermory and Sault Ste. Marie. In early 1913, a station was under construction in Sarnia, and work soon started on wireless facilities at Port Stanley, Port Colborne, Kingston, and Toronto. Once all nine stations on the Canadian side of the Great Lakes were in operation, the contract with the Canadian government gave the Marconi Company a subsidy of $31,500 a year for 20 years.

No sooner did the Marconi companies control the wireless industry on the Great Lakes than they raised their fees considerably. Great Lakes newspapers reported, on February 19, 1913, that "the Marconi Wireless Telegraph Company has given notice that 1913 contracts [for wireless service on Great Lakes vessels] will be made at an advance of from 50 to 75 per cent in rates. It is asserted that the reason for the lack of profit is that so few steamship lines have adopted the wireless system on their ships. This advance affects only fresh water vessels. A vigorous protest has been made against the increase.... As the Marconi people control practically all wireless service in the country, the only retaliation that can be made, it is claimed, is for the companies to withdraw.... Of course boats that are compelled by law to carry wireless apparatus have to stand for it."

Great Lakes freighters, by and large, found themselves exempt from the wireless requirement because their carrying capacity was fewer than 50 passengers or crew. The announced price increases for Great Lakes wireless made more than a few ship owners grateful that they were not obligated to carry wireless. Within a year, they would have reason to recant.

On November 9, 1913, the worst storm in recorded Great Lakes history struck, lasting three days, and many frightened crews on these very freighters undoubtedly wished they carried wireless. Eight enormous steel ships on Lake Huron alone disappeared with all hands. Wireless would have given a storm warning and kept some of these ships from venturing forth. In all, 19 ships were total losses on all of the Great Lakes during this storm; not so much as a single one of them carried wireless. Just before the storm, three ships cleared from Detroit upbound, one with wireless, two without. The former received the severe weather warning and, after trying to alert the other two, returned to port and was saved, while those without wireless were lost.

Whether wireless would have saved their crews' lives once the ships had steamed well into the lake is doubtful, but their crews would not have gone to their graves silently. To this day, more mysteries of the gales of November linger unsolved; two of those eight Lake Huron ships remain unlocated on the vast bottom of this inland sea.

By 1915, Great Lakes ship companies had grown intolerant of what they claimed were the Marconi Company's increasing rates and inadequate service. Small wireless stations at various Great Lakes ports signified a desire to cooperate with the passenger lines to inaugurate an independent service. The independent station in Detroit, operated by the Goodrich Rubber Company, communicated with their headquarters in Akron, Ohio, but they were willing to work with other independent wireless stations to create a network covering the inland seas. A.A. Schantz, general manager of the D&C Line in Detroit, was the driving force behind this rebellion against Marconi services.

"When we install a service of our own, we will have stations at all the ports of any size and will keep them open all the time," claimed Schantz. "The shore from Mackinac down to Detroit will be well supplied with stations." The plan went ahead, although the Marconi stations, under contract to the government, continued operations. The competition, however, forced them to improve their services and fees.

♦   ♦   ♦   ♦   ♦   ♦   ♦   ♦

Progress on voice wireless, or wireless telephony as it had also been called, had stalled since the early part of the century, with no reliable method being registered with the patent office. The earliest move in establishing what was to be called the radiotelephone on the Great Lakes began in 1933, when representatives of the pioneering Lorain County Radio Corporation applied to the Federal Communications in Washington, D.C., for a license for a ship-to-shore radiotelephone station in Lorain, Ohio; it became operative within a year.

By 1935, at the peak of wireless telegraphy activity on the Great Lakes, 195 ships carried wireless equipment. Ironically, from that point on, the wireless telegraphy system began to be replaced by the voice system of transmitting and receiving. The first Great Lakes ship equipped with a radiotelephone system was the Wilson Marine Transit Company's flagship steamer, the *William C. Atwater,* in April, 1934.

In 1936, the Lake Carriers' Association adopted this technology for the Great Lakes and coordinated the radiotelephone system.

On October 14, 1939, officials of the U.S. Federal Radio Commission (forerunner of the Federal Communications Commission) and the Canadian Department of Transport met at Ottawa, Canada, and adopted the frequency of 2182 KHz as the "common" channel restricted to safety and related uses, the Canadians relinquishing the 1630 KHz which they had been using.

Airway clutter was still a problem, as one dramatic incident on the Great Lakes showed. A Mayday call on the night of November 7, 1939 was picked up by the land station at Lorain, Ohio. It came from Captain A. Pearse of the steamer, *Carl D. Bradley*, which was standing by the disabled tug, *Badger State*, in a severe northwest Lake

Michigan gale. The *Bradley* did not yet have the new 2182 KHz, but would have had difficulty using it anyway, since the shore station in Chicago was broadcasting weather and hydrographic reports on that channel. This, in fact, prevented the Lorain station from using 2182 KHz for its intended purpose of notifying the Coast Guard and alerting nearby vessels of the *Badger State's* predicament. Fortunately, there was no major delay when the Lorain station used a regular telephone to call the Coast Guard station at Charlevoix. Lifeboats were immediately dispatched from the South Manitou and Charlevoix stations, along with the cutter, *Escanaba*. The *Badger State* also did not carry 2182 KHz, and it became a matter of juggling channels on the part of the Lorain station before it could finally put the *Bradley* in communication with the *Escanaba*. The tug sank with the loss of its captain, but the crew was rescued, thanks to the co-ordinated efforts of ship and shore stations.

The lessons learned were that every ship had to carry a radiotelephone system with 2182 KHz, and there could be no lengthy transmissions of weather or hydrographic reports, etc. on that frequency.

An emergency call three years later firmly established 2182 KHz as the distress medium on the Great Lakes. At 1:00 A.M. on September 3, 1942, a Mayday call was received at Duluth from the 258-foot-long *Steelvendor*, loaded with steel billets destined for war (World War II) material production. Nearby ships responded to the *Steelvendor's* broadcast. The ship had developed a severe list when her cargo shifted in heavy seas near Manitou Island in Lake Michigan. Subsequent flooding of the engine room prevented her crew from accessing the ship's diesel engine controls. The *Steelvendor* circled out of control for over two hours while the nearby ships could only stand by helplessly. The crew launched their lifeboats under extreme difficulty at 3:45 A.M., and the ship sank only six minutes later. The ships standing by picked up all of the survivors (one life had been lost). Meanwhile, as the *Steelvendor* sank, her radio transmitter continued to operate automatically from a voice control relay. The Duluth operator reported that he actually heard the rush of water into the pilothouse as the ship went down.

In the early 1950's, the Lorain station developed an eight-channel marine VHF/FM radiotelephone which centered around 156.8 mHz (now channel 16) for safety and distress purposes. This channel became official in 1974.

Wireless telegraphy, created by the wizard named Marconi, threw invisible lifelines across the saltwater oceans and the freshwater seas. His invention evolved considerably since the days when *Titanic's* sinking pushed it into a universal spotlight and affected every ship in the world, including the many which sailed the inland waters called the Great Lakes.

13 Icebergs and Lifesaving Legislation

The chance of an oceanliner striking an iceberg and sinking as a result was calculated by British underwriters to be one in a million. Yet what happened to *Titanic* prompted a general and worldwide outcry for global marine safety reform. The public's sore spots included concern over insufficient lifeboats, lack of round-the-clock wireless surveillance by all ships, inadequately trained seamen, no speed limits in ice fields, absence of bow searchlights, and missing binoculars for the lookouts, but overlooked the fact that *Titanic's* design flaws, such as incorporating an antiquated rudder and a central propeller that could not be reversed, were the real errors which caused the tragedy.

Evaluations and insights regarding *Titanic's* ice damage came from a variety of Great Lakes sources. In Toronto, John Martin, of 48 East Adelaide Street, mingled his theory with reminiscences about working as a steward on board the *Baltic* under Captain Smith.

"Capt. Smith was the most careful man I ever sailed under," Martin revealed, "but he was also the most unlucky. Soon after the arrival of the *Baltic* at Liverpool, with her hold full of bales of cotton, on Nov. 1, 1906, the cotton took fire, and but for the prompt action of the crew and the early arrival on the scene of the Liverpool fire department, the ship might have been destroyed.

"In the summer of 1906 the *Baltic* under Capt. Smith came very near being wrecked. The steamship was heading for Queenstown [Ireland] in a heavy fog, which suddenly lifted and showed the vessel to be steaming directly towards Daunt's Rock, a few thousand feet away. Including the crew, there were over a thousand persons on the *Baltic* at the time.

"I never knew a captain to take greater care than Capt. Smith did at the time I was with him. Every Sunday morning sharp at 10:30 a bugle would be sounded and the crew of the *Baltic* assemble on the deck and answer to the roll call. A fire bell would then be sounded and the crew would be divided into three sections, one party of which put blankets on the lifeboats, another brought out the chemical fire extinguishers and a third manned the hose. This was done when the boat was in mid-ocean.

"When in port the usual lifeboat drill of lowering the boats on to the water was undertaken by the crew. In port the lifeboats and life-preservers are overhauled and inspected for defects, new life-preservers being supplied when any are found with straps loose, etc.

"The captain was always on the lookout for the welfare of the crew. He took great interest in sports and athletics among them and would personally donate prizes for running races and other contests.

THE BIGGEST SHIP EVER BUILT!

Editorial artists seized the drama of an iceberg being the cause of *Titanic's* demise as material for their work. Here, the powerful hands of fate strongly grip the iceberg and thrust the doomed ship head-on into the ice. This inaccurate rendition appeared in the *Chicago Inter-Ocean* on April 17, 1912, prior to the details of the collision being made public.   AUTHOR'S COLLECTION.

"I feel confident that the passengers would have been saved if the *Titanic* had been in service 12 months. For about the first six months after a steamship is put in commission, the plate rivets keep loosening. This is especially the case on the first trip. For this reason the steamship does not leave the hands of the builders until twelve months after she is built, and during this period men in the employ of the shipbuilding company accompany the steamship on all her trips.

"The *Titanic* being on her first trip would have a large number of loose rivets on her plates, and for this reason the shock of the collision with the iceberg would much more easily knock the plate off. This accounts for the *Titanic* having sunk in four hours. Had she been in service twelve months none of her plate rivets would have been loose and she would not have been damaged so greatly by the iceberg.

HOW PUNY IS MANKIND!

In this personification of a spectral iceberg as towering villain, *Titanic* is sinking on an even plane with a strong starboard list. Again, the artist would not have known the actual details of the ship's sinking at this early date: *Port Huron* (MI) *Times-Herald*, April 18, 1912.   AUTHOR'S COLLECTION.

"Had this been the case, she would probably have floated eight hours until the arrival of *Carpathia*, and perhaps until the arrival of some of the other vessels, and no loss of life would have occurred."

THE RIVAL TITANS.
By John T. McCutcheon.

[Copyright. 1912. By John T. McCutcheon.]

Mother Nature as the Mother-Of-All-Icebergs, contemplative yet detached, gazes down, disinterested and emotionless, upon the sinking *Titanic,* symbol of man's futile efforts to be total master of his fate. This message, in the April 20th, 1912, *Cleveland Leader*, is clear: impersonal and pervasive nature ultimately triumphs over mankind's technology.　　AUTHOR'S COLLECTION.

Inman Sealby, former captain of the White Star Line's *Republic* which sank in a collision in 1909 on the North Atlantic, commented on *Titanic's* loss the day after the ship sank. At that time, Sealby was a senior law student at the University of Michigan in Ann Arbor, but his 26 years of maritime experience gave his observations authority.

"The most dangerous thing that the captain of a large steamer has to contend with are icebergs," explained Sealby. "The reason for this is because they so closely resemble water. I have seen icebergs which at one time look so much like the water that they cannot be distinguished a short distance off. A few minutes later, when seen at a different angle, they would reflect a different color and be very distinguishable.... On a very dark night, even though clear, an iceberg looks much like the horizon and ships can get very close to them before they are discernible."

Sealby recognized well in advance of any publicized eyewitness testimony that *Titanic* tried to dodge the iceberg, but instead gave it a glancing blow. "There is no danger of losing a large boat if it strikes [an object] head-on," he elucidated. "The most it could do in that case, would be to cave in 50 or 100 feet of the bow. That is what the *Florida* did when she rammed me. It was just the same to the *Florida* as though the *Republic* was an iceberg. Forty feet of the *Florida's* bow was stowed [sic] in, but she did not sink. The *Republic* sank because the glancing blow which the *Florida* gave her stove in many of the bulkheads."

One man from Pittsburgh was an iceberg expert. Obadiah Hodder, president of the Great Northern Copper Company, was born and raised in Newfoundland. "There is no safer place on the ocean than on a cake of ice if a person is provided with food or is picked up within a reasonable time," he stated. "I know of fishermen wrecked off the coast of Newfoundland to live for days on a piece of ice.... It is not an unusual thing for a fisherman to strip himself of his wet clothing in zero weather for the purpose of wringing the water out of each garment. The only precaution to keep

CAPT. INMAN SEALBY
AUTHOR'S COLLECTION.

from freezing to death on a piece of ice is to exercise the arms and legs constantly. Give a Newfoundland fisherman a seal and piece of ice and he will sustain his life for days.... I am surprised that the sailors and male passengers on the *Titanic* did not jump from the ship and swim to the floating ice. Many lives would have been saved, as everybody would have been rescued who had been able to swim the necessary distance. The *Carpathia* came up before many of them would have succumbed to the cold."

Fate as a robed, armed skeleton stands in complete control on an iceberg while savagely dashing a helpless mankind to death on the ice. A paltry *Titanic* life ring is all that remains afloat of the ship in this grim artwork from the *Cleveland Plain Dealer* on April 17, 1912.   AUTHOR'S COLLECTION.

The Great Lakes themselves were no strangers to ice destroying their vessels. One of the earliest losses was the schooner, *Dolphin*, holed by ice in Lake Ontario off Putneyville, New York, in 1818; her crew was saved. A 62-foot two-masted schooner named the *Brothers* sank off Goderich, Ontario, in Lake Huron in the early spring of 1869, crushed by ice. The wooden steamer, *George L. Dunlap*, sank after ice punctured her hull in Lake Huron on October 15, 1880. The *Dan Allan*, a 117-foot wooden barge built in Canada in 1872, was wrecked by ice in the Black River at Port Huron, Michigan, on April 9, 1885. The 218-foot wooden steamer, *William H. Barnum*, fell victim to floating sheets of ice cutting her hull on April 3, 1894, in the Straits of Mackinac; her crew was saved, but she was a total loss. The 231-foot schooner, *George W. Adams*, was crushed by ice on Lake Erie near Colchester shoal on December 11, 1895. At the mouth of the St. Clair River, the schooner *Fostoria*, sank after ice broke through her wooden hull on May 10, 1901. The tug, *Buffalo*, was sunk by ice near the mouth of Duluth Harbor on April 29, 1907. The year 1909 was a particularly bad year for ice on the Great Lakes. It arrived early and stayed late. On April 20th, the steamer, *Eber Ward*, her wooden hull punctured by ice, sank in the Straits of Mackinac, which connects Lake Michigan to Lake Huron; five lives were lost. Nine days later, the steel steamer, *Aurania*, succumbed to ice twisting her hull in Lake Superior. The ship and her coal cargo were lost, but the entire crew was saved. Later that year, at Toledo, Ohio, on Lake Erie, the tug, *Blazier*, sank after being holed by ice on December 9th. On December 19th, the steamer, *F.A. Meyer*, hit the bottom of Lake Erie in 80 feet of water and stayed there after ice punctured her hull; a passing steamer removed her entire crew.

Even ships on the freshwater seas proved as vulnerable to destruction by ice as their ocean counterparts.

◆   ◆   ◆   ◆   ◆   ◆   ◆   ◆

After *Titanic* sank, a worldwide public screamed its demands for maritime review and reform, for updated requirements reflecting modern tonnage, and for unheard-of passenger safety considerations.

Life preservers fell in the shadow of the globe's safety concerns, as there had been enough life belts for the passengers and crew on board *Titanic*. In fact, since May, 1906, when Congress made it law, all vessels that carried passengers for hire, even those ships in the Great Lakes, had to be equipped with one life preserver for each passenger.

But the number of lifeboats was a different matter altogether.

The lifeboat had evolved considerably since English coachmaker Lionel Lukin built the first one in 1780. The initial intent of the lifeboat was for picking up people from other wrecked ships, and not for the purpose of saving those on board in case of accident. But that concept was gradually altered, and by 1912, voices universally decried the fact that modern ships failed to carry "lifeboats for all."

Lifeboats, instead, would have saved every soul!

Titanic's luxuries did nothing to comfort the mourning figure of Grief lamenting the lack of lifeboats in this image from the *Cleveland Leader*, April 19, 1912.　　AUTHOR'S COLLECTION.

Canadian newspapers, with their proclivity to publish more British-based news than did their U.S. counterparts, were the first in North America to report the comments of Alexander Carlisle, Harland and Wolff's chief designer who worked on both *Titanic* and *Olympic*.

"I never thought there was such a thing as an unsinkable ship," Carlisle confessed. "When the news first came that the *Titanic* was sinking by the head I thought it likely that she would reach port. The fact that she sank within four hours after the impact with the ice indicates that her side was torn out.... I am of the opinion that the large ships of the present day do not carry anything like a sufficient number of [life] boats, but until the board of trade and the governments of other countries require sufficient boats to be carried, ship owners cannot afford such extra top weight. As a matter of fact, both the *Titanic* and the *Olympic* were fitted with davits designed for and capable of carrying four times the number of boats actually fitted in the ships when they went to sea."

Roy L. Peck, the federal inspector of steam vessels at Chicago, declared, "Most of the passenger steamers that ply Lake Michigan are inadequately provided with lifesaving apparatus. Laws referring to provisions for lifeboats and rafts are entirely inadequate, and, as applied to some of the lake boats, are absurb. For instance, there is one boat that carries nearly every day in the summer season more than 2,000 persons, and it has been known to carry nearly 4,000 [this was possibly the *Christopher Columbus*]. Only lifeboats enough for 156 persons are required, and only enough for 180 actually are carried."

"MORE LIFEBOATS!"

Titanic's ghosts point accusatory fingers at the symbolic figure of all ship owners responsible for the construction of vessels with too few lifeboats in this stark drawing from the *Chicago Inter-Ocean*, April 19, 1912.   AUTHOR'S COLLECTION.

Sydney Buxton, President of the British Board of Trade, warned, a few day's after *Titanic's* loss, against passing legislation in a panic. "If you overload the vessel with boats," he cautioned, "the real danger in the case of emergency would be that the very number of boats themselves might lead to disaster."

The Marine Engineer and Naval Architect journal, dated July, 1912, admonished"...there is a danger of making ships too tender if extra weights are placed on the boat decks...."

Maritime professionals and regulatory authorities alike opposed the wholesale belief that "lifeboats for all" was ideal or desirable. One marine publication of note pointed out that troops, trained in strict discipline, could fill and launch lifeboats at a maximum rate of 1,100 people every hour. Ordinary seamen loading untrained and uncoordinated passengers would take considerably longer, so a ship would likely sink before all the lifeboats could be launched.

Ships' captains, if not ships' owners, would give lingering thoughts to the availibility of lifeboats on the vessels in their command. This drawing, originally from the *Cleveland News*, appeared in the *Detroit News* on April 23, 1912.   AUTHOR'S COLLECTION.

Over the next few years, in dramatic instances at sea while lifeboat legislation was hotly debated on land, ships sank too quickly for lifeboats to be used as effective lifesaving devices.

The *Empress of Ireland*, massively holed in a collision on a foggy night on May 29, 1914, in the St. Lawrence River, sank within 14 minutes with the loss of over 1,000 people. Only six of her lifeboats were able to be launched during that brief time (Fireman William Clarke, who survived both tragic sinkings, stated, "The *Titanic* went down like a little baby going to sleep, while the *Empress of Ireland,* much as I hate to admit it, rolled over like a hog in a ditch.")

The *Lusitania,* torpedoed by a German U-boat off Ireland's coast on May 7, 1915, carried 22 lifeboats and 26 collapsible boats, more than enough for the nearly 2,000 people on board. But the ship sank within 18 minutes, taking with it over two-thirds of the 1,959 on board. Only six lifeboats of survivors were found.

This art, from the *Chicago Daily Tribune* of April 24, 1912, speculated how the *Titanic* tragedy would shift the concerns of ships' passengers. Instead of rushing to the purser to be assigned good dining table seats, they would line up for lifeboat seat assignments.   AUTHOR'S COLLECTION.

There were cases where a ship carried enough lifeboats to save all persons on board, but, even if time had not been a pressing factor, not all of those lifeboats could have been utilized. A case in point is again the *Empress of Ireland*. The *Empress* survivors told of their ship capsizing to starboard, rendering the port lifeboats useless because they could not be launched due to the angle of the list. There were lifeboats enough for all, but conditions were adequate for saving only thirty percent of the people on board. With over 1,000 lives lost, the *Empress of Ireland* became Canada's worst maritime catastrophe.

In more modern times, the *Andrea Doria* stayed afloat for 12 hours after a collision with the *Stockholm* off New York on July 25, 1956. The fatally wounded vessel also listed heavily to starboard, rendering all portside lifeboats unlaunchable, and hence useless.

IN CASE OF DISASTER ON LAKE MICHIGAN

IS THIS THE WAY THE OWNER EXPECTS TO SEE THE PASSENGERS RETURN TO LAND?

This artwork from the *Chicago Daily News,* April 26, 1912, depicts impossibly overcrowded lifeboats while an "excursion steamer" sinks in the distance, sparking concern that Great Lakes passenger ships lacked lifesaving equipment.   AUTHOR'S COLLECTION.

On the Great Lakes, several post-*Titanic* instances clearly showed that lifeboats-for-all did not ensure everyone's survival. The steel steamer, *Kiowa,* seriously took on water during a Lake Superior blizzard on November 30, 1929. Soon those waters extinguished the boiler fires, and the hull bobbed at the mercy of the wind and waves. The captain and ten of his 23 crewmembers launched a lifeboat into the raging seas, but the powerful waves overturned it. Only six of the crew succeeded in struggling back to the helpless vessel. By the next day, the ship had stranded in the shallows just off shore and the remaining men were safely removed. Five men had perished.

The steel steamer, *Sevona,* ran aground and broke in two during a storm on Lake Superior on September 2, 1905. Most of the 17 crew and passengers were on the stern section with the two lifeboats. They made it safely to shore. The seven men on the bow, including the captain and the two mates, could not be reached by a lifeboat from the stern through the pounding seas and howling winds, and they all perished. A forward lifeboat had been temporarily removed during the ship's rebuild the previous year, but someone forgot to return it.

"THE MOVING FINGER WRITES AND HAVING WRIT, MOVES ON"

Amidst flotsam, a dying *Titanic* passenger leaves but a single message for the rest of the world in this stark art from the *Columbus* (OH) *Evening Dispatch*, April 19, 1912.   AUTHOR'S COLLECTION.

The April, 1926 issue of *The Great Lakes Vesselman* contained this information about the burning of the wooden steamer, *Majestic,* off Long Point in Lake Erie on September 19, 1907, in an article entitled "Calling to Mind Some Notable Wrecks on the Great Lakes":

"...Captain Ellis [of the steamer, *Charlemagne Tower Jr.*] reported that the fire spread rapidly and that before the steamer was abandoned by the crew, one of the lifeboats was burned. That left only one boat for the entire crew and but for the timely arrival of the *Tower,* some of the *Majestic's* men might have been lost....Captain Hagen [of the *Majestic*] reports that the forward lifeboat could not be reached because of the fire and that the after boat was burned after being swung out. The *Tower* came alongside and made fast...."

There were clearly enough lifeboats on board the *Majestic* to carry the ship's entire crew, but the flames damaged or destroyed them to the point where they were rendered useless, and lives would have been lost had a passing ship not hastily steamed to the rescue. The assurance of "lifeboats for all" was clearly a hollow warranty, but this evidence did not mellow the demands of an outraged public.

Insufficient lifeboats were not the public's only concern. A speed-crazed pilot steers his ship dementedly while women on deck, their scarves blowing furiously in the wind, try to stay warm and protect their babies in this *Cleveland Plain Dealer* drawing, April 20, 1912. AUTHOR'S COLLECTION.

In Canada, those managers and agents of the various companies doing business on the Great Lakes cautiously evaluated the precautions they were using in protecting the lives of their passengers.

"We carry lifeboats and life preservers, in accordance with the law, and beyond that I cannot say anything," was the only comment from the Toronto agent of the R&O Navigation Company. He was undoubtedly aware that not so much as a single passenger boat sailing between ports on the lakes around Toronto carried wireless.

B. F. Folger of the Niagara Navigation and Hamilton Steamboat Company shrugged. "I would prefer not to discuss this subject while the public is in its present excited state."

However, he continued to discuss this subject: "No one realizes more fully than reputable steamboat owners the responsibility of their position, and no one welcomes more gladly than they any practical suggestion that tends to the safety of passengers. Such matters, however, must be treated calmly and intelligently by bodies specially

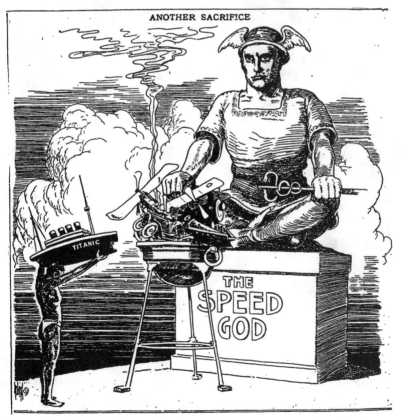

The "Speed God" demanded many sacrifices from modern man in relentless pursuit of faster trains, faster cars, faster aircraft and faster ships. *Titanic* is offered as the newest sacrifice in this April 20, 1912, drawing from the *Columbus* (OH) *Evening Dispatch*.   AUTHOR'S COLLECTION.

All of *Titanic's* virtues amounted to nothing without the most important one, here being added to the billboard by the personification of "Humanity." This drawing appeared in the *Cleveland Plain Dealer* on April 18, 1912.   AUTHOR'S COLLECTION.

commisioned to safeguard the people. The Niagara Navigation Company stands prepared at all times to meet the criticism and adopt the recommendations of such a tribunal."

Owners' expectations placing pressure on *Titanic's* officers to establish a speed record on this maiden voyage, in spite of serious ice warnings from other ships, is the theme of this *Chicago Daily Tribune* artwork from April 20, 1912 .   Author's Collection.

"We carry a life preserver to accommodate every passenger," offered James Bell of the Inland Line. "Our lifeboats, I think, could take off all passengers on the vessel at any time. Our crew is drilled once a week in launching boats." He then added, almost apologetically: "We only run one passenger boat; the rest are freighters."

The Goodrich Transportation Company of Chicago took steps immediately after *Titanic's* loss to put on their steamer covering the Georgian Bay route two small motor boats as lifeboats.

At Chicago on May 9, 1912, the local Federation of Labor adopted resolutions by the Lake Seamen's Union demanding that legislation be enacted for the safety of passengers travelling in passenger carrying ships on the Great Lakes. This meant providing a sufficient number of lifeboats to accommodate the passenger list and crew in case of accident, as well as holding regular lifeboat drills and ensuring that 75 per cent of the deck crew are experienced seamen.

The public pounds a fist on the desk of the ship owner, demanding a greater margin of safety on vessels. This rendition appeared in the Toronto *Globe* on April 20, 1912.   AUTHOR'S COLLECTION.

Senate hearings on a proposed bill designed to safeguard the lives of passengers on steamboats received testimony and suggestions from numerous maritime men during the spring and summer of 1912. Noted marine architect Frank E. Kirby of Detroit commented upon his return from Washington, D.C., "If passenger ships are required to carry enough lifeboats for all on board, some new method of building ship superstructures will have to be found to make room for them. Lifeboats...are so apt to be swamped in heavy seas that life rafts are far preferable.... In the case of the *Titanic*, the sea was very calm and the passengers who escaped in lifeboats survived. What chance would they have had if a heavy sea had been running at the time?"

WHY?

This figure representing the public, pointing out the several human weaknesses that caused the loss of the largest ship in the world, made the ship owner cast down his eyes in shame and/or guilt as mourners grieve the loss of their loved ones in the background. This drawing appeared in the *Chicago Inter-Ocean* on April 20, 1912. AUTHOR'S COLLECTION.

On December 15, 1913, Edward Dustin, President of the Ashley & Dustin steamship line of Detroit, testified to the Senate committee in Washington. "If this proposed bill is passed," Dustin stated, "we would have to carry a crew of 402 men and 187 lifeboats on each ship. Those 187 lifeboats would weigh, exclusive of the davits and other apparatus, 175 tons. No shallow draft boat could stand up with this weight on her top deck. No steamer could find room on her total deck space for such a number. There would not be room for davits on the sides for more than one-tenth of that number of lifeboats. And we would have to convert our passenger cabins into sleeping quarters for the additional seamen. Some suggest that we tow the lifeboats behind. It would mean a string of lifeboats a mile long. Passage of the bill means the elimination of the excursion business out of Detroit."

T.F. Newman, the general manager of the Cleveland & Buffalo Transit company, added, "In the recent storm [November 9-11, 1913, which destroyed a total of 19 ships on the Great Lakes], lifeboats were of absolutely no use, and when lifeboats from the lost vessels finally did come to shore, they were empty or carried dead bodies."

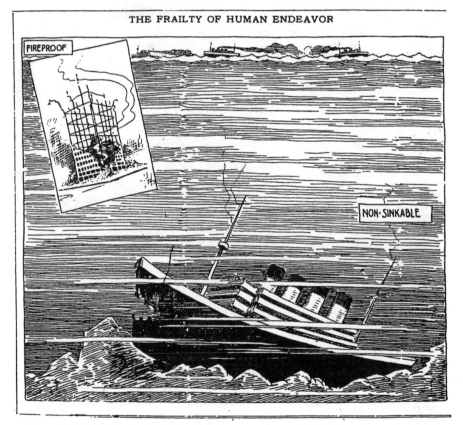

THE FRAILTY OF HUMAN ENDEAVOR

Among the idealistic goals of modern technology are quests to make buildings fireproof and ships unsinkable. Both ambitions have proven elusive. The *Columbus* (OH) *Evening Dispatch* published this artwork on April 17, 1912.   AUTHOR'S COLLECTION.

An International Conference on Safety of Life at Sea met in London, England, in late 1913 and early 1914. One Great Lakes delegate was Andrew Furuseth, President of the International Seamen's Union of America. For two decades, Furuseth had been lobbying for improved working conditions and for seamen's rights by increasing the strength of their unions. The Conference ended on January 20, 1914, with several articles established. Wireless became mandatory. Double bottoms were required on at least the forward portion of ships over 200 feet in length. Ships would be required to pass through ice fields at moderate speeds. An international ice patrol was established. Ships built after July 1, 1915, had to have bulkheads and watertight decks and doors. Most importantly, no ship could carry more people than could be placed into its lifeboats and liferafts.

A GRIM TEACHER.

[Copyright: 1912: By John T. McCutcheon.]

We supposedly learn from our mistakes, but sometimes those errors are so enormous that they make the student wince with shock and terror. In this drawing, from the *Chicago Daily Tribune* of April 20, 1912, a skeletal scholar points out lessons learned the hard way to an alarmed pupil. Chicago's terrible Iroquois Theater fire on December 30, 1903, left 603 people dead (about twice the number of lives lost three decades earlier in the more infamous Chicago Fire of 1871); building codes standardized fire safety measures as a result of the theater conflagration. The passenger steamship, *General Slocum*, on a Sunday school outing comprising mostly women and children, burned in the East River at New York on June 15, 1904, with the loss of 1,200 lives; excursion boats saw more stringent safety rules apply to them. What was going to be the outcome of the lesson learned from *Titanic's* loss? AUTHOR'S COLLECTION.

Furuseth, seeking to create more sailors' jobs, lobbied for "boats-for-all," with two recognized seamen required to man each lifeboat.

But the summer of 1914 saw the outbreak of World War I and a delay in the implementations of the Conference's articles.

In the U.S.A., proposals for making shipping safer manifested itself as Wisconsin Senator La Follette's Senate Bill 136. It was hotly debated, with strenuous objections loudly voiced from American vessel owners. The managers of four fleets of Detroit excursion ships protested that the light construction of their shallow draft ships did not allow for the placement of additional heavy lifeboats. Also disputed was the proposed number of additional crew that each ship would be required to hire for the dispatching and manning of the lifeboats if there were an emergency. Ship operators viewed the proposals as sympathizing with the Seamen's Union for more job creation.

A.A. Schantz, general manager of the Detroit & Cleveland Navigation Company, the main operator of overnight steamers on Lake Erie, appeared again before the Senate committee in Washington, D.C., on September 14, 1914, representing the independent Great Lakes ship operators (those not owned or leased by the powerful steel firms). He sought exemptions to the Act for Great Lakes vessels. The policies had been formulated with ocean-going ships in mind, and were inappropriate for Great Lakes ships, he reasoned. His convincing facts included the unlikelihood of any Great Lakes ship sinking in isolation, with vessels on the Detroit River, Lake Erie and Lake Huron passing each other within 15 minutes at most.

He added,"The extra weight of lifeboats and rafts would make [Great Lakes passenger ships] top-heavy and unseaworthy, and in our judgment, we believe some of them would turn turtle if you attempted to navigate them with this additional weight on the upper decks."

The U.S. result of the universal cry for maritime safety reform, the La Follette Seamen's Act, was signed into law by President Wilson on March 4, 1915, taking effect for American operators on November 4, 1915. Concessions were made for the concerns of Great Lakes passenger ships. Between May 15 and September 15, these ships had to provide lifeboats for 40% of their passengers and crew, with the remaining 60% accommodated in life rafts or collapsibles. At other times of the year, 75% had to be accommodated in lifeboats, with the other 25% on rafts. The act did not require that all lifeboatmen be able-bodied sailors, e.g. they could be engine room workers.

However, Schantz's prediction that the La Follette Seamen's Act would cause a Great Lakes ship to turn turtle lurked menacingly in the background as shipowners made moves to meet the legislation.

It struck with monstrous fangs in the summer of 1915.

14 Great Lakes Death Ship: The *Eastland*

One of the world's most appalling maritime disasters occurred on the Great Lakes three years after *Titanic* sank. Fingers of blame pointed in many directions, even at the new shipping safety legislation that came about only because of the tragic drama and the overwhelming publicity in the case of *Titanic* and the resulting emotional response of the world to this ocean tragedy.

In the entire history of the merchant marine in North America, there is no story more heartbreaking than this one. Over 800 men, women and children died when their excursion ship tipped over while at dock within a few small steps of the shoreline of a river that flowed into Lake Michigan half a mile away.

The Death Ship, called "the most ill-fated vessel on the Great Lakes," was named the *Eastland*.

◆　　◆　　◆　　◆　　◆　　◆　　◆　　◆

The steamer, *Eastland,* one of the most popular excursion ships on the Great Lakes, was built at Port Huron, Michigan, on lower Lake Huron's shores where the swift-moving fresh waters cram themselves into the funnel called the St. Clair River in a seemingly frantic race to the saltwater sea via the Great Lakes and the St. Lawrence River.

The Jenks Ship Building Company launched the 265-foot steel vessel on May 6, 1903. Her owner, the Michigan Steamship Company, immediately moved the ship to Lake Michigan, where she carried passengers and cargoes of fruit between Chicago and South Haven, Michigan. In 1907, the *Eastland* travelled to Lake Erie under the new ownership of the Lake Shore Navigation Company. The *Eastland* Navigation Company owned the ship from 1909 until 1915, during which time the vessel busily and safely carried thousands of excursionists from Cleveland to Cedar Point, a popular amusement park. During these half dozen years, the *Eastland* became so popular as a passenger ship that she appeared in local newspaper cartoons.

The ship was built for speed on the water, sleek and slim with fine lines, but she gained a bad reputation early in her existence because of her tendency to roll. From the time she was built in 1903, up until the disaster, there were five reports of her seriously listing. While some modifications were made, she continued to be unstable. In fact, some people feared her and would not travel on the *Eastland* at all.

Finally, in early 1915, the *Eastland* returned to Lake Michigan, purchased by the Chicago-St. Joseph Steamship Company. They paid $150,000 for the 12-year-old ship, a high price by 1915 standards, indicating that the ship was considered to be in topnotch condition.

Steamship Eastland and Chicago River.

The *Eastland* sailed out of Chicago for the first four years of her life (1903-1907) before spending eight years on Lake Erie. This postcard, postmarked July 18, 1906, shows the speedy steamer racing past docked schooners at the mouth of the Chicago River, heading towards the open waters of Lake Michigan for her usual run to South Haven, Michigan.   AUTHOR'S COLLECTION.

◆   ◆   ◆   ◆   ◆   ◆   ◆   ◆

Early on the morning of Saturday, July 24, 1915, the *Eastland*, tied to a shoreline dock in the shallow Chicago River in the heart of the largest city on the Great Lakes, capsized onto her port side. More than 800 of the over 2,400 people on board died, the majority of them women and children.

The Western Electric Company, expecting 7,000 people consisting of their employees, their families and their friends, had chartered five steamers for this massive round-trip day excursion to the beaches and dunes of Michigan City, Indiana. The first people to arrive at the south bank of the Chicago River just west of the Clark Street bridge at 6:30 A.M. crowded their way onto the *Eastland,* popular because she was the largest and the fastest of the bunch. Besides, the *Eastland* was contracted to be the first ship out due to timing difficulties the year before. The other four steamers, the *Theodore Roosevelt*, the *Petoskey*, the *Racine*, and the *Rochester,* awaited the overflow crowd.

The *Eastland's* ballast tanks were empty in order to let her ride a foot or two higher in the water so the gangway incline would not be dangerously steep for the boarding passengers. The ship, originally built as a cargo freighter but now modified for the passenger trade, had boarding ports in the railing awkwardly lower than the dock level.

Exactly 2,408 adult tickets were collected from *Eastland* boardings (but children under five needed no ticket, and children aged five to twelve boarded on a two-for-one basis). The dark, drizzly morning proved ill-omened. As hundreds upon hundreds of people poured onto the *Eastland,* the engineer below deck several times juggled the flow of water into the ballast tanks, first into the port side to correct a starboard list, then into the starboard side to remedy a port tilt.

Finally, at 7:27 A.M., the *Eastland* listed suddenly and heavily to port more than she had ever done before, an estimated 30 degrees. Deck chairs began to slide. An icebox in the ship's bar toppled over. The vessel hung there as if suspended for about a minute. Then the great ship went over onto her port side, sinking immediately to the bottom of the muddy, shallow river with about six feet of her starboard side exposed and gleaming above the surface.

Minutes after the capsizing, hundreds of passengers and crew scrambled along the starboard side of the *Eastland's* overturned hull while hundreds inside were dying.   AUTHOR'S COLLECTION.

The *Eastland* disaster, where 812 men, woman and children perished within a few feet of shore, was bizarre, bewildering, and inexplicable. Firemen recovered the body of a young woman which had just been brought to the surface by a hardhat diver.   AUTHOR'S COLLECTION.

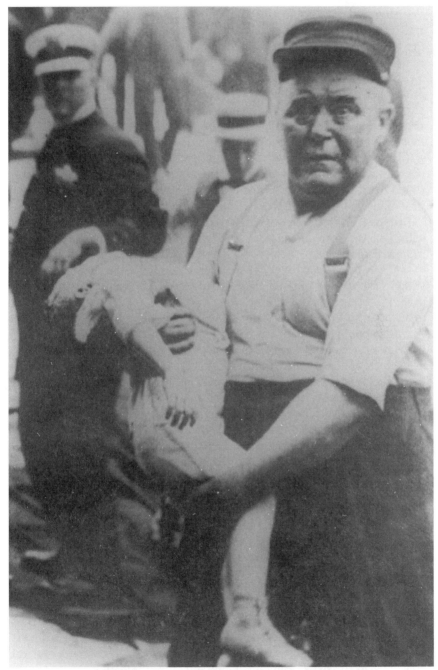

Horror had many faces on July 24, 1915, in Chicago. This fireman could not conceal his anguish as he carried the dead body of a child recovered from the hull of the *Eastland*. Newspapers across the USA and Canada published this emotional photo by Jun Fujita. AUTHOR'S COLLECTION.

Hundreds of people on the upper decks were thrown into the dirty river. Hundreds more inside the dark, steel ship were crushed under the weight of fixtures, chairs, tables and other people. Hundreds likely perished within the first minute of their terrifying ordeal.

Nineteen-year-old Anna Fredericks, who survived when two men pulled her to the high side of the capsized ship, described the horrible sounds at that moment. "I heard 500 women and babies scream at once. It was the most terrible thing one could imagine. The hold [sic] must have been full of people who could not escape."

Before the accident, Willie Guenther tapped on deck to the beat of the ragtime tune played by the *Eastland's* orchestra. When the ship rolled over, 23-year-old Willie did not drown; ironically, the amateur musician who played mandolin was crushed to death by a piano.

Mamie Maratz, a women saved from the disaster, praised the action of the men on board the *Eastland* in words which echoed the *Titanic* experience.

"The men were everywhere trying to help the women, " she stated. "Truly they proved their courage and kindness. It was another case of 'women and children first' wherever there was a chance to give them an opportunity to be saved."

But apparently many of these opportunities were lost, since sixty percent of the dead were women, according to one deputy coroner. The faces of the women bore the appearance of a desperate struggle for life. Some were scratched and clawed, their clothing was torn and their faces were bruised.

The Reid-Murdock Building across the river (today Chicago's Traffic Court) was conscripted as a makeshift morgue, the bodies being placed in neat rows on the floor as quickly as they were pulled from the river or the hull of the steamer. Later that day, crews transferred the many unidentified bodies to the Second Regiment Armory, which in recent times became home to Oprah Winfrey's Harpo Studios where her talk show was taped.

It took two weeks before all recovery and identification efforts of the *Eastland* victims ceased.

As on board *Titanic,* lovers were separated by the *Eastland* disaster. Among them, Peter Vehan, a survivor, witnessed his sweetheart, Mary Kesel, carried to her death in spite of his efforts to rescue her.

As with *Titanic*, the *Eastland's* captain was a man of much experience and no major nautical accidents. Capt. Harry Pederson, of Benton Harbor, Michigan, had spent 37 of his 57 years working on ships.

"I was on the bridge and was ready to pull out when I noticed the boat begin to list," Captain Pederson described the start of the catastrophe. "I shouted orders to open the gangway nearest the dock and give the people a chance to get out. The boat continued to roll and shortly afterward, the hawsers broke and the steamer turned over on its side and was drifting toward the middle of the river. When she went over, I jumped and held on the upper side. It all happened in two minutes. The cause is a mystery to me. I have sailed the lakes for 25 years and previous to that I sailed on salt water 12 years, and this is the first serious accident I ever had. I do not know how it happened."

Everyone on land jumped to the rescue as soon as the huge ship tipped over. Police officers, firemen, bridge tenders, doctors, nurses, passengers and bystanders helped rescue many people who splashed for survival in the river. Many more lives would have been lost had it not been for this group of impromptu heroes. A large number of people and businesses provided materials, help, and support.

For days following the disaster, hardhat divers worked ceaselessly removing bodies from the muddy river and from inside the steel hull.

John Elbert, a surviving *Eastland* gauge tender, attested that the capsizing resulted from most of the passengers rushing to the ship's port side to see a launch go by. But he was below deck at the time, and his credibility really disappeared when he claimed to be a *Titanic* survivor as well. Then, as today, his name graced no *Titanic* list.

HUMAN BALLAST.

[Copyright: 1915: By John T. McCutcheon.]

Artist John T. McCutcheon, who had drawn political commentary of the *Titanic* tragedy in 1912, did the same for the *Eastland* disaster in 1915.   AUTHOR'S COLLECTION.

The *Eastland* disaster wiped out 22 families (mother, father and children) and hundreds of ordinary people, commonplace individuals, many of Czech, Polish and Hungarian descent, who would never have placed among the passengers of distinction found aboard *Titanic*. The *Eastland* carried no notables: no Astors or Guggenheims, no Futrelles or Steads, no Peuchens or Molsons, no Millets or Stantons. The press searched in vain for famous names. These *Eastland* passengers were just simple, real people who went to work, raised their families, and indulged in the occasional boat ride. But many of them turned out to be heroes of *Titanic* caliber. Their tales could fill volumes.

Had the *Eastland* passengers booked onto *Titanic,* they would have been traveling steerage, and there was socioeconomic discrimination in 1915 just as there had been in 1912. For that reason, identification of the deceased seemed less urgent, and later academic research into the disaster stalled. The number of *Eastland* victims varied from 803 to 844, for one reason, because foreign names appeared in both their original spelling and in their anglicized version.

Great Lakes headlines blasted readers with the vital facts about the *Eastland* disaster just as they had done with the *Titanic* tragedy (with similarly varying degrees of accuracy). This is the evening edition, July 24, 1915, of the *London* (Ontario) *Advertiser*.   AUTHOR'S COLLECTION.

Undertaker Otto Muchna resided on the west side of Chicago in a neighborhood where many Western Electric employees lived. At the same time that a telephone call told him of the disaster, relatives knocked on his door with the first of many identified *Eastland* bodies. By noon, they filled the entire funeral chapel. Corpses were then lined up in the enclosed driveway. While Otto mustered all his skills as an embalmer, his wife worked on hair, make-up and other cosmetic touches. They toiled continuously all day Saturday, all that night, and all day Sunday before taking a rest. The work continued to keep them occupied all day Monday and Tuesday. The Muchnas were not the only ones working overtime; even the horses were worn out from the many trips between the morgue and the cemeteries.

As was the case after the _Titanic_ disaster, composers went right to work producing emotional music and touching lyrics for the masses. One song available in sheet music published by the Frank K. Root and Company, Chicago and New York, was called, "Helpless There the _Eastland_ Lay, The Boat That Never Left Town."

◆   ◆   ◆   ◆   ◆   ◆   ◆   ◆

The _Eastland_ capsized for a number of reasons, foremost among which were the ship's initial design, an overburdened capacity on the day of the accident, top heaviness, recent structural modifications, and improper use of the ballast system.

The _Eastland_ was constructed as a freighter, not as a passenger excursion ship. She was built quite narrow, sleek and tall in order to be swift in the water carrying as much cargo as possible below her decks. She carried a high center of gravity (or balance point), yet the ship's gangways appeared low and close to the waterline, a situation which allowed water to enter the hull easily when the ship tilted.

Overcrowding was the first suspected cause of the _Eastland_ accident, but the ship carried no more people on the day of the accident than her legal limit established by government inspectors. In fact, the ship had often carried a greater number of passengers without mishap. Yet, with the vessel's known stability problems (she had tilted and swayed on several past occasions), the number of passengers was likely more than should have been permitted on board. Early in the 1915 season, the _Eastland_ had been certified to carry 2,183 passengers and 70 crew. An increase in the number of liferafts by July officially increased the total capacity to 2,570 people. It must be kept in mind that initially, the _Eastland_ was licenced to carry 2,800 passengers when her design allowed for only six lifeboats capable of carrying a total of 120 passengers. In 1915, as proof of change in safety factors following _Titanic's_ loss, she carried a total of 11 lifeboats, 37 liferafts, and a workboat, all loaded onto the hurricane deck. The total capacity was about 800, still considerably short of the "boats-for-all" call, but a vast improvement from earlier conditions.

Almost immediately, the new maritime legislation became suspect, as one Great Lakes newspaper reported the day after the disaster, "...it is said the seaman's law which was claimed to be a safety measure on the basis of its piling up added lifeboats on the upper deck, will come in for a severe scrutiny as being a possible source of danger rather than of safety...." "Boats-for-all" was termed "inefficacious."

Additional lifeboats and liferafts added to the _Eastland's_ danger-ous topheaviness. The 37 liferafts, weighing 1,100 pounds each, were piled up on the stern of the hurricane deck. They alone added over 20 tons of weight to the top of the ship. Lifejackets weighing six pounds each were available for each of the 2,500 passengers and the 70 crew.

As it was, the disaster happened too quickly for even a single lifeboat or liferaft to be launched, or a lifejacket to be donned. Had the *Eastland* carried boats for all, not so much as a single life would have been saved from the 800+ who perished when the ship capsized.

It has been argued that the universal "lifeboats-for-all" cry was counterproductive, pointing to the *Eastland* disaster as an example, but a singular examination of this Great Lakes tragedy defies the reality of maritime losses. Like *Titanic*, the root of these new maritime rules, the accident which befell the *Eastland* was a one-in-a-million occurrence, not at all representative of maritime mishaps, neither before nor since, from which to draw general or universal conclusions.

Some physical modifications to the *Eastland* also affected her weight distribution and center of gravity. Steel was removed from the lower portion of the ship's hull to allow the ship to navigate shallower waters. A heavy air conditioning system was installed, and in 1915, at least 30 tons of concrete (and possibly as many as 57 tons) were poured in between the deck and the main floor for repairs, adding to the topheaviness of the ship and increasing its instability in the water.

The *Eastland's* ballast system consisted of 12 separate tanks capable of carrying 800 tons of water ballast. The system, however, was not quick enough to respond to changes in weight distribution, such as when two thousand passengers boarded ship. The water in the ballast was brought in and pumped out through the same hole in the boat's hull, so the ballast system could not bring water into one side of the *Eastland* while simultaneously pumping water out of the other.

◆   ◆   ◆   ◆   ◆   ◆   ◆   ◆

The capsizing of the *Eastland* was the worst disaster of any kind, not only in the history of Chicago, but in the history of the entire Great Lakes. There were certainly some tragic contenders. The Iroquois Theater fire of December 30, 1903, left more than 600 people dead in Chicago. The Chicago Fire of October 8-9, 1871, killed approximately 350 people. The worst maritime accident on the Great Lakes, after the *Eastland,* was the sinking of the steamer, *Lady Elgin,* in a collision with the schooner, *Augusta,* off Winnetka, ,Illinois, on September 8, 1860, with the resulting deaths of about 300 people.

But fires and collisions could be understood. A dockside ship tipping over in shallow water and killing 812 people was hard to reason.

Angry citizens of Chicago filed hundreds of lawsuits and litigation lingered for decades. Legal action was taken against the captain and the chief engineer of the ill-fated vessel, against the President and Vice President/General Manager of the company which owned the *Eastland,* and against the local government inspector of hulls and the inspector of boilers. Lawyers argued about whether the accident had occurred "upon the high seas," which would merit federal jurisdiction (which it did not), or upon any of "the waters of the Great Lakes or waters connecting the Great Lakes" (which it also did not).

Finally, in August, 1935, the United States circuit court of appeal upheld a lower court ruling that the St. Joseph-Chicago Steamship Company, former owner of the *Eastland*, was not liable for the deaths caused by the disaster. The company was liable only to the extent of the salvage value of the vessel. The court held that the boat was seaworthy, that the operators had taken proper precautions and that the responsibility was traceable to an engineer who neglected to fill the ballast tanks properly with water ("if a sufficient number of the [ballast] tanks had been filled with permanent water ballast, she would not have been topheavy with any load she was authorized to carry...").

Application for another appeal was filed, but in 1936, the United States Supreme Court refused to review these decisions. Case closed.

     ◆   ◆   ◆   ◆   ◆   ◆   ◆   ◆

The *Eastland* was righted and removed from the accident scene within three weeks, but the wrecking company was not paid for years. The wreck was offered for sale, but it had become a pariah. No one would buy it. Nobody wanted the ship in which 812 people had died.

The steel hull of the *Eastland* was finally sold by the Central Trust Company of Illinois to the Naval Reserve on November 21, 1917 for $42,000, of which $38,000 went to the wrecking company which had removed the shipwreck from the river. Now a government ship, the *Eastland's* upper deck and part of one side were cut away, and she was rebuilt, renamed the *Wilmette* and used as a training gunboat for the Navy. Although commissioned late in World War I (September 20, 1918), she was used as a training vessel for the final months of that war, and again a generation later during World War II.

On June 6, 1921, several miles off Chicago in Lake Michigan, the *Wilmette* provided the gunfire that sank the *UC-97*, a World War I German submarine, one of the spoils of war, which was towed into the Great Lakes and sunk to fulfill a provision of the Treaty of Versailles.

Even the ship's public appearances in positive roles failed to erase her catastrophic past. The *Eastland's* ghosts of screaming people haunted the *Wilmette*, and sailors felt uneasy about sailing on her. She was decommissioned on November 28, 1945 and sold to the Hyman Michaels Company on October 31, 1946, for scrapping. In 1947, the ship was again offered for sale, but there were no takers.

On November 2, 1948, the *Wilmette* was quietly towed to a wrecking yard on the South Branch of the Chicago River and the scrappers' torches removed her quickly and unobtrusively from sight and existence. Thirty-one years earlier, her name had been changed, her contours had been altered, and her purpose was completely switched, but her disguises failed to keep her away from Chicago's hateful eyes. Too many people had lost friends and family because of this ship.

Her scrapping made front page news in Chicago.

In 1989, the first ever marker placed in Chicago's Loop district by the Illinois State Historical Society told the story of that dreadful maritime disaster, the worst in the history of the Great Lakes.

$\bullet$ $\bullet$ $\bullet$ $\bullet$ $\bullet$ $\bullet$ $\bullet$ $\bullet$

The *Eastland* had been a wonderful excursion boat for many people on Lake Erie prior to the ship's tragic episode in Chicago in the summer of 1915. In fact, just three years earlier, the *Cleveland Leader* had published cartoons celebrating the arrival of spring on the inland seas, and it included the popular steamer in its lined tapestry of eagerly anticipated warm weather activities treasured by its readers.

This *Eastland* drawing appeared in the Sunday edition of that newspaper. The date, coincidentally, was April 14, 1912, the day *Titanic* struck the iceberg.

IN THE SPRING A YOUNG MAN'S FANCY - ETC.

15 The Captain

Catherine Crosby claimed to have felt *Titanic* jar several times as the ship struck huge pieces of ice long before the iceberg was encountered. Despite this, the speed of the steamship was not slackened.

"I calculate that we are travelling at a speed of 26 miles an hour," her husband had informed her prior to the collision.

Mr. and Mrs. Crosby had booked luxurious First Class accommodations for themselves in cabin B-22, while their daughter, who had just spent the last two years living in Europe studying music (and perhaps getting over a failed marriage), occupied cabin B-26. Both rooms were close to the First Class salon.

"All of us had retired early on Sunday night, as it was very cold and unpleasant outside, and even our staterooms were uncomfortable. We fell asleep with the clinking of glasses and the hilarity from the party in the salon ringing in our ears," Mrs. Crosby later complained.

"We were awakened at about 11:40 by a crash," she continued. "Mr. Crosby at once arose, and after dressing fully, went out to see what had happened."

Meanwhile, their daughter, Harriette, had partly dressed and, hearing some commotion and talk outside about having struck an iceberg, went out to see what it looked like.

Mr. Crosby hastily returned and, eyeing his wife still in bed, snarled at her as if she should know what was happening outside.

"You would lie in bed even though you knew you were about to drown! Put on your clothes and get up on the deck as soon as possible."

Catherine Crosby was only partly dressed when her daughter rushed in and urged her to hurry.

"The crew are lowering the lifeboats!" Harriette clamored.

With her husband gone off someplace, Catherine and Harriette Crosby headed towards the lifeboats, knocking on stateroom doors of acquaintances, many of whom had not yet risen, as they walked past.

"We reached the deck just as the first boat containing passengers was being lowered. Some of the deckhands had already taken several of the boats. We were assigned to the second boat, and if Mr. Crosby had only remained with us, he might have been saved, as men were allowed in those first two boats," recalled Catherine. "My daughter tried to jump out of the boat to get him, but she was pushed back by an officer."

No sooner had their lifeboat been launched, as they slowly moved away from the sinking ship, one of the officers groped for a plug in the bottom of the boat. He feared that it had not been driven properly, and that their lifeboat would swamp. This contagious anxiety soon infected everyone on board, and they spent a horrible night in dread.

Their boat, like the others, carried no light, so they were forced to drift in utter darkness. They suffered terribly from the cold night air.

"I shall never forget the sight of the *Titanic* going down," Catherine announced later. "We could hear music faintly, but were so far away that we could not tell what was being played. All around us it was still, and every one of the 36 persons in our boat was watching. [They were in Lifeboat 7, which actually contained only 28 people, all from First Class or the crew, including the Bishops from Dowagiac, Michigan, and the Snyders from Minneapolis.] Suddenly the prow of the big vessel began to sink. None of us believed even then that she would disappear completely, but before we realized what had happened, the stern rose high in the air and then settled, leaving everything in utter darkness."

The men at the oars, fearing that suction from the sinking *Titanic* would pull their lifeboat under water, began pulling with all their might. There appeared, however, only a slight swell.

"In the distance we could hear the cries of those who had lost dear ones on the vessel, but in our boat, there was nothing but quiet sobbing."

"The hours from then until daylight I will never forget."

Later, on board the *Carpathia*, Catherine and Harriette Crosby tried to locate Mr. Crosby, but he was not among those rescued. Several people had seen him on *Titanic,* assuring passengers that the ship was so well built that it could not sink for at least eight hours. He wore the same smile with which he greeted his friends every day, recalled witnesses later, and his coolness calmed dozens of people who otherwise would have become frantic with anxiety.

Several survivors told Catherine Crosby that they had seen her husband struggling in the water just before the ship went down. One of the lifeboats passed him and attempted to pick him up, but he, seeing that the boat was already crowded, turned away.

"Never mind me," he told them, "I guess I'll come out all right."

Not too long afterwards, Captain Edward Gifford Crosby, president and general manager of the Crosby Transportation Company of Milwaukee, Wisconsin, a man who had sailed many ships across the vast, fresh waters of the inland seas with few difficulties, lost consciousness as the icy salt water of the North Atlantic Ocean numbed him into eternal sleep.

◆ ◆ ◆ ◆ ◆ ◆ ◆ ◆ ◆

Captain Edward Gifford Crosby
of Milwaukee, Wisconsin

From HISTORY OF WISCONSIN, VOL. 7, 1914

Harriette Crosby (1872-1941), the only daughter of Captain Edward and Catherine Crosby.   AUTHOR'S COLLECTION.

Mother and daughter clearly felt that the blame for the accident rested entirely with the company. In New York, the newly-widowed Catherine Crosby condemned *Titanic's* master.

"Capt Smith was giving a party to some of his friends just before the crash came. Wine was flowing free as water, and the group was hilarious," she claimed.

She also pointed out that, despite the fact they were in a dangerous region, the speed of the boat was not slackened.

The crew's disclipine, she felt, also deserved castigation.

"Even on our Great Lakes steamers, we have a rule that whenever the danger signal is sounded, every man in the crew has his place, and must stick there until relieved."

Catherine Crosby filed a sworn statement in Wisconsin for the Senate Inquiry. In her written and notarized testimony, she admitted that much of her negative information (e.g. a dinner party given for Captain Smith where "the wine flowed freely" at the time of the collision) had been "common talk" which she heard from other *Titanic* survivors while they were on board the *Carpathia*.

◆   ◆   ◆   ◆   ◆   ◆   ◆   ◆

The body of Captain Crosby, wearing a green tweed suit and overcoat, with his pipe, a memo book and $500 U.S. and £80 ($400 U.S.) cash in the pockets, was recovered from the deep by the *MacKay-Bennett*. Frank Walsh, the Crosby Transportation Company's passenger agent in Milwaukee, took it upon himself to make tentative arrangements for the captain's homecoming.

"...As it would be utterly impossible for anyone to travel from Milwaukee to Halifax in time for the landing of the ship *MacKay-Bennett,* we have telegraphed H. J. Kelly, vice-president of the Grand Trunk railroad, who is in Halifax arranging for the sending home of the remains of Mr. Hays, president of the Grand Trunk line, to arrange for the shipment of Mr. Crosby's body to Montreal...."

As it turned out, Walsh himself journeyed to Halifax to identify and bring home the corpse of his old employer.

♦   ♦   ♦   ♦   ♦   ♦   ♦   ♦

Born of Scottish, and historically connected, lineage (his mother was cousin to Abraham Lincoln) on February 18, 1842, in Perrinton Township, Monroe County, New York, Edward Gifford Crosby passed his boyhood days in Ontario County, New York before his family moved to Lenawee County, Michigan in 1856. The eighteen-year-old Crosby, full of youthful patriotism, enlisted in the First Michigan Cavalry on August 21, 1861, to serve in the War between the States. And serve he did: the Wilderness Campaign, Bull Run, Antietam and Gettysburg.

Crosby did not receive his military discharge until April 14, 1866. It was the first anniversary of the assassination of his relative, President Lincoln, and the Civil War had been over for a year. The 14th of April 46 years later would also prove to be significant for Crosby.

After his distinguished military service, Crosby tried his hand at a number of trades: as a railroad man in Michigan, a brick manufacturer in Kansas City, Missouri, and as a lumber driver at Whitehall, Muskegon County, Michigan. Between jobs, he married Catherine Elizabeth Halstead on April 18, 1868, at Hudson, Michigan.

By 1873, he had saved enough money to purchase a tugboat, which he promptly placed into commission in the towing of logs. Business prospered, and in 1881, he established the E. G. Crosby Company, engaged in pier and drydock construction as well as government contracting for navigation-related jobs on Lake Michigan.

Before long, Crosby operated a line of tugboats, scows, and scow-ferries. He supervised the construction of many government piers on the eastern shore of Lake Michigan, as well as building the breakwaters at Milwaukee, Kenosha and Racine on the western shore.

Crosby saw a bright future in package freight transportation across Lake Michigan, a part of the Great Lakes with which he was by now quite familiar. With several other businessmen from Muskegon, he purchased the steamer, *Nyack,* which the group placed into service running between Milwaukee and Chicago. For the next 21 years, the *Nyack* was the flagship of the fleet. Captain Crosby established the Crosby Transportation Company, and soon took a controlling interest among his associates due mainly to his business acumen and surpassing energy. Soon, the steamer, *Fremont,* joined the *Nyack* on the same prosperous run.

In 1896, Crosby purchased the 15-year-old, 209-foot iron steamer, *Wisconsin,* which he, casting aside all superstitions about not changing the name of a ship without encountering bad luck, renamed her *Naomi.* That bad luck was slow in coming, but it hit hard. On May 21, 1907, a memorable and tragic fire virtually destroyed the ship on

Lake Michigan off Grand Haven. Four lives were lost, and the burned-out hulk was towed to Manitowoc, Wisconsin. Undaunted, Crosby borrowed one hundred thousand dollars (with virtually no security other than his word) and rebuilt the *Naomi*. He then changed the ship's name again -- to his own!

The rebuilding and the change in names from *Naomi* to *E.G. Crosby* became final on May 18, 1910. Less than two years later, Captain Crosby went down with *Titanic.* Perhaps there is some substance to the superstition about not changing a ship's name.

The *E.G. Crosby* sailed for many more years, enduring three more name changes, coincidentally ending up with her final name being the very same as her first: *Wisconsin!* The *Wisconsin* sank in a severe gale on Lake Michigan off Kenosha, Wisconsin, with the loss of nine lives on October 29, 1929. That happened to be the day later known as "Black Tuesday" because the stock market crashed and the world fell into the depths and despair of the decade-long Great Depression.

The wreck of the *Wisconsin,* incidentally, rests in 90 to 130 feet of water, upright and intact, with three vintage 1920's automobiles in the rear cargo hold. This deep site is popular with advanced scuba divers.

There were actually three ships in all named the *E.G. Crosby*. The first was an 89-foot wooden tugboat built by Duncan Robertson at Grand Haven, Michigan, in 1892. It spent its entire 22-year lifespan named after the captain. This 310-horsepower vessel, official number 136320, was dismantled, its final enrollment surrendered at Buffalo on July 25, 1914, and endorsed "Abandoned." Its engines were rebuilt and placed in the steel tug, *Illinois* (official number 212542).

The other ship named the *E.G. Crosby* began life as the *City of South Haven* when it was launched on March 21, 1903 at Toledo, Ohio. This 247-foot steel steamer became the *City of Miami* in 1920 when it sailed between Florida and Cuba, but returned to the Great Lakes, three years later, and was renamed, as a continuing tribute to the late captain, the *E.G. Crosby*. It was abandoned in the early 1930's when the Great Depression took root. The remains of this ship accidentally burned in the "bone yard" (ships' graveyard) at Sturgeon Bay, Wisconsin, on December 3, 1935. The steel hull was scrapped in 1942 to build bullets for the war effort.

In addition, a small tug simply named *Crosby* (official number 126617) was built at Benton Harbor, Michigan, in 1889 for Captain Crosby. He sold it out of his fleet in 1891 when he commissioned the larger tugboat. The *Crosby* was abandoned due to age in 1930.

As an added career victory, Captain Crosby obtained the contract with the Grand Trunk Railway Company to operate their steamboat service between the ports of Milwaukee, Grand Haven, and Muskegon, Michigan. That business capacity led to Edward Crosby and Charles Hays becoming intimate friends. Hays was another Great Lakes con-

Great Lakes Ships Named *E.G. Crosby*

The Tugboat, *E.G. Crosby* (1892-1914)

The Iron Steamer, *E.G. Crosby* (1881-1929)

The Steel Steamer, *E.G. Crosby* (1903-1935)

GREAT LAKES MARINE COLLECTION OF THE
MILWAUKEE PUBLIC LIBRARY/WISCONSIN MARINE HISTORICAL SOCIETY.

nection who lost his life on *Titanic*.

Captain Crosby's ice problems began long before he left the Great Lakes for Europe on a combined business and vacation trip, and returned on a ship named *Titanic*. During the winter of 1898-1899, the Crosby Transportation Company chartered a ship, the *John V. Moran,* to carry package freight across Lake Michigan. This 214-foot wooden steamer was less than ten years old, but the ship could not withstand the exceptionally cold winter conditions on the Great Lakes that year. In February, 1899, caught in heavy ice which punctured her hull, the *Moran* sank twelve miles off Muskegon, Michigan. No lives were lost, as the crew had abandoned ship, but the ship, valued at $35,000, was a total loss, as was the $55,000 cargo.

The Crosby Transportation Company fleet during Captain Crosby's lifetime included the wooden steamer *Conestoga,* acquired in 1906, sold Canadian in 1920, and burned to a total loss on May 21, 1922, on the St. Lawrence River canal at Cardinal, Ontario; the 67-foot wooden harbor tug, *O.M. Field* (ex-*Cora Fuller*; official number 126007); the 306-foot steel railroad car ferry, *Grand Haven*, (official number 200007) built in 1903 at Toledo and scrapped at Hamilton, Ontario, in 1970; the 56-foot passenger and freight ship, *Carrie A. Ryerson* (official number 126156), built at Grand Haven in 1883, destroyed by fire at Willow Springs, Illinois, April 23, 1921; and a number of other ships that the company would charter when needed.

◆   ◆   ◆   ◆   ◆   ◆   ◆   ◆

Out of respect for the late Captain Crosby, all operations in the Crosby transportation offices ceased for five minutes on Thursday morning, April 25, 1912, from 10:30 to 10:35. Even the Crosby ships steaming across the lake stopped their engines for five minutes. Memorial services were held all around Lake Michigan: at the Grand Army Posts in Milwaukee, in Grand Haven and in Muskegon, and on board the company's flagship, the *Nyack*, at Grand Haven, as well as aboard his namesake, the passenger steamer, *E.G. Crosby*, on April 28.

On May 7, 1912, Captain Crosby's funeral was held on board one of the company steamers and his body was afterwards cremated and interred in Fairview Mausoleum in Milwaukee.

One Wisconsin eulogy to Captain Crosby combined the victim's Great Lakes connections and his demise, trailing off into purely Victorian phrasing, imagery and sentiment:

"...He was long one of the most prominent and influential figures in connection with navigation interests on the Great Lakes, was president and general manager of the Crosby Transportation Company at the time of his death, and in the entire marine circles of the great inland seas came a deep sense of personal loss and bereavement when it became known that Captain Crosby had paid the final debt to nature under circumstances tragic in the extreme,--- circumstances that proved anew that he was the veritable captain of his soul in the hour of peril, the hour of death. He had long had fellowship with those that 'go down to the sea in ships,' and in view of the results of his final voyage, which terminated on the shores of eternity, we may well recall the heartfelt question of time, 'Life-giving, death-giving, which shall it be, oh breath of the merciful, merciless sea?'"

Fortunately the Crosby legacy remains visible in the wide and colorful realm of Great Lakes maritime history.

◆　　◆　　◆　　◆　　◆　　◆　　◆　　◆

Newspapers reported that "Captain Crosby was returning from a European tour taken to gather ideas for a new lake vessel when he met his death." The new Crosby company ship, it was also reported after his death, would carry "lifeboats and life rafts ...[to] accommodate 520 persons, although the vessel will only have accommodations for 476 passengers and crew...." It was a lesson learned at great cost.

Frederick G. Crosby (1882-1966), Captain Edward Crosby's only son, succeeded him as president and general manager of the Crosby Transportation Company. He tried hard to follow in his father's footsteps, but the world was a different place than it had been 30 years earlier, and Frederick Crosby was not like Captain Crosby. In 1927, he sold the family business and became an insurance executive.

Catherine Crosby remained in Milwaukee until her death at the

A tree in Graceland Cemetery, Milwaukee, with this granite marker at its base, commemorating the Crosby family, was made possible by the *Titanic* Historical Society.　　PHOTO BY CRIS KOHL.

Crosby home, 474 Marshall Street, on July 29, 1920, only eight years after *Titanic* sank. She was 72. Her body was interred beside the cremated remains of her husband in Fairview Mausoleum.

Harriette Crosby pursued her musical interests in California, where she died on February 11, 1941, at the age of 68. Her cremated remains were returned to Milwaukee, as Harriette had wished, for interment with her parents in Fairview Mausoleum.

But by 1995, Fairview Mausoleum had fallen into disrepair, so badly in fact that the building was collapsing. Each of the approximately 1000 human remains inside its weakening walls were transferred to a special section of Graceland Cemetery in northern Milwaukee. There the Crosby family rests in peace today, under a special marker that reads, "Passengers on the *Titanic*," with a *Titanic* drawing carved into one corner, while in the opposite is etched the seal of the *Titanic* Historical Society, which supplied the gravestone and a special marker at the base of a tree planted in the Crosbys' memories.

An etching of *Titanic* decorates the lower left corner of the Crosby headstone, set up by the *Titanic* Historical Society. All three members of this Milwaukee family who experienced the tragic sinking of this ship rest in peace together.   PHOTO BY CRIS KOHL.

◆   ◆   ◆   ◆   ◆   ◆   ◆   ◆

On August 19, 1912, four months after Captain Edward Crosby died on *Titanic,* a young couple, Mr. and Mrs. Frederick Reincke of Muskegon, Michigan, crossed Lake Michigan enroute to Milwaukee on board the steamer, *E.G. Crosby.* During the crossing, and while still 18 miles from Milwaukee, Mrs. Reincke gave birth to a healthy baby boy. The proud parents named him Frederick Crosby Reincke.

One way or another, the Crosby name would live on.

16 The Artists

Two famous artists with Great Lakes connections were on board *Titanic* when the great ship sank.

Mr. Francis Davis Millet, the older of the two, was 65 years of age when he boarded *Titanic*. Years before, during the Civil War, he had served as a drummer boy in a Massachusetts regiment, and later assisted his surgeon father. Although he excelled at Harvard and rose in journalism to the position of city editor with the *Boston Courier*, his real interest was in lithography. He returned to school, this time in Europe (Antwerp's Royal Academy of Fine Arts) where he again excelled in his pursuits and won several medals for his artwork.

Not one to burn bridges behind him, Millet worked as a war correspondent during the conflict between Russia and Turkey in 1877. His courage, medical assistance, and ability to dodge bullets earned him two decorations from Russia.

An avid traveller, Millet published accounts of his travels. Adding to his image as a Renaissance Man, Millet also wrote essays and short stories, and even a translation of Leo Tolstoy's story, "Sebastopol."

In 1893, when he was 46 years old, Millet made a strong connection to the Great Lakes region by taking the position of Superintendent of Decora-

Francis Davis Millet, noted artist, war correspondent and "soldier of fortune" sailed on *Titanic*. AUTHOR'S COLLECTION

tion for the World's Columbian Exposition in Chicago. He had been teaching at the Art Institute of Chicago at the time.

In December, 1892, half a year before the Exposition in Chicago opened, Millet boldly announced that the only color for most of the classic Roman and Greek influenced buildings was white, establishing the "White City" style of architecture. In fact, the white paint was quickly applied by means of a new invention used for the first time, compressed-air squirt guns.

Originally conceived in 1889 as an occasion to celebrate the upcoming 400th anniversary of Columbus' discovery of America in 1892, the World's Columbian Exposition of 1893 (the vast number of buildings and the 633 acres of grounds could not be completed in time for 1892) turned out to be one of the most intense and impressive displays of human energy and talent ever assembled.

A prize boat at the Chicago Columbian Exposition of 1893 was named the *F. W. Millet*, after its Superintendent of Decoration, who, 19 years later, boarded *Titanic*. The Exposition's celebrated nine-member Emergency Crew manned the boat for this publicity photo.   AUTHOR'S COLLECTION.

The 200 buildings included structures representing 38 U.S. states and 79 foreign countries, plus a vast assortment of industries. The Chicago World's Fair of 1893 displayed a number of "firsts," including Thomas Edison's Kinetoscope (an early forerunner of motion pictures), the original Ferris wheel and the Midway, the first time that a vast amusement area was created separately as a part of a world's fair. However, the main attraction was the Exposition's breathtaking architecture. The undeniable success of the Columbian Exposition was proven by the fact that over 27,000,000 people visited the grounds between May and October of that year.

The Columbian Exposition of 1893 was a chance to show Easterners that Chicago, the phoenix midwest metropolis which had risen from the ashes of the Great Fire of 1871 only 22 years earlier, was not just a cattle town in the wild west.

A British firm named the White Star Steamship Company had a strong presence at the Exposition. The company, already famous in 1893 for Atlantic Ocean transportation, and which, years later, commissioned the construction of the ill-fated *Titanic*, drifted from the severely classical and built a free-standing circular pavilion in the shape of an ocean liner's pilot house to enthrall many of the Chicago Exposition's visitors. The verandah was noticeable because of its nautical motif: the pillars were wound with rope, and the rings above and below were life preservers.

The White Star Line had been among the shrewd companies looking early for space on the Exposition grounds; all the other ocean steamship lines were compelled to display their models and wares in the general Transportation Building.

The round pavilion constructed by Britain's White Star Steamship Company in Chicago for the 1893 Columbian Exposition resembled the pilot house of an ocean liner, in stark contrast to the classic white buildings prevalent on the grounds. There is little doubt that both Francis Davis Millet and Samuel Ward Stanton visited this pavilion nearly two decades before they traveled on board the White Star Line's largest ship, *Titanic*.   AUTHOR'S COLLECTION.

Millet's refined artistic talents, coupled with his administrative skills as he worked on the shores of Lake Michigan in the capacity of Superintendent of Decoration at the Columbian Exposition of 1893 were recognized and appreciated (he won a medal for his art exhibit): his labors in Chicago added to his stature as a master of the arts.

Millet's other artwork includes impressive murals in the state Capital Buildings of the Great Lakes states of Wisconsin, at Madison, and Minnesota, at St. Paul.

Francis Davis Millet was a resident of East Bridgewater, Massachusetts, when he boarded *Titanic* at Southampton into First Class accommodations in the company of his friend, Major Archibald Butt. The two of them had been in Europe for six weeks, Millet on business in Rome as director of the American Academy, and Butt as an escape from the intense quarrel in Washington between his two friends Theodore Roosevelt and President William Taft (although less kind sources of information indicate that he needed escape to ponder his upcoming plans for marriage to two different women).

While on board *Titanic,* sailing between Southampton and Queenstown, Millet wrote a letter to a friend. His disapproval of the class system, in particular the pretentious women of the "upper class" of society, showed in his barbed pen:

"Queer lot of people on the ship. There are a number of obnoxious, ostentatious American women, the scourge of any place they infest and worse on shipboard than anywhere. Many of them carry tiny dogs, and lead husbands around like pet lambs."

Millet's letter left *Titanic* at Queenstown and ultimately reached its destination. He should have done the same.

The letters, "F. D. M." on a gold watch and chain identified the body of Francis Davis Millet when it was lifted from the ocean by the crew of the ship, *MacKay-Bennett*. From Halifax, his body was sent to Boston and interred at East Bridgewater Central Cemetery. In the Detroit Museum of Art, black crepe-paper draped Millet's painting, "Reading the Story of Oenone." An eight-foot-tall marble fountain memorial, located at the Ellipse in Washington, D. C., commemorates Millet and his friend, Major Butt, who also lost his life in the sinking.

◆　　◆　　◆　　◆　　◆　　◆　　◆　　◆

The artwork of both Francis Davis Millet and a younger marine artist named Samuel Ward Stanton graces the U.S. Customs House at Baltimore, and it was not entirely coincidental that both men ended up on *Titanic* together.

Ships had played a prominent role in the young Samuel Ward Stanton's life. His father, Samuel Stanton (1839-1899), opened the Ward, Stanton and Company shipyard in Newburgh, New York, with a partner named Luther C. Ward. Their construction specialty was ferries, tugboats and other vessels peculiar to the Hudson River.

Samuel Ward Stanton was remembered as "the foremost authority in this country on the history of steam navigation" and described as "spare, rather tall, well formed, of gentle dignity, and dressed in perfect taste. His countenance reflected a beautiful intellect and the artistic temperament -- his every action was that of the born gentleman."
PHOTO COURTESY OF JOAN STICKLEY, SAMUEL WARD STANTON'S GRANDDAUGHTER.

All three of Samuel Stanton's sons entered maritime professions. William Henry Stanton (1861-1918) ran away from home at 15, sailed the oceans of the world for three years, later working as a captain for Tampa, Florida's, Favorite Line Steamers. In 1884 (when Samuel Ward Stanton was only 14), the senior Stanton had moved the family to Braidentown (today's Bradenton), Florida, near Tampa. Curtis Henderson Stanton (1865-1892), the middle son, a skilled engineer and machinist, worked on ships cruising between Tampa, Florida, and Havana, Cuba, but he died at 27 from typhoid fever.

The youngest (born on January 8, 1870, in Newburgh, New York, on the shores of the Hudson River), Samuel Ward Stanton, enjoyed writing about and drawing ships. He had been collecting early drawings and postcards of Hudson River vessels since he was ten, keeping them in scrapbooks.

Young Stanton lived with his family in Florida from 1884 until 1888, when, at the age of 18, he moved to New York City and found work at *Seaboard Magazine*, which had begun as the *Nautical Gazette* in 1871. This publication gave Stanton the opportunity to work as a reporter and illustrator, his dream combination vocation since he had

Attention to nautical detail and ornate decoration and scrollwork characterized the pen-and-ink marine drawings of Samuel Ward Stanton. The *Christopher Columbus*, built specially for the Columbian Exposition in Chicago in 1893, and the only passenger whaleback ever constructed, carried over two million visitors at the Exposition. Stanton undoubtedly took a short trip out into Lake Michigan on her.   FROM "AMERICAN STEAM VESSELS" (1895) BY SAMUEL WARD STANTON.

been a child. His marine artwork graced not only the covers and pages of this periodical, but also the calendars and advertisements of shipping companies.

In 1893, his nautical pen-and-ink drawings, many of which had appeared in *Seaboard Magazine,* and which now numbered over 300, were exhibited at the World's Columbian Exposition in Chicago. He displayed his portfolio of artwork in chronological order depicting the history and development of American steam vessels, from the Clermont of 1807 to the whaleback steamer expressly constructed on the Great Lakes for the 1893 World's Exposition, the *Christopher Columbus.* Stanton won a bronze medal and a diploma which read, "A very finely illustrated and interesting collection of drawings which show with great skill and cleverness various types of war ships, mercantile ocean steamers, lake and river steamers and yachts. They are of general interest and show artistic merit and historical value."

Two years later (during which time Stanton had produced many more maritime illustrations), these drawings formed the bulk of the approximately 500 illustrations reproduced in his 498-page book, *American Steam Vessels.* By then, he was viewed as an expert on steamships and their histories. He was 25 years old.

Samuel Ward Stanton exhibited 300 of his pen-and-ink sketches of steamships at the World's Columbian Exposition in 1893 at Chicago on the shores of Lake Michigan. He received a bronze medal and a diploma for "a very finely illustrated and interesting collection of drawings...[which] show artistic merit and historical value."
PHOTO COURTESY OF JOAN STICKLEY, SAMUEL WARD STANTON'S GRANDDAUGHTER.

After his book's success, Stanton was asked to do illustrations for others, which he did for Beer's *History of the Great Lakes* in 1899, Morrison's *History of American Steam Navigation* in 1903, and Buckman's *Old Steamboat Days on the Hudson River* in 1907.

In 1898, Stanton and his brother, William, bought *Seaboard Magazine* and returned it to its old name, *Nautical Gazette*. Samuel bought out his brother's share in 1899.

The last half of the 1800's and the early 1900's were the years when good illustrators were eagerly sought by newspapers and magazines to satisfy the public's hunger for images to accompany the text. The technology to easily and affordably publish photographs did not develop until about 1910, so, until then, a high-quality talent such as Stanton's, was in great demand.

Stanton did more than provide detailed illustrations for the magazine. He visited waterfront towns and shipyards, he witnessed ship launchings, he interviewed old sailors, he travelled on board steamers -- and he wrote about all of these experiences, soon making the *Nautical Gazette* the most popular maritime journal in the U.S.A.

But in 1903, Stanton sold the *Nautical Gazette* and moved his wife, Cornelia (1874-1956), whom he had married in 1897, and his daughters, Elizabeth Henrietta (1899-1992) and Marguerite Fuller (1900-1961), to a home in Bradenton, Florida, constructed on the land where his family originally ran a sawmill. Today, the city library stands there. Stanton, perhaps seeing the writing on the wall for the old-style pen-and-ink illustrators who used to be hired by newspapers and magazines, hoped to devote himself full-time to marine painting.

But in 1904, the *Nautical Gazette* was struggling to stay alive, so Stanton returned to New York City to nourish it back to health. In 1910, Stanton became consulting editor of *Master, Mate and Pilot* magazine in New York. His family, including son Samuel Ward Jr. born in 1908, travelled often between Florida and New York then.

Like Millet, Samuel Ward Stanton was a Renaissance Man. An accomplished pianist with a proclivity for Mozart and Beethoven, Stanton also wrote compositions and illustrated them in color. His interest in the theater compelled him to organize a theatrical society in 1890. Even after 1899, Stanton continued his artistic education at New York's Art Student's League.

The Hudson River Day Line hired Stanton as the interior designer for their proposed ship, *Washington Irving*, named after the famous American writer. The company's owners wanted the ship's writing room to be embellished with murals reflecting themes from the writer's works. As a result, in February, 1912, they sent Stanton by steamer to Spain to make sketches of the Alhambra and other locations eminent in Irving's writings. Stanton then journeyed to Paris for additional art training at the Julien Academy.

Samuel Ward Stanton had booked return passage on board the *Baltic*, but a chance encounter with his old colleague, Francis Davis Millet, in Paris changed his mind. The two knew each other from their Columbian Exposition days in Chicago in 1893, and Millet was returning to the United States on *Titanic*.

"That is the best chance in the world for you to get a wonderful marine piece on the world's largest unsinkable ship," Millet argued, knowing Stanton's position with a marine magazine back home. "You are missing a chance of a lifetime if you don't go."

Millet talked his artistic colleague into scrapping an intended visit to London and returning home with him earlier than planned on board the "unsinkable" *Titanic*. Samuel Ward Stanton boarded the new ship at Cherbourg, France, on the evening of April 10, 1912.

Neither man survived the ship's sinking five days later.

The Hudson River Day Line President, E. E. Olcott, accompanied by Captain George A. White, waited on the New York pier when the *Carpathia* arrived, hoping to greet Stanton, but he never disembarked.

A survivor later visited Stanton's family, informing them that he had last seen Stanton walking on deck after the collision, but that he did not know what happened to him.

The commemorative plaque outside the Manatee County Central Library in downtown Bradenton, Florida, reads in part, "...In 1903 the western half of the property was sold by Samuel Stanton to his son Ward who was a marine artist lost in the *Titanic* disaster of 1912. The property had been sold by him in 1910...." PHOTO BY CRIS KOHL.

According to an October, 1966, interview with Stanton's nephew, Curtis Stanton (who was 21 when his uncle died on *Titanic*), "...They found a man frozen, partly frozen, decomposed, floating in the waters with a coat on. He didn't have any identification. He had been there so long that they couldn't tell who he was. But inside the coat pocket was a letter. But the water had obscured the address and everything on it. But they could make out 'W anton.' Since his name was S. W. Stanton, they just figured that was him. But his body was so badly decomposed, and gone to pieces, that they had to leave it. They couldn't take it out of the ocean, had to leave it there. But they got the coat. And they brought the coat back and gave it to his wife."

The *New York Tribune* eulogized Stanton: "People prominent in shipping circles and artists both here and abroad heard the news of the *Titanic* disaster with a sense of personal loss because of the death of S. Ward Stanton... the foremost authority in this country on the history of steam navigation...."

Stanton's daughter, Elizabeth, was only 13 when her father died, but she had already developed an interest in art and she later studied at the Art Student's League. Beginning in the early 1960's, Elizabeth organized the reprinting of portions of her father's drawings in a series of ten books based on ships in various U.S. geographical regions. She enjoyed locating her father's original drawings and researching these ships. His drawings attracted public notice at exhibits in Detroit, Chicago, and Cleveland in 1961 and 1962.

"He was a devoted and delightful family man," she stated. "He was a hard-working man of great self-discipline, admired by all his friends, never drank alcohol in all his life, smoked cigars only in his last year. He was a genial man with a delightful sense of humor. Beyond his nautical interests, he was fond of literature and collected fine and numbered editions. In describing his methods, he prescribed 'constant application.' He had no interest in sports; he played the piano well and attended the opera and concerts regularly."

Alexander Brown said about Stanton's passing, "...the world has been the poorer for it," but present-day Virginia historian William A. Fox, added, "But we have also been the richer for all that he left us."

The Central Library in Bradenton, Florida, is dedicated to the memory of Stanton, the man who once owned the land where the library now sits. The plaque outside that building, and the Customs House mural in Baltimore, act as the only public memorials to the uniquely talented marine artist, Samuel Ward Stanton. Regrettably, no marker exists to commemorate him in the Great Lakes region.

◆   ◆   ◆   ◆   ◆   ◆   ◆   ◆

Two well-known Great Lakes marine artists have strong *Titanic* connections.

Jim Clary grew up along the shores of the Detroit River, closely observing the many ships that travelled up and down that busy waterway. When his family relocated to Richmond, Michigan, Jim spent most of his free time in the nearby waterfront town of St. Clair, on the shores of the St. Clair River, where he eventually took root, devoting his talents to drawing and painting ships, collecting maritime history, and operating his marine art studio.

In a recent interview with the author, Clary talked about *Titanic*. "It's the biggest piece of marine lore that there is. Living near the water, my first big interest was the *Titanic*. I was probably ten or eleven years old."

In the summer of 1983, Jim Clary, selected as team historian and artist, participated in the third expedition mounted by Texas oil millionaire Jack Grimm to an area in the North Atlantic Ocean dubbed "*Titanic* Canyon," about 660 miles from Halifax.

"I knew that any underwater cameras would not be able to see *Titanic* in a panoramic view down there," recalls Clary. "They might have great visibility at that depth, but I knew it was impossible to see the whole wreck at once. I said to Jack Grimm, 'I could give you panoramic views of the *Titanic*.' I did 464 computer drawings of the *Titanic* on the bottom from every possible angle, because we didn't know how it lay then, for on-site study, and that really was my ticket to go on the mission."

Sonar readings indicated that the expedition had located "a ship the size of the *Titanic* in an area where the ship went down, based on its S.O.S. signal and where the first lifeboats were." Unfortunately, the underwater photography equipment malfunctioned, and no pictures could be taken to back up the wreck's identity.

A sketch of the shipwreck lying upright and intact, but with a port list, appeared in the *Detroit News* on August 2, 1983.

Jim Clary pointed out to the expedition members an important historical point unfamiliar to them (and which he later told to a *Detroit Free Press* reporter):

"After she hit the iceberg, the captain started up again and ran ahead, gushing water into the hull. The 300-foot gash on her side sort of wrapped around the bow, where there was a hole, and going ahead would move water right into the hull.... The captain had no way to know for sure the length of the gash, and he was probably going by the book,... but it made the *Titanic* sink faster."

This fact (although the estimated length of time that *Titanic* continued to move forward under steam power after the collision varies from ten to 30 minutes) became the premise of Jim Clary's

1998 book, *The Last True Story of Titanic,* which the author dedicated to the late Jack Grimm, "who first found the *Titanic."*

When *Titanic* was found, identified, and photographed on September 1, 1985, by the joint American-French expedition led by Robert Ballard, Grimm expedition participants felt frustrated, convinced that Ballard had used their "$3 million road map" to the wreck site. Their opponents argued that the Grimm expeditions had located the wrong wreck. This issue is still hotly debated.

Marine artist Jim Clary views one of his excellent works, the Great Lakes passenger steamer, *SeeandBee,* largest on the lakes when launched in 1913, and the only four-stacker on the inland seas (and all four worked; none was a dummy like *Titanic's* fourth stack).   PHOTO BY CRIS KOHL.

Jim Clary's superb artwork, although leaning towards historic Great Lakes ships, includes many paintings of *Titanic* and numerous other saltwater vessels.

He has also written three other books, containing many color photos, on marine topics: *Ladies of the Lakes* and *Ladies of the Lakes II* (about famous Great Lakes vessels and events) and *Superstitions of the Sea.*

Jim Clary can be contacted at his studio, Maritime History in Art, 201 North Riverside, St. Clair, Michigan 48079, telephone (810) 329-7744. His web site is http://www.jclary.com

◆   ◆   ◆   ◆   ◆   ◆   ◆   ◆

Bob McGreevy, noted Great Lakes marine artist, operates a studio out of his home in a Detroit suburb. His interest in *Titanic* and all things nautical was evidently inherited.

"My grandfather, Hugh Robert McGreevy, was one of the thousands of men who built the *Titanic* and her sister ships, the *Olympic* and the *Brittanic,* in 1909-1912 at the Harland and Wolff shipyards in Belfast, Ireland."

Bob's grandfather, who started working in the shipyards at age 14, was in his 20's when he did carpentry work on the *Olympic's* interior. Three months later, work commenced on *Titanic's* hull, but Hugh Robert McGreevy had to wait until *Olympic* was finished before he could begin work on *Titanic*.

Bob's father, Robert Hugh McGreevy, also worked for Harland and Wolff, beginning in 1939, at the time when his father retired from the firm. "So there was still a McGreevy there," quips Bob, aware that skilled positions were often passed down through families. Robert Hugh at first repaired damaged British warships during World War Two, but later shifted to the company's

Hugh Robert McGreevy, seated in the first row, second from the left, arms folded and wearing a light-colored cap, posed with many other Harland and Wolff workers. He helped build *Titanic*; his grandson painted her.
PHOTO COURTESY OF BOB MCGREEVY.

aircraft division until 1950 when he relocated his family to the Detroit area and did aircraft fastening work there.

Bob is carrying on the family marine connection, but instead of building today's ships, he paints yesterday's vessels. Bob's detailed painting of *Titanic,* the only non-Great Lakes ship he has produced commercially and offers as a limited edition print, stands as a tribute, particularly to his grandfather and father.

"I was born in Belfast," continues Bob, "which is built around the shipyard, and have always been interested in the *Titanic*. The shipyards had a great deal of influence on me as I was growing up. A lot of kids in Detroit drew cars; I drew ships and airplanes."

Bob studied *Titanic's* history, examined as many of the photographs of the ship that he could find, and combined that knowledge and evaluation with the stories handed down through family members to produce his *Titanic* painting, a two-year project.

"The *Titanic* was sleek and yacht-like in appearance," Bob points out. "What you don't see in the black-and-white photographs of the ship is a gold stripe across the hull, which was a trademark of the White Star Line." Bob's *Titanic* print includes an embossed gold stripe running from bow to stern.

Although Bob prefers to paint ships when they are sailing, and he tries to keep away from tragedies, he is well-known at scuba diving shows for his prolific sketches of Great Lakes shipwrecks. Scuba diving colleagues show Bob underwater photos and videotapes of newly-discovered wrecks, and he produces exquisitely detailed drawings along the style of Samuel Ward Stanton's pen-and-ink marine drawings of a century ago. His wreck drawings of the schooners, *Emme Neilson, Dunderberg*, and *City of Milwaukee,* and the freighters *John McGean* and *Daniel J. Morrell,* are among his fine works.

Great Lakes marine artist Bob McGreevy applying a remarque to one of his *Titanic* prints at his studio. Bob's specialty is models and prints of Great Lakes ships.   PHOTO BY CRIS KOHL.

Bob's commercial color prints, more than two dozen to date, include fine, original renditions of the *Edmund Fitzgerald*, the Bob-lo steamer *Ste. Claire*, the Great Lakes' White Star Line steamer, *Tashmoo,* a night view of the latter ship at Port Huron, the steamer *William Clay Ford,* and the *Greater Detroit* in the Detroit River.

Examples of Bob McGreevy's *Titanic* artwork can be found on the back cover of this book, and on the half title page.

Bob McGreevy can be contacted at his studio, Marine Art, C.T.M. Associates, P.O. Box 36441, Grosse Pointe, Michigan, 48236, telephone (313) 882-0827. His web site is www.mcgreevy.com

17 The Prophet

In 1898, fourteen years before the *Titanic* disaster, a struggling writer living in New York City concocted a dramatic story about the largest passenger steamer in the world, luxurious and reputed to be unsinkable, crossing the North Atlantic Ocean on her maiden voyage one April, striking an iceberg, and sinking with enormous loss of life.

His name was Morgan Robertson, his novella was published as *Futility*, and his doomed ship was called the *Titan*.

This small book remains to this day the most astonishingly prophetic tale ever written about the sea.

This prophet, the author, was born and raised along the shores of Lake Ontario, the son of a Great Lakes captain.

♦　　♦　　♦　　♦　　♦　　♦　　♦　　♦

Morgan Andrew Robertson came into this world on September 30, 1861, at Oswego, New York, a few hundred feet away from the waters of Lake Ontario. He left this world 53 years later while gazing eastward across the Atlantic Ocean in the direction where *Titanic* sank.

His parents were Captain Andrew Robertson, a well-known master of Great Lakes vessels, and his wife, the former Ruth Glassford (1837-1875) of Prescott, Ontario. Morgan was named after his father's ambitious Oswego friend, Morgan Miles Wheeler, who married a sister of Ruth Glassford and later owned a fleet of Great Lakes schooners. Morgan frequently accompanied his father on lake trips during his summer vacations and "could steer his trick with the best of the men when the weather wasn't too heavy." By the time "Morg" (the nickname used by his friends) reached his early teens in the 1870's, he "knew every stitch of canvas and line on the fore-and-aft canallers and barkentines that made Oswego a port of call."

The first schooner acquired by Captain Robertson was the *Lucy J. Latham* in 1863. Later acquisitions included the *Grenada*, the *Norwegian*, and the *T.S. Mott*. The young Morgan learned sailing upon all of them. His father also skippered vessels like the schooners _Jamaica_ and _Samana,_ owned by Morgan's uncle, Morgan Wheeler.

Another ship owned by Captain Robertson, and upon which the young Morgan often trod as a child, was the _Thomas Kingsford._ This 136-foot schooner, built at Oswego in 1856, was cut by an ice floe and sunk in 26 feet of water about 100 feet off Waugoschance Point, in Lake Michigan just west of the Straits of Mackinac, on April 8, 1871. Her anchors, chain, and items of rigging were salvaged, but the hull, split in two, was a total loss. Although Morgan was only nine years old at the time and far away from it when the ship actually sank, the experience of a familiar vessel being destroyed by ice stayed in the back of his mind, emerging 27 years later when he wrote about a huge ship which sank after hitting ice.

Morgan Robertson's boyhood home on West Fifth Street, near the rough Lake Ontario and Oswego River waterfronts in Oswego, NY, built circa 1860, still exists.　　PHOTO BY CRIS KOHL.

Morgan Robertson was a restless 16-year-old. His widowed father had remarried the year before, and a half-sister was born in 1877. Feeling out of place, Morgan left Oswego in December, 1877, for a life on the high seas. Captain William Bray, master of the clipper ship, _Ringleader,_ out of New York, offered Morgan a job as cabin boy. Before the ship reached China, Morgan had grown to dislike Captain Bray, a brutal man who proved to be unlike the free and easy skippers of the Great Lakes, many of whom the lad knew and who had made a fuss over him because he was "Captain Andy's boy."

But Morgan continued to sail the salt seas, experiencing the work of learning navigation, the sweat of raising anchors, the adventure of sailing to foreign lands, the thrill of exploring wild-and-tumble ports, and the danger of being in a shipwreck, But the glamor of being a full-fledged sailor began to pall, even though he had reached the rank of First Mate. Robertson's efforts to arouse public support for the reform of maritime laws and practices remained a lifelong activity.

Morgan returned to land in 1886 and was hired by Tiffany's in New York as a diamond setter. He stored his nautical knowledge and experiences in the back of his mind for later retrieval.

In love with the outdoors and in awe of femininity, Robertson was never comfortable indoors or in the company of women. He feared that his rough sailor's characteristics would offend females, but, in contrast, they found him attractive and appealing. In 1894, he married Alice M. Doyle and they resided at 149 West Thirty-fifth Street. Later that year, Morgan's sight began to fail. His career was in jeopardy. He left the diamond-setting business and drifted for two years.

Oswego-born and raised writer Morgan Robertson, in a formal portrait taken in New York circa 1899, not long after he began writing.   COURTESY OF THE OSWEGO HISTORICAL SOCIETY.

In 1896, a friend introduced him to a book of sea stories written by Rudyard Kipling. The very evening he finished reading this book, Robertson sat down and wrote his first story on the backs of flyers that he had been paid to deliver. An overturned washtub served as his table. He sold his story, called "The Destruction of the Unfit," to a magazine for $25.00 (which was almost a month's salary for the average worker in 1896).

Thus a writer was born.

Morgan Robertson wrote scores of lively and nautically accurate sea tales among the 200+ stories he penned between 1896 and 1915, most of which appeared in magazines before they were collected and published in book form. The *Dictionary of American Biography*, Volume XVI (p. 27), stated of him: "His stories deal with sailing ships, steam vessels and the long steel men-of-war. They treat of mutiny and bloody fights, shipwreck and rescue, brutality, shanghaiing, courage and wild daring, telepathy, hypnotism, dual personality, and extraordinary inventions."

Booth Tarkington, in the October, 1915 issue of *McClure's Magazine*, wrote that "[Robertson's] stories are bully, his sea foamy, and his men have hair on their chests."

Famed author Joseph Conrad, himself a sailor-turned-writer and the author of books such as *Lord Jim* and *The Heart of Darkness*, corresponded with Robertson: "Indeed, my dear sir, you are a first rate seaman -- one can see that with half an eye."

But Robertson totally surprised his old friends back in Oswego. In their youth, they had noticed absolutely nothing bookish about him. In fact, they remembered his rough voice, his broad shoulders and his stocky build, and thought of him more as a sailor than as anything else. His alternating brushes with wealth and poverty were also recalled in Oswego. It was said that he had fashioned buttons for his coat out of five-dollar gold coins -- an immediate hit with the young ladies in town -- but the "buttons" gradually disappeared over that winter as his need to return them into circulation increased.

In 1905, Morgan Robertson turned inventor, devising a periscope which grew out of an imaginary instrument that he used to embellish one of his submarine stories. The Holland Torpedo Boat Company purchased his invention.

He fitted his New York studio like a ship's cabin with nautical decor. He positioned a cushioned window seat beneath a porthole. He could cover his bathtub and use it as a table. His room was papered with illustrations of his stories.

Robertson's story, "Masters of Men,' dedicated "To my wife, a good woman," told the tale of an orphan lad who works his way up in the navy just prior to the Spanish-American War. This story was made into a silent film in 1923 and shown at Oswego's Orpheum Theater.

Morgan Robertson wrote sea stories, and many of them were tales of the freshwater seas, products of his origins.

"Where Angels Fear to Tread," an early Robertson marine tale, involves a lively bunch of "fresh water" (Great Lakes) sailors who sign up with an ocean sailing rig. The men are all from Oswego, and

Robertson took their nicknames from real-life characters he knew or met during his youth in Oswego or on Great Lakes ships. Some of the colorful nicknames include Turkey Twain, Sorry Welch, Ghost O'Brien, Shiner O'Toole, and Sinful Peck, all very capable fighters who love a good row. The tale's tongue-in-cheek bottom line is that Great Lakes sailors are better men than their saltwater counterparts.

Another of his short stories appears to be a thinly disguised description of a Great Lakes voyage with his father. "A Yarn Without a Moral" relates with a sense of humor the relaxed relationship that existed between captain and crew on the inland seas (contrasting with the strict discipline on ocean ships). Morgan poked some good-spirited fun at the beloved captain, his father.

In 1898, Morgan Robertson wrote a story which would turn out to be eerily prophetic. Published in New York by M.F. Mansfield and Company, the short novel, just over 20,000 words in length and selling for seventy-five cents, was called *Futility*. In it, Morgan envisioned and described the maiden voyage of the largest passenger ship in the world. His imaginary ship was 800 feet long; *Titanic* was 882.5 feet in length. The fictional ship was built with 19 watertight compartments; *Titanic* was constructed with 16 watertight bulkheads. Each ship had three propellers. Both ships were British. The fictional ship was owned by an unspecified steamship company whose major stockholder was a wealthy American named Mr. Selfridge. The real-life *Titanic* was owned by the White Star Line whose major stockholder was the wealthy American, J. P. Morgan. The fictional ship carried 24 lifeboats; *Titanic* had 20. Both ships were deemed "unsinkable." In the story, 2000 lives were lost when the ship sank after striking an iceberg. *Titanic* lost over 1,500 lives when she sank after hitting an iceberg. The name of Morgan Robertson's ship was *Titan*, unbelievably close to the real-life *Titanic*.

Robertson's story often seemed to hit the nail squarely on the head, beginning with the opening words: "She was the largest craft afloat and the greatest of the works of men." Later, "From the bridge, engine room and a dozen places on her deck, the ninety-two doors of nineteen water tight compartments could be closed in half a minute by turning a lever...." and "Unsinkable, indestructible, she carried as few lifeboats as would satisfy the laws," as well as "...She would steam at full speed in fog, storm and sunshine and on the northern lane route, winter and summer,...."

The *Joliet News* in May, 1912, referred to Morgan Robertson as the man with "the eyes that pierced the future," and called his novella, *The Wreck of the Titan*, "the most sensational prophecy of modern times." The newspaper then continued with a glaring misuse, by today's standards, of one of the most common and overused words in the English language: "It was a wonderful forecast of what was to happen, and what did happen, to the steamship *Titanic* off the banks of Newfoundland, when more than 1,500 lives were lost."

Some Great Lakes newspapers, excitedly announcing this upcoming serialization, chose their words poorly (by today's standards and meanings) in advertising Morgan Robertson's 14-year-old tale which prophesied, with shocking accuracies, the loss of *Titanic*.   AUTHOR'S COLLECTION.

Robertson's 1898 story found eager serialization in numerous newspapers in the spring of 1912, including several in the Great Lakes region, such as the *Joliet* (Illinois) *News* and the Fond du Lac, Wisconsin, *Daily Commonwealth*. Preliminary comments advertising this timely publishing event included lines like "Read the graphic narrative of the loss of the *Titan*... and you will see and really live through the eventful night when the palatial *Titanic* crashed into an iceberg and sank two miles to ocean bottom" and "It is a sea story of absorbing interest, full of action and adventure, and... well worth reading---a far better story in fact than the average 'best seller.'"

Robertson frightened people who had just met him or who knew him only as an acquaintance when his story about the loss of the *Titan* was serialized in newspapers in the spring and summer of 1912.

But no one, including Robertson, seems to have recorded his reaction to the tragic loss of *Titanic* in 1912.

"Something ahead, sir. Can't make it out."

Examples of the artwork that enhanced the newspaper serialization of Morgan Robertson's "The Wreck of the *Titan*" in 1912. They are similar to the *Titanic* story.   AUTHOR'S COLLECTION.

Two other prophetic tales received considerable publicity in the spring of 1912. Mayn Clew Garnett was the author of a story called "The White Ghost of Disaster," about an 800-foot passenger liner crashing into an iceberg and sinking with half the lives on board because there were not lifeboats for all. However, the well-publicized *Titanic* was being fitted out for her maiden voyage when this story was written, so it hardly qualifies as fortunetelling. In fact, it appeared in print after *Titanic* sank, in the May, 1912, issue of *Popular Magazine*.

William Stead's 1893 novel, *From the Old World to the New*, showcased a large oceanliner which sank after a collision with an iceberg. If Stead had clairvoyance, he ignored the warning, for he was one of the more than 1,500 people lost when *Titanic* sank.

Morgan Robertson's autobiography appeared in the March 28, 1914, issue of *Saturday Evening Post*. He described his life, so full of ups and downs, and experiences ranging from sailing the Great Lakes to circumnavigating the globe, from cow-punching in Texas to learning a jeweller's art, from attaining financial success as a writer to later living a hand-to-mouth existence in New York City, having few possessions but many friends, always on the move and forever experimenting. He named his story "Gathering No Moss." It told of the fate of a writer of sea stories when he became written out.

Morgan Robertson felt that he had reached the end of his life. One writer described him during this time as keeping busy "autographing books and visiting bars." Definitely an alcoholic, Robertson also suffered from rheumatism, insomnia and depression.

In December, 1914, Robertson's "The Closing of the Circuit," was filmed by the Vitagraph Company of America, with Morgan serving as technical advisor for the marine sequences. In early 1915, the same company filmed a second Robertson story, "The Enemies," which ironically deals with the consequences of alcoholism.

But Morgan Robertson never lived to see the film.

◆   ◆   ◆   ◆   ◆   ◆   ◆   ◆

One of the top headlines on the front page of the March 25, 1915 issue of the *New York Times* announced boldly, "Morgan Robertson Dies Standing Up."

> "ATLANTIC CITY, N. J., March 24 -- Morgan Robertson, of New York, the writer of sea stories, was found dead this afternoon in his room in a hotel here. He was standing when found, leaning against a bureau, on the top of which his head rested. On the bureau was a bottle containing paraldehyde, which Mr. Robertson had been using to induce sleep, and it was at first thought that death had resulted from an overdose. A physician, however, said that heart disease was the cause. Mr. Robertson came here some time ago to recover from a nervous breakdown...."

The *Titanic* prophet had passed into the Great Unknown.

18 Aftermaths

Titanic's sinking obviously affected a great many people, more individuals than ever strolled its decks. There were relatives and friends of the survivors and the deceased, and there were even people who had absolutely nothing to do with *Titanic*.

In Detroit, an 18-year-old man grew morbid from reading the newspaper accounts of *Titanic's* sinking and swallowed poison. Administered an antidote, he was hospitalized in serious condition.

In Chicago, a young man, formerly a bellboy at the Auditorium Hotel, reportedly became mentally unbalanced when he read about the *Titanic* disaster. He marched out into the icy waters of Lake Michigan at the foot of Foster Avenue, waving a long saber and proclaiming, "No ship leaves the shore. I am a-gonta stop these shipwrecks." Police quickly rushed him to a detention hospital.

In Boissevain, Manitoba, a man with a history of heart trouble dropped dead when he heard of the disaster the day after *Titanic* sank.

However, Trans-Atlantic crossings remained popular, with only small pockets of concern. Forty Chicagoans had booked passage on *Titanic* for spring crossings (the majority for the vessel's return trip). After the disaster, half of them sought refunds instead of booking on another vessel, "deciding to risk their lives in 'seeing America first' rather than in dodging icebergs," as one Chicago newspaper put it.

The *Titanic* tragedy did not dampen the wanderlust of many. In Duluth, Minnesota, almost 100 Norwegian residents had planned to take *Titanic* back to Europe in May, 1912, so they could attend the Olympic games in Christiana, Norway, that summer. None of them changed their minds about making the voyage after the tragic sinking.

"The majority favor making a slower voyage than usual, looking toward safety rather than speed," acknowledged group organizer, Fred Erickson, after *Titanic* sank. "The list of those going has been increasing and that before the date of leaving Duluth on May 8, I expect that the number will be between 100 and 150."

◆   ◆   ◆   ◆   ◆   ◆   ◆   ◆

A month after *Titanic* sank, on May 13, 1912, the White Star Line ship, *Oceanic*, while crossing the Atlantic, spotted something bobbing at latitude 39.56 N., longitude 47.01 W. It was one of *Titanic's* collapsible lifeboats carrying a cane with the name "Duane Williams" on it (Charles Duane Williams, 51, a lawyer travelling First Class with his son to Pennsylvania, was killed when *Titanic's* funnel toppled onto him), a coat with letters addressed to Richard N. Williams (who was Charles Duane William's 21-year-old professional tennis player son, on his way to attend Harvard; he survived the sinking and went on to a successful career in tennis and banking until his death in June, 1968), a ring inscribed "Edward and Gerda," and a grisly cargo of three badly decomposed male bodies. The corpses were those of Thomson Beattie of Winnipeg and two unidentified crewmembers, one a sailor and the other a fireman. It was Beattie who had told Arthur Peuchen about the orders to don lifebelts and lower the lifeboats. Bits of cork appeared on and in the mouths of the deceased, lending credence to the theory that they had been starving to death and, in desperation, broke open their lifejackets to eat the cork interior. This was the conclusion of Dr. French of the *Oceanic's* medical staff. The public was aghast at the thought of these unfortunate individuals' suffering.

The White Star Line quickly and repeatedly responded to this news: "With reference to the boat picked up by the *Oceanic*, the White Star Line repeats what it stated yesterday, that Officer Lowe, before the senate investigating committee at Washington, testified that he took from the boat 20 men and one woman, leaving in it the bodies of three men, who all the passengers said were dead, and who, he was certain, were dead some time before he abandoned the boat."

Another company official quickly added an explanation for the cork bits. "The sea was full of floating cork, and the finding of these particles does not, in my view, lend credence to the starvation theory."

The bodies, taken aboard the *Oceanic* and sewn into canvas with steel weights at their feet, were buried at sea. Coincidentally, Thomson Beattie was buried at sea in the exact location where his mother had been born on a ship 82 years earlier, to the day.

The finding of these *Titanic* bodies recalled a strange coincidence in the Great Lakes. Captain Edward Martin, master of the Anchor Line steamer, *Octorara,* told the press that it was entirely possible for shipwreck bodies to wind up in unusual locations at odd times. Using a local example, he told about the steamer, *Clarion,* which had caught fire and burned to the waterline off Point Pelee in western Lake Erie just three years earlier with tragic loss of life.

"One morning about two months after that disaster," Captain Martin recounted, "someone notified the Anchor Line offices in

Buffalo, New York, that a body wearing a lifebelt from the *Clarion* had floated ashore four miles down the Niagara River. It was found to be indeed the corpse of one of the ill-fated passengers and had floated the 244 miles in just 55 days, averaging almost four and a half miles per day, showing among other things, that there is a pretty good current heading seawards in Lake Erie."

Stranger still was the location where the body washed ashore. It was at the foot of the street where the dead man had lived with his family when he was alive, in a house only two blocks away.

He had simply come home.

◆　　◆　　◆　　◆　　◆　　◆　　◆　　◆

In the 1930's and '40's, many survivors declined invitations to attend *Titanic* reunions. The pain was still too fresh, so the idea appalled them. But the 1950's saw the "second wave" of public interest in *Titanic* with the release of the 1953 film called "*Titanic*," starring Clifton Webb and Barbara Stanwyck, followed in late 1955 with the publication of lawyer Walter Lord's first book, *A Night to Remember*, which was turned into a successful motion picture in 1958. Lord's attention to detail and accuracy, and his ability to spin a good tale in few, well-chosen words, propelled his book to the bestseller lists. He switched professions and enjoyed an incredible career as an historian.

From then on, interest in *Titanic* never waned. The *Titanic* Historical Society was formed in the early 1960's, other similar groups followed, and *Titanic* reunions became increasingly popular, in many instances offering good therapy. Survivors who had never talked about their experiences that tragic night came out of their shells ---and found that they enjoyed relating their recollections to appreciative audiences. However, public fascination with *Titanic* did hit another incredible "high," or its "third wave," when Robert Ballard located and photographed the remains of *Titanic* under two-and-a-half miles of ocean on September 1, 1985, spawning several subsequent expeditions to the site. Walter Lord wrote a successful sequel to his original book called *The Night Lives On*.

The most recent, the "fourth wave" (and likely the last; can one climb higher than Everest?) of public absorption with *Titanic* arrived in late 1997 and early 1998 with the mass popularity of James Cameron's film, "*Titanic*," which became the highest grossing film of all time, garnishing over one billion dollars worldwide. So intense was the resulting surge of public interest in all things *Titanic* that Walter Lord found his 1955 book, *A Night to Remember*, on the bestseller charts again!

◆　　◆　　◆　　◆　　◆　　◆　　◆　　◆

Some *Titanic* survivors remained emotionally plagued by the tragic sinking for the rest of their lives, while others put this tragedy behind them and went on with their existences.

Titanic survivors bound for the Great Lakes area lived varied lives:

Helmina Nilsson resided in Joliet, Illinois, for a few years, married a fellow Swede in 1918, and eventually returned with him and their family to Sweden. She died there in the town of Hillefällan, Rörvik, in May, 1971. The Joliet press reported in 1912, "...Her inability to understand English kept many of the horrible details of the accident from her, and for this reason she has suffered little from nervousness."

Six-year-old **Nina Harper**, was travelling with her father, Reverend John Harper, from London to Chicago. He died in the sinking and little Nina returned to England with her aunt, Jessie Leitch, a week after arriving in New York. Nina was raised by her father's brothers, and she later married a minister. She died in England in 1986 without ever having visited Chicago.

Jessie Leitch, Nina Harper's aunt, returned to England after *Titanic's* sinking, and died there about 50 years later.

Ida Hippach returned to her comforting husband, Louis, in Chicago, where she had been born. Tragedy struck in 1914 when her son, Howard, was killed in an automobile which flipped into a pond. Ida then devoted herself to children's welfare work. She also belonged to the Audubon Society, the Chicago Humane Society and the German Altenheim. In later life, she enjoyed the company of her daughter and her three grandchildren. She died in Chicago at the age of 72 on September 22, 1940, outliving her husband by five years.

Jean Hippach returned to Chicago with her mother and married Swedish businessman Hjalmar Unander-Scharin in 1920, with whom she had three children, two daughters and a son (whom she named after her late brother, Howard) before their divorce in 1929. Jean moved to a beautiful home on the ocean in Osterville, Massachusetts, just west of Hyannis, after her mother's death in 1940, and she relocated again to nearby Barnstable, Massachusetts, where she died at the age of 79 on Nov. 14, 1974. Both Jean and Ida are buried in Chicago's Rose Hill Cemetery.

Anna Katherine Kelly took a train to Chicago with fellow survivor Annie McGowan after leaving a New York City hospital in April, 1912, and eventually became a nun until her death in December, 1969, in Adrian, Michigan. She returned for a visit to Ireland once in her lifetime.

Annie McGowan left St. Vincent's Hospital in New York City after a few days and made her way with Anna Kelly to Chicago where she later married a man named Straube. She died there at the age of 92 on January 30, 1990.

Norwegian **Karl Albert Midtsjø** made it to Chicago on April 26, 1912, and married Anna Paulson from Wisconsin in 1913. In the early 1920's they moved back to Norway, but returned to Illinois a year later. Hereditary heart disease killed Karl at the age of 48 on January 25, 1939. His wife died two decades later, and they are buried in Mount Olive Cemetery in Chicago.

Miss **Velin Öhman** travelled to the home of her uncle, Henry Forsander, in Chicago, as she had claimed, but the "uncle" turned out to be her fiancé, and they were soon married. She lived in Chicago for the next 54 years, until her death on November 19, 1966. "Vivian" Forsander was buried at Chapel Hill Gardens in Elmhurst just outside Chicago.

Hilda Maria Hellström stayed with her widowed aunt in Evanston, Illinois, married John Larson in that city on December 7, 1915, and lived most of her life at 1870 Green Bay Road in Highland Park, a Chicago suburb. She remained terrified of water for the rest of her life, and never again crossed any ocean or lake. She died at the age of 72 at her daughter's house in Streator, Illinois, on March 16, 1962 (her husband had died in 1948), and she was buried in Skokie.

Franz Karun remained in Galesburg, Illinois, operating a boarding house, until 1914, when he and his family, including daughter, **Manca Karun,** who was travelling with him when they survived *Titanic's* sinking, returned to his home town of Milje, Slovenia. He died there on July 7, 1934, while his daughter passed away in the 1970's.

Dagmar Bryhl, completely shaken by the loss of her brother and fiancé in *Titanic's* sinking, reached Rockford, Illinois, but returned home to Sweden within a month and eventually married there. She died in Sweden in the summer of 1969 at the age of 77.

Albert and **Sylvia Caldwell**, both from Roseville, Illinois, survived, but their marriage did not, ending in 1930. Both remarried. Albert died in Richmond, VA, on March 10, 1977, while Sylvia passed away in Normal, Illinois, on January 14, 1965. Their son, **Alden Caldwell,** born in Bangkok 10 months before *Titanic* sank, became a chemical engineer in Pennsylvania. Although he sometimes talked about *Titanic,* the subject held little interest for him; he had been too young to remember the sinking. A lifelong bachelor, he died on December 18, 1992, at his winter residence in Largo, Florida.

Alice Johnson and her two children, **Harold Johnson** (4) and **Eleanor Johnson** (1), returned to St. Charles, Illinois. Alice died there on December 19, 1968, at the age of eighty-three, while Harold predeceased her by eight months, dying on April 10, 1968, at the age of sixty just a year after he retired from the International Harvester

Company. Eleanor married Delbert Shuman. In later years, her living room was filled with *Titanic* photos, books, a model and other memorabilia, and she attended two conventions for *Titanic* survivors in Delaware and Boston. In 1996, she returned to the wreck site when salvage attempts were made on some of the wreckage. She passed away on March 7, 1998, one of the last seven *Titanic* survivors, only a month after seeing the film, *Titanic,* at a special screening with director James Cameron and others from the production. The realistic film revived memories, and Eleanor cried considerably during the film, but she was cheered up when Cameron told her that she reminded him of Rose, a main character in his film. She was buried in Elgin, Illinois.

After Wilhelm Ström, who had remained at home in Indiana Harbor, Indiana, lost his wife, Elna, and daughter, Selma, on *Titanic*, he obtained work for his late wife's brother, **Ernst Persson**, who had survived the sinking. Ernst (who later changed his name to Ernest Pearson) worked and lived in Indiana for the rest of his life. He died in Hammond on October 17, 1951, at the age of 65.

Nellie Becker and her children, **Ruth** (12), **Marion** (4), and **Richard** (1), returned to Benton Harbor, Michigan. Nellie, who became upset whenever the discussion turned to *Titanic,* died at the age of 84 on February 15, 1961, and was interred in the Becker family plot at Princeton, Illinois with her missionary husband, Reverend Allen Becker, who had died in 1956. Marion died of tuberculosis in California at 36 on February 15, 1944, and was buried in the family plot at Princeton. Richard, the youngest, who was married in St. Louis in 1943, died at the age of 65 on September 6, 1975, exactly a year and a week after his wife passed away. He was buried in Peoria, Illinois. Ruth went to school in Ohio, taught high school in Kansas, and married former classmate Dan Blanchard. For years, Ruth tried to put *Titanic* out of her mind, but began talking freely about her experiences after she retired and moved to California. She became a regular at *Titanic* conventions. When she died at the age of 90 on July 6, 1990 (earlier that year, she had taken her first ocean trip since 1912, a cruise in Mexico), her cremated remains were taken to the site of *Titanic's* sinking and scattered over the rolling waters.

Theodoor De Mulder reached his destination, Detroit, worked at the Ford Motor Company plant, later tried farming in Canada, but, in 1931, returned to Belgium where he set up a café named after *Titanic*. When he died on April 19, 1954, he was 72 years old.

Emily Goldsmith and her son, **Frank Goldsmith, Jr.** (9), settled in Detroit as planned after the death of Frank Goldsmith, Sr., on *Titanic*. Emily married Harry Illman. She died on a train in Ohio on September 22, 1955, at the age of 72. Frank, Jr., operated a photography store in Mansfield, Ohio, until he retired in 1979. He died in Florida on January 27, 1982, at 79. His cremated remains were strewn into the waters over the *Titanic* site.

This impressive *"Titanic* Monument" marks the final resting place of Michael Peter "Ty" Joseph and his wife, Catherine, in section 26 of the Resurrection Cemetery in the Detroit suburb of Clinton Township, Michigan. In the white column base are etched the words, "Michael P. Joseph, nicknamed 'Ty' and recognized as a miracle child by the Nuns of Sts. Peter & Paul Jesuit Church after surviving the sinking of the *Titanic* on April 12 [sic], 1912." PHOTO BY CRIS KOHL.

Catherine Joseph and her children, **Michael Joseph** (4) and **Anna Mary Joseph** (2), luckily survived the sinking, but were followed by misfortune. Anna died when her clothing caught on fire from her bedroom stove at their Detroit home at 134 Congress Street East on March 22, 1914, when she was only four. Catherine died a year later from her old foe, tuberculosis; she was a mere 27. Only Michael lived to old age, dying in Detroit on May 18, 1991, at the age of 84, after enjoying 24 years of retirement. He had been a soft drink driver for Vernor's in Detroit, and he never lost enthusiasm for telling the story of his rescue from *Titanic*. Throughout his life, the story he enjoyed telling the most was that he would never have lived if not for a guardian angel that saved him when the giant vessel sank. A beautiful, impressive depiction of *Titanic* steaming towards the iceberg is etched onto his huge marble headstone at Resurrection Cemetery in Clinton Township northeast of Detroit, and these words are emblazoned on the base: "Michael P. Joseph, nicknamed 'Ty' and recognized as a miracle child by the Nuns of Sts. Peter & Paul Jesuit Church after surviving the sinking of the *Titanic* on April 12 [sic], 1912." The nickname, "Ty," came from "*Titanic*," and was bestowed on him by the nuns. Michael's wife, Catherine, who died on March 3, 1998, rests beside her husband beneath the same monument.

Jane Quick and her daughters, **Winifred Quick** (8) and **Phyllis Quick** (2), remained in the Detroit area, residing at 1497 Roslyn Road, Grosse Pointe Woods, Michigan. Phyllis, who had married William Murphy, with whom she had four children, died on March 15, 1954, at the age of 45, while Jane passed away on February 24, 1965 at the age of 86 (her husband, Frederick, had died six years earlier). Winifred married Alois Van Tongerloo, and their family grew to include three sons and two daughters. They enjoyed camping, and did so in almost every state of the union. Alois died in the summer of 1987. Winifred is the only remaining *Titanic* survivor from the Great Lakes region, residing in a retirement home near Lansing, Michigan. She is 96.

Jean Scheerlinckx, unable to find farm work in the Detroit area, accepted the White Star Line's offer of free return transportation to Europe. In Belgium, he quickly married, served in the military during World War I, then spent the remainder of his life in farming. His popular firsthand *Titanic* tales kept his glass full from appreciative listeners in local cafés. Jean died in his home town at the age of 73 on June 25, 1956.

Julius Sap went to Detroit, but in 1914 was doing farmwork in the Toronto area. He returned to Belgium to enlist in the army during World War I, married after the war, and travelled with his wife to Winnipeg, Manitoba, for farm work in 1924. A year later, they returned to Belgium for good. After a lifetime of farm work, Julius passed away on December 15, 1966, at the age of 79.

The wealthy newlyweds, **Dickinson** and **Helen Bishop**, delayed when they gave testimony at the Senate inquiry, returned to Dowagiac, Michigan, to considerable misfortune. Their baby, a son whom they named Randall Walton Bishop was born on December 8, 1912 (less than eight months after *Titanic* sank), but died within two days.

The couple escaped for a visit to California, where they experienced an earthquake. To fulfill the final Egyptian prophecy, Helen suffered a serious automobile accident outside Kalamazoo, Michigan, on November 5, 1913. With her husband's cousin at the wheel, the car struck a tree head-on. Helen flew from the front seat over the windshield and through the tree's branches before striking her head on the concrete. Emergency surgery in Kalamazoo removed a portion of her skull and some brain tissue, and installed a silver plate. The *New York Times* hastily proclaimed that Helen Bishop was "fatally injured" in the accident, but she did recover. However, her personality changed radically. After a two-month recovery spent in the hospital, she was about to go home when an attack of appendicitis and subsequent surgery kept her in the hospital for another three weeks, prompting a local newspaper to describe her as belonging to "the class immune from fatal results." Later that year, on September 18, 1914, she escaped injury when she accidentally drove her electric coupe into a taxicab in Battle Creek, Michigan. The taxi was badly wrecked and the driver seriously injured.

By then, many elements combined to work against the Bishops, and they announced their divorce on January 18, 1916. Dickinson, who had paid a $100,000 settlement to Helen, was in Palm Beach, Florida at the time, and Helen decided to take a cruise to Panama. Upon her return, she visited a friend in Danville, Illinois, where emergency surgery upon her old head wound resulted in her death on March 15, 1916. After an intense 23 years, her adventurous life was over. The former "belle of Sturgis, Michigan, society" was buried beside her infant son in the town where she grew up.

Dickinson Bishop struggled against false rumors that he had disguised himself as a woman to escape the sinking *Titanic*. He suffered more than he let on when his infant son died and when his wife was almost killed in the car accident. He had already been widowed once, when his first wife, Mary Lee, died in childbirth, with the infant dying too, on September 28, 1910, two years after they were married and a year after they returned from their year-long, round-the-world honeymoon. The fact that Mary Lee's will left her husband over half a million dollars did not assuage his loss. One account indicated that Dickinson, deluged with these many personal tragedies, sought solace in alcohol after Helen's accident, and that this only inflamed the Bishops' relationship. However, less than two months after their marriage ended, Dickinson remarried for his third and final time. He had experienced the extremes of fortune and misfortune; he was not yet 30. He married his third wife, Sydney Boyce, a daughter of the American Boy Scout movement founder (a monument to that effect towers over his gravesite), in Atlanta, Georgia, on March 14, 1916. Ironically, the front page of the *Dowagiac Daily News*, in two articles poised like boxers in their respective corners, tactlessly announced the gleeful news of Dickinson's remarriage opposite the tragic tidings of Helen's death.

Headlines of the *Dowagiac Daily News*, March 14, 1916, featured stories of very opposite moods about each of the estranged Bishops who had survived *Titanic's* sinking.   AUTHOR'S COLLECTION.

On the day Helen's short life ended, Dickinson and Sydney Bishop sped westward-bound by train for a two-to-three-month honeymoon in Honolulu. They arranged for their chauffeur, Earl Patterson, to meet them with their car in San Francisco, where they all, car included, boarded a ship to Hawaii.

Dickinson enlisted and served in World War I when the U.S.A. entered it in 1917. After the war, he lived in Ottawa, Illinois, working as general manager of the utility company. He and Sydney had two sons and a daughter, but still engaged in one of their favorite activities: travel. In the summer of 1923, for example, the family cruised aboard the steamer, *Lapland* (coincidentally the same vessel which carried *Titanic's* surviving crew back to England in 1912.) Dickinson died of a stroke at the age of 73 on February 16, 1961, and was buried near the Boyce family plot next to Sydney, who had predeceased him in 1950. His headstone lists him as "Husband of Sydney Boyce," perhaps because his third marriage was the start of a hitherto unknown happy or virtually problem-free life, and the legacy he wished to leave behind excluded previous wives and *Titanic*.

Helen Walton Bishop was laid to rest at the tender age of 23 in her home town of Sturgis, Michigan (left). The child that she was already carrying on board *Titanic,* a boy whom the parents named Randall Walton Bishop, lived for only two days and also lies in Sturgis with his mother (below). Dickinson Bishop's headstone in Ottawa, Illinois, hints that life, for him, began with his third marriage (below left). PHOTOS BY CRIS KOHL.

Hanna Touma (who later anglicized her name to Anna Thomas) and her two children, **Maria Touma** (9) and **Georges Touma** (7), joined husband Darwis Touma in Dowagiac, Michigan, and lived there from 1912 until 1920, when the family moved to Michigan City, Indiana, on the shores of Lake Michigan. In 1923, they moved one final time to Burton (just outside Flint), Michigan. Hanna died in a Flint hospital at the age of 91 on June 28, 1976. Maria passed away on August 12, 1953 at 50, while Georges died at 87 on December 9, 1991, also in Flint. Although all five passengers bound for the little town of Dowagiac, Michigan, survived *Titanic's* sinking, the Toumas (Third Class passengers) and the Bishops (First Class passengers) never met, neither before nor after the tragedy, indicative of the strong and distinct separation of the classes in the existing social structure.

Maude Sincock joined her miner father in Hancock, Michigan, and recounted the story of her rescue on various Upper Michigan community stages to attentive audiences. In 1918, she married Arling Roberts, who worked loading and unloading ships at the docks in Ripley, Michigan. He died in late 1969. In her later years, Maude often visited her sisters in Chicago, but she never stepped aboard an ocean liner again. She became a popular source for *Titanic* interviews on radio and television until her death on May 21, 1984, at Hancock.

Elizabeth Agnes Davies and her youngest son, nine-year-old **John, Jr.,** joined her other son from a previous marriage and her daughter-in-law in Calumet, in Michigan's Upper Peninsula. Elizabeth remarried and died 20 years later on August 4, 1933, at the age of 70. Although John had moved to Detroit, after he died on December 16, 1951, his body was returned to Calumet, Michigan, for interment at Lakeview Cemetery where his mother was buried.

Borak Hannah arrived at Port Huron, Michigan, on the southern shores of Lake Huron, and within three months married Miss Elizabeth Hassey. Over the years, he worked in factories, anglicized his name to Bert Johns, ran a fruit store on Quay Street, and ultimately operated a tavern, but never left Michigan. He died at the age of 66 on February 2, 1952, at his home at 216 Broad Street, Port Huron.

Nicola Lulich landed in New York and headed straight to his uncle's residence in Chicago while enroute to Chisholm, Minnesota, where he had worked in the mines for almost a decade before his visit to Croatia in late 1911-1912. After World War I, he returned to Croatia and died there at the age of 79 in 1962.

Alice Silvey returned to her home in Duluth, Minnesota, without her husband who had gone down with *Titanic*. She remarried six years later to Richard Patrick and she died on May 2, 1958, in Duluth at the age of 85.

Another Duluth native, **Constance Willard**, moved from Minnesota to California in 1934, apparently to be close to her sister. Constance, who never married, died at the age of 73 on April 25, 1964.

Hedwig Turkula had been a widow for ten years when she decided, at the age of 63, to move to America from Finland and settle in Minnesota, where half of her many children and grandchildren lived. She died there ten years later on April 3, 1922.

Olaus Abelseth headed to Minneapolis, Minnesota, after surviving *Titanic's* sinking, and worked in Canada and Montana before returning to his South Dakota farm, where he married Anna Grinde in the summer of 1915. They retired in 1946 and moved to Hettinger, North Dakota. Anna died at the age of 100 in 1978, and Olaus passed away at the age of 94 on December 4, 1980.

Sixteen-year-old **Karen Abelseth** travelled to Minneapolis after a short stay in a New York City hospital upon arrival on board the *Carpathia*. She died in California on July 27, 1969, at the age of 73.

Johan Asplund joined his brother, Fred, in Minneapolis, for a few years, but in 1923 returned to Oskarshamn, a seaport city in Sweden, and died there on August 14, 1943.

Mahala Dutton Douglas returned to her mansion at Lake Minnetonka outside Minneapolis, Minnesota. Her husband had perished on *Titanic,* and she never remarried. She died on April 21, 1945, at the age of 81, and was buried beside her husband in Oak Hill Cemetery, Cedar Rapids, Iowa.

Newlyweds **John** and **Nelle Snyder** returned to Wayzata, a suburb of Minneapolis, Minnesota, where they raised three children. John, who served with the armed forces in World War I, died of a heart attack at the age of 71 while playing golf on July 22, 1959. Nelle died at the age of 94 on December 9, 1983, and was buried next to her husband in Lakewood Cemetery in Minneapolis.

Joseph Dequemin, bound for Albion, New York, ended up returning to Guernsey in the Channel Islands, England. His legs never recovered from the cold during the night *Titanic* sank, and both of them were amputated years later. He died some time in the mid 1960's.

Grace Bowen, the Ryerson's governess, returned to Cooperstown, New York, where she taught at a girls' school and where she succumbed to a cerebral hemorrhage in 1945 at the age of 78.

Emily Ryerson and her children, **Suzette Ryerson** (21), **Emily Borie Ryerson** (18), and **John Borie Ryerson** (13), returned home to Cooperstown, New York. Suzette went to France in 1916 during World War I to work as a bacteriologist in a field hospital, where she was decorated with the Croix de Guerre. There she met the man she later married, Lieutenant George Patterson (who also had been awarded the Croix de Guerre). After the war, they settled in Morristown, New Jersey. On January 13, 1921, Suzette died of heart failure at the age of

30 after an operation for appendicitis. She was buried in the family plot at Cooperstown. Their daughter, Emily, was married twice before she died in 1960 at the age of 66. The Chicago-born John graduated from Yale in 1921, and was an investor, as well as owning and operating a golf course. He died at the age of 87 at his winter home in Palm Beach, Florida, on January 21, 1986. Single until his mid-50's, when he eventually married, he and his wife had no children.

Victorine Chaudanson, the Ryerson maid, married a man named Henry Perkins and lived in Delaware County, Pennsylvania, where she died on August 17, 1962, at the age of 86.

Another Ryerson/*Titanic*/Great Lakes connections was one of the ship's Second Class Saloon Stewards, a distant Ryerson cousin named **William Edwy Ryerson**. He had been born in the small harbor town of Port Dover, Ontario, in 1879, on the shores of Lake Erie (this perhaps influenced his decision to work at sea). It is not likely that he and the Ryerson family were aware of each other's presence on board *Titanic,* as he had left North America many years earlier. After *Titanic's* loss, he and his English wife moved to Ontario, Canada, to try their hand at farming, but upon retirement, they returned to England, where William died on December 9, 1949, at the age of 70.

A gravestone in Holley, New York, near Lake Ontario, marks empty ground, but serves to commemorate two local male passengers, William Doughton and Peter McKain, who were lost at sea when *Titanic* sank. The date of "April 14, 1912" is a bit askew.   PHOTO BY CRIS KOHL.

Norman and **Bertha Chambers** returned home to Ithaca, New York. Bertha died on October 16, 1959, at the age of 80, while Norman passed away at a hotel in Portugal on February 9, 1966, at 81.

Edward and **Ethel Beane,** another of *Titanic's* honeymoon couples, both survived the sinking and travelled on to Rochester, New York, where Edward worked as a bricklayer. Edward died at the age of 68 on October 24, 1948, and Ethel passed away at the age of 90 in a nursing home on September 17, 1983. They are buried together at White Haven Memorial Park in Perinton, New York. Neither of them stepped aboard a ship again after their *Titanic* experience.

Lillian Bentham, born in Holley, New York, but returning to her family in Rochester, New York, married John Black in 1918 and they resided at 11 Kay Terrace in Rochester. She died on December 15, 1977 at the age of 84.

Elizabeth Hocking lived at 195 Gale Street, Akron, Ohio, for two years until April 9, 1914, when she was accidentally killed in a streetcar accident. She was 54 years old.

Elizabeth Hocking's sister, **Ellen Needs Wilkes,** made it to her nephew's residence in Akron, Ohio, and remained in that city for the rest of her life. She died a recluse at the age of 90 on April 27, 1955. She lived in squalor without heat or running water in winter, and she slept sitting in a chair surrounded by years worth of unopened mail. Frostbitten feet were partially the cause of her death.

Elizabeth Hocking's older daughter, **Emily Hocking Richards,** and her two young children, **William Rowe Richards** (3) and **George Sibley Richards** (1), rejoined Emily's husband and the boys' father, James Sibley Richards, in Akron, Ohio, where they remained for several years before returning to England. Emily died at Penzance, England, on November 10, 1972, at the age of 85. William died at Penzance on January 9, 1988, at the age of 78, while George had passed away there a month earlier on December 4, 1987, at 76.

Elizabeth Hocking's younger daughter, **Ellen "Nellie" Hocking,** married George Hambly as planned, and they lived their lives briefly in Akron, Ohio, until moving to Schenectady, New York. She died on October 14, 1963, at the age of 71.

Addie Wells and her two children, **Joan Wells** (4) and **Ralph Wells** (2) were met in New York by their husband/father, Arthur Wells, and they all travelled together to Akron, Ohio, where Arthur had been living and working. They resided at 613 Euclid Avenue, and later at 712 Patterson Avenue. Another son, Arthur, was born in 1918. Addie died at Akron on May 28, 1954, at the age of 71. Joan started working for the B.F. Goodrich Company when she was 17 in 1925. She underwent two operations, but died of peritonitis on July 10, 1933, at the age of 25. Her fiancé, William F. Lachman, was on a fishing trip far in the Canadian north woods and sadly could not be reached in time to return to her side. Ralph married Colina Troutman Wells and they resided at 260 Madison Avenue, Akron. He died at the age of 62 on September 27, 1972.

Anna Turja was given a train ticket to Ashtabula by the White Star Line in New York City so she could reach the home of her sister and brother-in-law at 81 Oak Street. In that city she met her future husband, Emil Lundi, and they had seven children. In later years, the widowed Anna lived with one of her sons in Long Beach, California, where she died on December 20, 1982, at the age of 89. She was buried in Edgewater Cemetery, Ashtabula, Ohio.

Martha Evelyn Stone died on May 12, 1924, in New York City, at the age of 75. Childless, she bequeathed her cash and personal possessions to **Amelia Icard**, who was her maid on board *Titanic*. Martha was laid to rest in Cincinnati, Ohio, next to her husband, George Stone, who had died in 1901.

Victor Sunderland travelled by train from New York to Cleveland after he left the *Carpathia*. He later married May McNaughton and in 1923, they moved to Toronto, where they resided at 63 1/2 Waverley Road. Victor, who worked as a plumber, died on August 21, 1973.

Banoura Ayoub travelled to Columbus, Ohio, to be re-united with her family. Eventually they relocated to Windsor, Ontario.

Fahim Leeni (Philip Zenni) reached his destination of Dayton, Ohio, where he worked as a machinist. He died on December 2, 1927, of pneumonia, at the age of 38.

Chicago-born **Caroline Bonnell**, a resident of Youngstown, Ohio, married Paul Jones, who became a federal judge, and they had two children. She died at Shaker Heights, Ohio on March 13, 1950, at 67.

After her husband's death on *Titanic*, **Mary Hitchcock Wick** of Youngstown, Ohio, kept herself very busy with volunteer work for organizations such as the Young Women's Christian Association and the Free Kindergarten Association. She died on January 29, 1920, at the age of 52. Her daughter, **Mary Natalie Wick**, married a military man from England named Thomas Nevinson in 1916, and she spent most of the remainder of her life living in England and France. She died in England at the age of 63 due to complications after surgery on October 13, 1944.

David Vartanian sojourned to Hamilton and Brantford, Ontario, with his compatriot and fellow *Titanic* survivor, Neshan Krekorian, for a short time. David immediately began work at contacting his wife, Mary, who had stayed behind in Armenia. Political oppression in that country, and people on the move from village to village because of government persecution, made it impossible for David to contact, or even locate, his wife. Months passed with only depressing news reports of massacres reaching David. He stubbornly refused to give up, and, with assistance from friends, he kept writing letters to churches, town councils, and newspapers in Armenia.

Years passed. People told David that Mary had likely been killed in one of the recurring waves of bloodshed in the old country. But

David maintained both his faith that she was alive and his correspondence to various agencies that could help him prove it.

Ten years after he commenced his campaign to find his wife, his endless allegiance met with reward when a letter arrived from Armenia stating that Mary was alive. Neither David nor Mary had remarried during their long, trying period of separation. But it was not until early 1924 that the two lovers-in-exile could, once and for all, overcome the geographic and political barriers which separated them. Mary Vartanian landed in Canada, and her husband, David, by this time, lived in the United States. As if arranged by fate itself, the nearest border crossing was that honeymoon capital for lovers, Niagara Falls, and only a churning river separated the couple. With Mary starting across the pedestrian bridge from the Canadian side, and David from the American side, the pace of their strides increased when they sighted each other. Years of anguish and separation ended the moment they embraced in the middle of that bridge which, for one brief moment unknown to the rest of the world, linked much more than two of the largest and most powerful countries in the world.

Eventually David and Mary Vartanian settled in Detroit, residing at 1563 Livernois, and raised three children. David worked for the McLouth Steel Corporation for many years and died on August 3, 1966, at the age of 76, while his wife, Mary, died on October 12, 1979, at the age of 84. They lie together forever in Woodmere Cemetery.

Theirs is one of the more powerful *Titanic* love stories.

David and Mary Vartanian struggled long and hard to overcome forces that sought to keep them apart. "*Titanic* David's" children proudly added the words, "*Titanic* Survivor" above his name on their exemplary parents' headstone in Detroit.   PHOTO BY CRIS KOHL.

Neshan Krekorian caught pneumonia after barely surviving *Titanic's* sinking, and when he arrived in Brantford, Ontario, he spent some time in the hospital recuperating. He moved to nearby St. Catharines six years later, married Persa Vartanian on July 12, 1924,

THE CORPORATION OF THE
CITY OF ST. CATHARINES
ONTARIO

T. ROY ADAMS
MAYOR

BOX 3012
POSTAL CODE L2R 7C2

May 23rd, 1978

The Krekorian Family

Dear Friends:

      The passing of your loved one, Mr. Neshan Krekorian, on Sunday, May 21st, at the age of ninety-two years, severs a link between our City and the past. I refer to the fact that Mr. Krekorian was the last known survivor of the tragic sinking of the Titanic so many years ago.

      Certainly he has left a great heritage to his family and friends. His being spared from drowing in that great tragedy was more than justified in that he was granted some twenty-two years in excess of what is considered man's normal span of life. I am confident that Mr. Krekorian used all the intervening years in being a good father and a good citizen who, though sadly missed, will long be remembered by all.

      I join with my colleagues on Council in extending to the members of the family our sympathy and understanding. May the memories of a fine gentleman inspire you to give of your best to family, community and country.

Yours very truly,

T. Roy Adams

T. Roy Adams
Mayor

The mayor of St. Catharines, Ontario sent this eulogizing letter to the family of *Titanic* survivor, Neshan Krekorian, after his death in 1978.   COURTESY OF ALICE SOLOMONIAN.

and they had four children. Neshan, who worked at General Motors until his retirement in 1954, never again travelled anywhere by ship, and, according to his daughter, Alice Solomonian, even the sight of a large body of water made him uneasy. Neshan, who arranged for his two younger brothers, Mgerdich and Edward, to escape the political troubles at home and come to Canada, was a founding member of the St. Gregory's Armenian Apostolic Church. He died on May 21, 1978 at the age of 92. Many members from several generations of his family made an emotional visit to the St. Catharines Museum in early 1995 to view the *Titanic* photographic exhibit on display.

Hudson Trevor Allison, who was one year old when he survived the sinking of *Titanic,* but lost his parents and his sister in that tragedy, was returned to Canada where an aunt and uncle raised him. He died of ptomaine poisoning at the age of 18 while on vacation in Maine on August 7, 1929, and was buried beside his father in Chesterville, Ontario.

Alice Catherine Cleaver, the Allison nursemaid, saw to it that baby Hudson Trevor Allison was taken off the sinking *Titanic* (while the rest of his family sadly perished). She returned to England, married Edward Williams, and had two daughters. She died at Winchester, Hampshire, on November 1, 1984, at the age of 95. Recent biographies have caused the kindly, respected Alice Catherine Cleaver a great disservice by confusing her with Alice Mary Cleaver, an Englishwoman convicted in 1909 of killing the infant she had borne out of wedlock.

Mariana Assaf returned to Ottawa, Ontario, where she continued to do so well for herself financially in the grocery business that she eventually retired and returned to Syria.

Major Arthur S. Peuchen developed a defensive posture against a society which generally ostracized him because he was a man who had survived the *Titanic* sinking while many women and children died. He saw active duty in World War One, but had to bear the added stigma of having returned from the war alive. In the 1920's, bad investments drained many of his finances. He spent considerable time during his last four years on his company's property at Hinton, Alberta. He rose in rank to Lieutenant-Colonel before he died after a one-month illness at his Toronto residence, 105 Roxborough Street East, on Saturday afternoon, December 7, 1929, at the age of 70, with his beloved wife, Margaret (Thomson) at his side. He was buried in Toronto's Mount Pleasant Cemetery. His obituary, hinting at either a lack of sentimentality or at his despondence, made a single request: "Kindly omit flowers."

Clara Hays, the widow of Charles Hays, President of the Grand Trunk Railway which ran interlaced among the Great Lakes, spent most of her remaining life along Maine's seaboard, which she surprisingly loved. She was 96 when she died in 1955.

Orian Hays Davidson died at the age of 93 in 1979 in Montreal. Twelve years after the *Titanic* tragedy claimed her husband, she married his business partner, Robert Hickson.

Helga Lindqvist Hirvonen and her two-year-old daughter, **Hildur Hirvonen,** were greeted in New York City by her husband, Alexander, who worked in the steel plant in Monessen (outside Pittsburgh), Pennsylvania. In the mid-1920's, they moved to Syracuse, New York. Helga died in 1961 at the age of 71. Daughter Hildur had passed away in 1959 at the age of 49.

The headstone of Lt.-Col. Arthur Peuchen (he rose in rank before his death in 1929) and his wife Margaret is ironically in central Toronto's busy Mt. Pleasant Cemetery; in his latter years, he avoided the questioning public.   PHOTO BY CRIS KOHL.

Eino Lindqvist, after arriving on the *Carpathia* in New York City, followed his older sister, Helga Lindqvist Hirvonen, and his brother-in-law, Alexander Hirvonen, to Monessen, Pennsylvania.

Elin Hakkarainen carried through her late husband's plans to reach Monessen, Pennsylvania, where she lived and worked for five years before moving to West Virginia. There, she married Emil Nummi and they had one son. Elin died in 1957 at the age of 69.

Marion Kenyon returned alone to her home in Pittsburgh after her husband, Frederick, died in the sinking. She never remarried, and died in California on October 3, 1958, at the age of 78.

Lillian Minahan returned to Fond Du Lac, Wisconsin, after her physician husband died on *Titanic,* but she relocated to California shortly thereafter. She married Dr. Lee Kaull in 1914 and they moved to Arizona in 1919, where he passed away unexpectedly. Lillian moved to Hollywood and married a man named Danielson. In 1947, she moved to Laguna Beach, where she died at 86 on Jan 13, 1962.

Daisy Minahan, who lost her physician brother on *Titanic*, returned to Wisconsin with her sister-in-law, Lillian Minahan. She planned to return to work as a school teacher, but was hospitalized with pneumonia. Ill health plagued her for the next seven years, in spite of relocating to her sister's home in California for its healthier climate. She died of tuberculosis in Los Angeles at the age of 40 on April 30, 1919.

Oscar Olsson Johansson, after surviving yet another shipwreck, this one in the Great Lakes, returned to Sweden in 1918, working for a while in a shipyard (on land!) before he and his wife settled down to operating a family hotel. He died on April 5, 1967, at the age of 87.

For information on Milwaukee's **Elizabeth Halstead Crosby** and her daughter, **Harriette Crosby**, see Chapter 15: "The Captain."

Anton Kink, his wife, **Louise Heilmann Kink**, and their four-year-old daughter, **Louise Gretchen Kink**, were sent money by Anton's uncle in Milwaukee to buy train tickets to get them there. Anton worked in a factory and leased a farm on the side. In 1919, after he and Louise divorced, he returned to Graz, Austria, married a woman half his age in 1920, operated a grocery store, then moved to Brazil, where they eventually went bankrupt. The family returned to Graz in 1939 only to be surrounded and ensnared by World War II. Anton died in 1959 at the age of 76, while his second wife passed away 25 years later. Louise Heilmann Kink remained in Milwaukee with her daughter, and eventually married a man named Kroepfl. She died at the age of 93 on October 9, 1979. Her daughter, Louise Gretchen Kink, took care of her mother in her last years. Daughter Louise married Harold Pope in 1932 and the had four children before they divorced. She spent the latter part of her life residing at 4329 North 60th Street, died of lung cancer on August 25, 1992, at the age of 88, and was buried next to her mother in Milwaukee.

Jennie Howard Hansen, who lost her husband of 12 years and her brother-in-law when *Titanic* sank, returned home to Racine, Wisconsin, and lived at her brother's home, suffering from violent nightmares for several years. Earlier, she had escaped death in the Blake Opera House fire which claimed five lives in 1884. In the summer of 1915, she married a considerably younger man named Elmer Emerson, and they resided at 1214 Center Street. She died at the age of 85 on December 15, 1952. Her second husband, Elmer, died eight years later and is buried beside her. Their headstone includes a memorial to Jennie's first husband, Peter Hansen, who died on *Titanic*.

◆　　◆　　◆　　◆　　◆　　◆　　◆　　◆

Giant shipbuilding continued after the loss of *Titanic*.

On May 23, 1912, Germany launched the 906-foot-long Hamburg-American Line steamship, *Imperator,* "the biggest vessel in the world." She boasted lifeboats for all, a lesson learned from *Titanic* (and in addition to her 84 lifeboats, she carried two large, self-propelling, high-speed launches each equipped with its own wireless telegraphic apparatus), as well as three full-time wireless operators, two First Officers, a great entertainment hall two stories high, a conversation room, a smoking room, a ladies' hall, a winter garden, a rathskeller, women's salons in different decorative periods and national styles, "universal" telephones, big gymnasium, running track, squash court, a reproduction of ancient Roman baths in bronze, marble and ivory, and a blunt bow decorated with an immense figurehead of the German Imperial eagle, wings spread, standing on the world. The immense ocean liner was utterly breath-taking.

Just as the wonderfully huge ship, *Imperator*, slid down the ways during her launch in Hamburg, Germany, a heavy block of wood flew out and almost killed the Kaiser.

Titanic's lesson hadn't gone too far.

◆   ◆   ◆   ◆   ◆   ◆   ◆   ◆

Today, the *Col. James M. Schoonmaker*, the largest ship on the Great Lakes when *Titanic* sank in 1912, is preserved as a museum in Toledo, Ohio, along the shoreline of the Maumee River, under the name she received in 1969, the *Willis B. Boyer*.

The largest freighter in the world in 1912 is today a museum ship at Toledo, Ohio. PHOTO BY CRIS KOHL.

◆   ◆   ◆   ◆   ◆   ◆   ◆   ◆

Today, artifacts from *Titanic's* passengers and crew, as well as actual parts of the ship itself, are preserved as touring exhibits, drawing huge crowds at places in the Great Lakes region such as St. Paul, Minnesota, Toronto, Ontario, and Chicago, Illinois.

Titanic photos and artifacts on travelling exhibit made their way to the large Great Lakes cities of Toronto (above) and Chicago (below), where thousands upon thousands of people found fascination with the story of the world's most famous shipwreck.   PHOTOS BY CRIS KOHL.

♦   ♦   ♦   ♦   ♦   ♦   ♦   ♦

A few people in 1912 found debris from the wrecked *Titanic* washed ashore in Newfoundland and realized that these items were keepsakes of the worst maritime disaster in history. Reportedly there are half a dozen *Titanic* deck chairs presently in Canada alone. One is on display at the Maritime Museum of the Atlantic in Halifax, and another, privately owned in Tecumseh, Ontario, drew much attention while on temporary exhibit at the Sci-Tech Museum in Windsor, ON.

Maritime history buff Joan Forsberg gazes emotionally at the *Titanic* deck chair on display at the Maritime Museum of the Atlantic in Halifax, Nova Scotia. The city set aside a special section in Fairview Cemetery for the *Titanic* victims recovered at sea in 1912.   PHOTOS BY CRIS KOHL.

♦   ♦   ♦   ♦   ♦   ♦   ♦   ♦

A collection of *Titanic* items recently came to light in Peoria, Illinois. A man was cleaning out his home in the winter of 1997-1998 when he turned up a scrapbook filled with authentic documents about, and photographs of, *Titanic*. It turned out to be the long-lost Dr. Frank H. Blackmarr collection.

A Chicago physician, Blackmarr was travelling on board the *Carpathia*, on April 14-15, 1912, when that ship steamed to the rescue of over 700 *Titanic* survivors. He busily took notes, borrowed a camera and shot some photographs, and spoke with survivors, from millionaires to uneducated steerage passengers, while he assisted in the medical treatment of the hurt and hypothermic. He gave up his own berth on the *Carpathia* to a *Titanic* survivor.

The grandfather of the scrapbook discoverer was Dr. Blackmarr's attorney, and Blackmarr had given him the scrapbook at some point.

The scrapbook opens with a typewritten letter composed and signed by Bruce Ismay, president of the White Star Line, who was on board *Titanic* and survived the sinking. The photographs include scenes of *Titanic's* recovered lifeboats on the *Carpathia's* deck, survivors comforting one another, and a variety of icebergs on the ocean. Included are two paintings of the disaster by Colin Campbell Cooper, one of the iceberg and the other one of survivors in a lifeboat. Three handwritten survivor accounts of the sinking precede Dr. Blackmarr's 22-page typewritten account of the vessel's loss.

Dunning's Auction Services of Elgin, Illinois, handled the sale of the historic scrapbook on Saturday, April 25, 1998. Dunning's own appraiser claimed that the 60-page scrapbook would normally be expected to bring about $2,500, but this was during the screening height of James Cameron's extremely popular film, *"Titanic."*

The scrapbook fetched $50,000 from Chicago area businessmen.

◆　　◆　　◆　　◆　　◆　　◆　　◆　　◆

The Green Bay (Wisconsin) Public Library's fragile *Titanic* scrapbooks are filled with hundreds of original 1912 newspaper clippings.　　　　　　　　　　　　　PHOTO BY CRIS KOHL.

In the Green Bay, Wisconsin, public library, two scrapbooks packed with original 1912 *Titanic* newspaper clippings rest safely. Some years ago, these *Titanic* scrapbooks were tossed into the garbage by a member of the library's Board of Directors. Fortunately a farsighted librarian retrieved them, and today, library personnel guard the originals zealously. Members of the public are allowed to read and handle photocopied versions of these scrapbooks.

♦   ♦   ♦   ♦   ♦   ♦   ♦   ♦

The Chicago Freemasons in late April, 1912, agreed to provide "the most beautiful floral tribute that Chicago might furnish in memory of the *Titanic* dead.... [and] 'to place this floral offering with the White Star line to be taken on ship and dropped in the sea as near as possible to the place where the heroes of the *Titanic* have found a grave.'... The wreath will bear the inscription 'At Rest --- *Titanic*.'"

Those final three words form quite an epitaph, but it has turned out to be wishful thinking. *Titanic* has not been at rest since her keel was laid. This shipwreck provided just the right amount of tragedy (with over 1,500 lives lost), drama (with over 700 survivors left to tell their tales), pathos (husbands and fathers lost), timing (remaining afloat for almost three hours after hitting the iceberg), and irony (the "unsinkable" largest ship in the world striking an iceberg and sinking on her maiden voyage) to keep her story in the forefront forever.

The *Lindsay* (Ontario) *Post,* on April 26, 1912, printed, "...In the absolute stillness of the depths of the ocean, where there is perpetual night, the *Titanic* must remain. Any attempt at salvage is utterly out of the question. At a depth of about 200 feet divers suffer great hardships. At the depth at which the *Titanic* is resting, diving is absolutely impossible. Only by some strange and mighty upheaval of nature can the lost liner ever be exposed again to the gaze of human beings."

The author of those speculative words lacked the imagination to picture how technology could develop over the next 73 years when, in the late summer of 1985, the remains of the mighty ship, *Titanic,* were located at a depth of about two-and-a-half miles. Within a year, personal items which had belonged to the passengers and crew, commonplace things in 1912, were now treasured artifacts, physical history mementos from what had been the world's worst maritime disaster. These were carefully picked up off the ocean floor and patiently deposited by a robot's arm into a basket beneath a small submersible. At the surface, they were gingerly conserved from their seven decades of saltwater immersion. Within a few more years, large pieces of the *Titanic* itself would see the light of day again.

Fortunately, these irreplaceable items did not disappear behind the haughty walls of private collections. Many thousands of people in the Great Lakes region, and elsewhere, have delighted at the sight of *Titanic* artifacts that are touring on public exhibit.

That "strange and mighty upheaval of nature" called modern technology has seen to it that *Titanic* can "be exposed again to the gaze of human beings," rather than being slowly devoured by bacteria and destroyed into nothingness, save memories.

We are all more fortunate for that.

TITANIC
Great-Lakes-Bound Passenger List

Ranked alphabetically according to destination by state and city.
TOTAL: 345 Great Lakes passengers (128 survived, 217
perished) from among the 1,343 passengers on board *Titanic*.
This is just over 25% of the total number of passengers.

Survivors' names are printed in *italics*.
The code for "boarded at" is S = Southampton, C = Cherbourg, Q = Queenstown
The code for "class" is 1 = First Class, 2 = Second Class, 3 = Third Class (steerage)

Name	Age /boarded at/class	Bound for	Date Died
Augustsson, Mr. Albert	23/S/3	Bloomington, IL	April 15, 1912
Andreasson, Mr. Paul Edvin	20/S/3	Chicago, IL	April 15, 1912
Angheloff, Mr. Minko	26/S/3	Chicago, IL	April 15, 1912
Bostandyeff, Mr. Guentcho	26/S/3	Chicago, IL	April 15, 1912
Bourke, Mr. John	28/Q/3	Chicago, IL	April 15, 1912
Bourke, Mrs. Katherine McHugh	32/Q/3	Chicago, IL	April 15, 1912
Bourke, Miss Mary	25/Q/3	Chicago, IL	April 15, 1912
Braf, Miss Elin Ester Maria	20/S/3	Chicago, IL	April 15, 1912
Cacic, Mr. Luka	38/S/3	Chicago, IL	April 15, 1912
Cacic, Miss Manda	21/S/3	Chicago, IL	April 15, 1912
Cacic, Miss Marija	30/S/3	Chicago, IL	April 15, 1912
Cacic, Mr. Grego (Jego)	18/S/3	Chicago, IL	April 15, 1912
Colcheff, Mr. Peyo (Peju)	36/S/3	Chicago, IL	April 15, 1912
Coleff, Mr. Fotio (Satio)	24/S/3	Chicago, IL	April 15, 1912
Dahlberg, Miss Gerda Ulrika	22/S/3	Chicago, IL	April 15, 1912
Danoff, Mr. Yoto	27/S/3	Chicago, IL	April 15, 1912
Dantchoff, Mr. Khristo	25/S/3	Chicago, IL	April 15, 1912
Foley, Mr. Joseph	26/Q/3	Chicago, IL	April 15, 1912
Harper, Rev. John	28/S/2	Chicago, IL	April 15, 1912
Harper, Miss Annie Jessie	6/S/2	Chicago, IL	1986
Hippach, Mrs. Ida Sophia	44/C/1	Chicago, IL	Sept. 22, 1940
Hippach, Miss Jean Gertrude	16/C/1	Chicago, IL	Nov. 14, 1974
Isham, Miss Anna Eliza	50/C/1	Chicago, IL	April 15, 1912
Johansson, Mr. Nils	29/S/3	Chicago, IL	April 15, 1912
Jonkoff, Mr. Lalio (Lazor)	23/S/3	Chicago, IL	April 15, 1912
Kelly, Miss Annie Kate	21/Q/3	Chicago, IL	Dec., 1969
Laleff, Mr. Kristo	23/S/3	Chicago, IL	April 15, 1912
Lemore, Mrs. Amelia Milley	34/S/2	Chicago, IL	?
Leitch, Miss Jessie W.	/S/2	Chicago, IL	1963
Lewy, Mr. Ervin G.	30/C/1	Chicago, IL	April 15, 1912
Mangan, Miss Mary	32/Q/3	Chicago, IL	April 15, 1912
Markoff, Mr. Marin	35/S/3	Chicago, IL	April 15, 1912

McGowan, Miss Annie	14/Q/3	Chicago, IL	Jan. 30, 1990
McGowan, Miss Katherine	36/Q/3	Chicago, IL	April 15, 1912
Midtsjo, Mr. Karl Albert	21/S/3	Chicago, IL	Jan. 25, 1939
Mionoff, Mr. Stoytcho	28/S/3	Chicago, IL	April 15, 1912
Myhrman, Mr. Per Fabian	18/S/3	Chicago, IL	April 15, 1912
Naidenoff, Mr. Penko	22/S/3	Chicago, IL	April 15, 1912
Nankoff, Mr. Minko	32/S/3	Chicago, IL	April 15, 1912
Nemaugh (Mernagh?), Mr. Robt.	26/Q/3	Chicago, IL	April 15, 1912
O'Donoghue, Miss Bridget	21/Q/3	Chicago, IL	April 15, 1912
Öhman, Miss Velin	22/S/3	Chicago, IL	Nov. 19, 1966
Oreskovic, Miss Jeka (Jelka)	23/S/3	Chicago, IL	April 15, 1912
Oreskovic, Miss Marijo	20/S/3	Chicago, IL	April 15, 1912
Oreskovic, Mr. Luka	20/S/3	Chicago, IL	April 15, 1912
Pålsson, Mrs. Alma Berglund	29/S/3	Chicago, IL	April 15, 1912
Pålsson, Miss Stina Viola	8/S/3	Chicago, IL	April 15, 1912
Pålsson, Master Paul Folke	6/S/3	Chicago, IL	April 15, 1912
Pålsson, Miss Torborg Danira	3/S/3	Chicago, IL	April 15, 1912
Pålsson, Master Gösta Leonard	2/S/3	Chicago, IL	April 15, 1912
Pecruic (Pokrnic), Mr. Mate	17/S/3	Chicago, IL	April 15, 1912
Pecruic (Pokrnic), Mr. Tome	24/S/3	Chicago, IL	April 15, 1912
Petroff, Mr. Nedeca (Nedialco)	19/S/3	Chicago, IL	April 15, 1912
Petroff, Mr. Pentcho	29/S/3	Chicago, IL	April 15, 1912
Petterson, Mr. Johan Emil	25/S/3	Chicago, IL	April 15, 1912
Radeff, Mr. Alexander	27/S/3	Chicago, IL	April 15, 1912
Sdycoff, Mr. Todor	42/S/3	Chicago, IL	April 15, 1912
Staneff, Mr. Ivan	23/S/3	Chicago, IL	April 15, 1912
Stoytcheff, Mr. Ilia	19/S/3	Chicago, IL	April 15, 1912
Strilic, Mr. Ivan	27/S/3	Chicago, IL	April 15, 1912
Todoroff, Mr. Lalio	23/S/3	Chicago, IL	April 15, 1912
Willer, Mr. Aaron	37/C/3	Chicago, IL	April 15, 1912
Hellstrom, Miss Hilda Maria	22/S/3	Evanston, IL	March 16, 1962
J(Y?)alsevac, Mr. Ivan	29/C/3	Galesburg, IL	?
Karun, Mr. Franz	37/C/3	Galesburg, IL	July 7, 1934
Karun, Miss Manca	4/C/3	Galesburg, IL	1970's
Elsbury, Mr. William James	47/S/3	Gurnee, Lake Co. IL	April 15, 1912
Carlsson, Mr. Carl Robert	24/S/3	Huntley, IL	April 15, 1912
Jonsson, Mr. Carl	32/S/3	Huntley, IL	?
Aronsson, Mr. Ernest Axel	24/S/3	Joliet, IL	April 15, 1912
Edvardsson, Mr. Gustaf Hjalmar	18/S/3	Joliet, IL	April 15, 1912
Nilsson, Miss Helmina Josefina	26/S/3	Joliet, IL	May, 1971
Bengtsson, Mr. John Viktor	26/S/3	Monee, IL	April 15, 1912
Dorking, Mr. Edward Arthur	19/S/3	Oglesby, IL	?
Ödahl, Mr. Nils Martin	23/S/3	Peoria, IL	April 15, 1912
Bryhl, Miss Dagmar Jenny	20/S/2	Rockford, IL	August, 1969
Bryhl, Mr. Kurt Arnold Gottfrid	25/S/2	Rockford, IL	April 15, 1912

Enander, Mr. Ingvar	21/S/2	Rockford, IL	April 15, 1912
Caldwell, Mr. Albert Francis	26/S/2	Roseville, IL	March 10, 1977
Caldwell, Mrs. Sylvia Mae	28/S/2	Roseville, IL	Jan. 14, 1965
Caldwell, Master Alden Gates	1/S/2	Roseville, IL	Dec. 18, 1992
Beavan, Mr. William Thomas	18/S/3	Russell, IL	April 15, 1912
Johnson, Mrs. Alice Backberg	27/S/3	St. Charles, IL	Dec. 19, 1968
Johnson, Master Harold Theodor	4/S/3	St. Charles, IL	April 10, 1968
Johnson, Miss Eleanor Ileen	1/S/3	St. Charles, IL	March 7, 1998
Gustaffson, Mr. Alfred Ossian	20/S/3	Waukegan, IL	April 15, 1912
Ecimovic, Mr. Jeso	17/S/3	Hammond, IN	April 15, 1912
Strom, Mrs. Elna Persson	29/S/3	Indiana Harbor, IN	April 15, 1912
Strom, Miss Silma Matilda	2 /S/3	Indiana Harbor, IN	April 15, 1912
Homer, Mr. Harry Haven	35/C/1	Indianapolis, IN	?
Persson, Mr. Ernst Ulrik	25/S/3	Indianapolis, IN	Oct. 17, 1951
Toomey, Miss Ellen	50/S/2	Indianapolis, IN	?
Crafton, Mr. John Bertram	59/S/1	Roachdale, IN	April 15, 1912
Becker, Mrs. Nellie Baumgardner	36/S/2	Benton Harbor, MI	Feb. 15, 1961
Becker, Miss Ruth Elizabeth	12/S/2	Benton Harbor, MI	July 6, 1990
Becker, Miss Marion Louise	4/S/2	Benton Harbor, MI	Feb. 15, 1944
Becker, Master Richard F.	1/S/2	Benton Harbor, MI	Sept. 6, 1975
Berriman, Mr. William John	23/S/2	Calumet, MI	April 15, 1912
Carbines, Mr. William	19/S/2	Calumet, MI	April 15, 1912
Lingane, Mr. John	61/Q/2	Chelsea, MI	April 15, 1912
Masselmany, Mrs. Fatima	17/C/3	Dearborn, MI	?
De Mulder, Mr. Theodore	30/S/3	Detroit, MI	April 19, 1954
Eitenmiller, Mr. George Floyd	23/S/2	Detroit, MI	April 15, 1912
Goldsmith, Mr. Frank John	33/S/3	Detroit, MI	April 15, 1912
Goldsmith, Mrs. Emily Brown	31/S/3	Detroit, MI	Sept. 22, 1955
Goldsmith, Master Frank John	9/S/3	Detroit, MI	Jan. 27, 1982
Hamalainen, Mrs. Anna	24/S/2	Detroit, MI	?
Hamalainen, Master Viljo	1/S/2	Detroit, MI	?
Hampe, Mr. Leo Jerome	19/S/3	Detroit, MI	April 15, 1912
Hiltunen, Miss Marta	18/S/2	Detroit, MI	April 15, 1912
Joseph (Peter), Mrs. Catherine	23/C/3	Detroit, MI	1915
Joseph (Peter), Master Michael	4/C/3	Detroit, MI	May 18, 1991
Joseph (Peter), Miss Mary	2/C/3	Detroit, MI	March 22, 1914
Lievens, Mr. René	24/S/3	Detroit, MI	April 15, 1912
Quick, Mrs. Jane Richards	33/S/2	Detroit, MI	Feb. 24, 1965
Quick, Miss Vera Winifred	8/S/2	Detroit, MI	
Quick, Miss Phyllis May	2/S/2	Detroit, MI	March 15, 1954
Rush, Mr. Alfred George John	16/S/3	Detroit, MI	April 15, 1912
Sap, Mr. Julius "Jules"	25/S/3	Detroit, MI	Dec. 15, 1966
Scheerlinckx, Mr. Jean	29/S/3	Detroit, MI	June 25, 1956
Stokes, Mr. Phillip Joseph	25/S/2	Detroit, MI	April 15, 1912
Theobald, Mr. Thomas Leonard	34/S/3	Detroit, MI	April 15, 1912

Van Melkebeke, Mr. Philmn	23/S/3	Detroit, MI	April 15, 1912
Vandercruyssen, Mr. Victor	47/S/3	Detroit, MI	April 15, 1912
Wittevrongel, Mr. Camille	36/S/3	Detroit, MI	April 15, 1912
Bishop, Mr. Dickinson H.	25/C/1	Dowagiac, MI	Feb. 16, 1961
Bishop, Mrs. Helen Walton	19/C/1	Dowagiac, MI	March 15, 1916
Touma (Thomas), Mrs. Hanna	27/C/3	Dowagiac, MI	June 28, 1976
Touma (Thomas), Miss Maria	9/C/3	Dowagiac, MI	Aug. 12, 1953
Touma (Thomas), Master Geo.	8/C/3	Dowagiac, MI	Dec. 9, 1991
De Pelsmaeker, Mr. Alphonse	16/S/3	Gladstone, MI	April 15, 1912
Sawyer, Mr. Frederick Charles	23/S/3	Halley, MI	April 15, 1912
Sincock, Miss Maude	20/S/2	Hancock, MI	Sept. 11, 1993
Andrew, Mr. Frank	25/S/2	Houghton, MI	April 15, 1912
Banfield, Mr. Frederick James	28/S/2	Houghton, MI	April 15, 1912
Davies, Mrs. Agnes Mary	48/S/2	Houghton, MI	Aug. 4, 1933
Davies, Master John Morgan	9/S/2	Houghton, MI	Dec. 16, 1951
Fillbrook, Mr. Charles Joseph	18/S/2	Houghton, MI	April 15, 1912
Jenkin, Mr. Stephen Curnow	32/S/3	Houghton, MI	April 15, 1912
Nicholls, Mr. Joseph Charles	19/S/2	Houghton, MI	April 15, 1912
Sobey, Mr.Samuel James Hayden	25/S/2	Houghton, MI	April 15, 1912
Henricksson, Miss Jenny Lovisa	28/S/3	Iron Mountain, MI	April 15, 1912
Pettersson, Miss Ellen Natalia	18/S/3	Iron Mountain, MI	April 15, 1912
Skoog, Mr. William	40/S/3	Iron Mountain, MI	April 15, 1912
Skoog, Mrs. Anna Karlsson	43/S/3	Iron Mountain, MI	April 15, 1912
Skoog, Master Karl Thorston	11/S/3	Iron Mountain, MI	April 15, 1912
Skoog, Miss Mabel	9/S/3	Iron Mountain, MI	April 15, 1912
Skoog, Master Harald	5/S/3	Iron Mountain, MI	April 15, 1912
Skoog, Miss Margrit	2/S/3	Iron Mountain, MI	April 15, 1912
Andersson, Miss Ida Augusta	38/S/3	Manistee, MI	April 15, 1912
Davies, Mr. Alfred J.	24/S/3	Pontiac, MI	April 15, 1912
Davies, Mr. John Samuel	22/S/3	Pontiac, MI	April 15, 1912
Davies, Mr. Joseph	17/S/3	Pontiac, MI	April 15, 1912
Lester, Mr. James	39/S/3	Pontiac, MI	April 15, 1912
Hannah (Bert Johns), Mr. Borak	20/C/3	Port Huron, MI	Feb. 2, 1952
Calic, Mr. Petar	17/C/3	Sault Ste. Marie, MI	April 15, 1912
Ahlin, Mrs. Johanna Larsson	40/S/3	Akeley, MN	April 15, 1912
Lulich, Mr. Nicola	29/S/3	Chisholm, MN	1962
Johansson, Mr. Karl Johan	31/S/3	Duluth, MN	April 15, 1912
Silvey, Mr. William Baird	50/S/1	Duluth, MN	April 15, 1912
Silvey, Mrs. Alice Munger	39/S/1	Duluth, MN	May 2, 1958
Stranden, Mr. Juho	31/S/3	Duluth, MN	?
Willard, Miss Constance	21/S/1	Duluth, MN	April 25, 1964
Carlsson, Mr. August Sigfrid	28/S/3	Fower, MN	April 15, 1912
Turkula, Mrs. Hedvig	63/S/3	Hibbing, MN	April 3, 1922
Abelseth, Mr. Olaus Jorgensen	25/S/3	Minneapolis, MN	Dec. 4, 1980
Abelseth, Miss Karen Marie	16/S/3	Minneapolis, MN	July 27, 1969

Asplund, Mr. John Charles	23/S/3	Minneapolis, MN	Aug. 14, 1943
Douglas, Mr. Walter Donald	50/C/1	Minneapolis, MN	April 15, 1912
Douglas, Mrs. Mahala Dutton	48/C/1	Minneapolis, MN	April 21, 1945
Humblen, Mr. Adolf Mathias	42/S/3	Minneapolis, MN	April 15, 1912
Johnson, Mr. Malkolm Joachim	33/S/3	Minneapolis, MN	April 15, 1912
Lahtinnen, Rev. William	30/S/2	Minneapolis, MN	April 15, 1912
Lahtinnen, Mrs. Anna Sylfven	26/S/2	Minneapolis, MN	April 15, 1912
LeRoy, Bertha (Douglas maid)	30/C/1	Minneapolis, MN	?
Moen, Mr. Sigurd Hansen	25/S/3	Minneapolis, MN	April 15, 1912
Silven, Miss Lyyli Karolina	18/C/2	Minneapolis, MN	?
Snyder, Mr. John Pillsbury	24/S/1	Minneapolis, MN	July 22, 1959
Snyder, Mrs. Nelle Stevenson	23/S/1	Minneapolis, MN	Dec. 9, 1983
Soholt, Mr. Peter Andreas L. A.	19/S/3	Minneapolis, MN	April 15, 1912
Salkjelsvik, Miss Anna Kristina	21/S/3	Proctor, MN	?
Salander, Mr. Karl Johan	24/S/3	Red Wing, MN	April 15, 1912
Nilsson, Mr. August Ferdinand	21/S/3	St. Paul, MN	April 15, 1912
Olsson, Miss Elida	31/S/3	St. Paul, MN	April 15, 1912
Vendel, Mr. Olof Edvin	20/S/3	St. Paul, MN	April 15, 1912
Alexander, Mr. William	23/S/3	Albion, NY	April 15, 1912
Dequemin, Mr. Joseph	24/S/3	Albion, NY	1966?
Howard, Miss May Elizabeth	24/S/3	Albion, NY	1957
Hale, Mr. Reginald	30/S/2	Auburn, NY	April 15, 1912
Kent, Mr. Edward Austin	58/C/1	Buffalo, NY	April 15, 1912
Thorneycroft, Mr. Percival	36/S/3	Clinton, NY	April 15, 1912
Thorneycroft, Mrs. Florence K.	32/S/3	Clinton, NY	?
Bowen, Miss Grace Scott	45/C/1	Cooperstown, NY	1945
Chaudanson, Miss Victorine	36/C/1	Cooperstown, NY	August, 1962
Ryerson, Mr. Arthur Larned	61/C/1	Cooperstown, NY	April 15, 1912
Ryerson, Mrs. Emily Maria	48/C/1	Cooperstown, NY	?
Ryerson, Miss Suzette Parker	21/C/1	Cooperstown, NY	Jan. 13, 1921
Ryerson, Miss Emily Borie	18/C/1	Cooperstown, NY	1960
Ryerson, Master John Borie	13/C/1	Cooperstown, NY	Jan. 21, 1986
Botsford, Mr. William Hull	25/S/2	Elmira, NY	April 15, 1912
Ford, Mr. Arthur	22/S/3	Elmira, NY	April 15, 1912
Douton, Mr. William James	54/S/2	Holley, NY	April 15, 1912
Chambers,Mr.Norman Campbell	27/S/1	Ithaca, NY	Feb. 9, 1966
Chambers, Mrs. Bertha Griggs	31/S/1	Ithaca, NY	Oct. 18, 1959
Drazenovic, Mr. Josef	33/C/3	Niagara Falls, NY	April 15, 1912
Goodwin, Mr. Chas. Frederick	40/S/3	Niagara Falls, NY	April 15, 1912
Goodwin, Mrs. Augusta T.	43/S/3	Niagara Falls, NY	April 15, 1912
Goodwin, Miss Lillian Amy	16/S/3	Niagara Falls, NY	April 15, 1912
Goodwin, Mr. Charles Edwin	14/S/3	Niagara Falls, NY	April 15, 1912
Goodwin, Mastr Wm.Frederick	11/S/3	Niagara Falls, NY	April 15, 1912
Goodwin, Miss Jessie Allis	10/S/3	Niagara Falls, NY	April 15, 1912
Goodwin, Master Harold V.	9/S/3	Niagara Falls, NY	April 15, 1912

Goodwin, Master Sidney L.	2/S/3	Niagara Falls, NY	April 15, 1912
Lockyer, Mr. Edward Thomas	21/S/3	Ontario, NY	April 15, 1912
Beane, Mr. Edward	32/S/2	Rochester, NY	Oct. 24, 1948
Beane, Mrs. Ethel Clarke	20/S/2	Rochester, NY	Sept. 17, 1983
Bentham, Miss Lillian W.	19/S/2	Rochester, NY	Dec. 15, 1977
Case, Mr. Howard Brown	49/S/1	Rochester, NY	April 15, 1912
Fox, Mr. Stanley Hubert	38/S/2	Rochester, NY	April 15, 1912
McKain, Mr. Peter David	46/S/2	Rochester, NY	April 15, 1912
Bailey, Mr. Percey Andrew	19/S/2	Akron, OH	April 15, 1912
Cotterill, Mr. Henry	20/S/2	Akron, OH	April 15, 1912
Hocking, Miss Ellen (Nellie)	20/S/2	Akron, OH	Oct. 14, 1963
Hocking, Mr. Richard George	23/S/2	Akron, OH	April 15, 1912
Hocking, Mrs. Elizabeth	53/S/2	Akron, OH	April 15, 1914
Richards, Master George Sibley	1/S/2	Akron, OH	Dec. 4, 1987
Richards, Master Wm. Rowe	3/S/2	Akron, OH	Jan. 9, 1988
Richards, Mrs. Emily Hocking	24/S/2	Akron, OH	Nov. 10, 1972
Wells, Master Ralph Lester	2/S/2	Akron, OH	Sept. 27, 1972
Wells, Miss Joan	4/S/2	Akron, OH •	July 11, 1933
Wells, Mrs. Adie Dart	29/S/2	Akron, OH	May 28, 1954
Wilkes, Mrs. Ellen Needs	45/S/3	Akron, OH	April 27, 1955
Turja, Miss Anna Sofia	18/S/3	Ashtabula, OH	Dec. 20, 1982
Davison, Mr. Thomas Henry	/S/3	Bedford, OH	April 15, 1912
Davison, Mrs. Mary Finck	/S/3	Bedford, OH	?
Abbing, Mr. Anthony	42/S/3	Cincinnati, OH	April 15, 1912
Icard, Amelia (Stone maid)	38/S/1	Cincinnati, OH	?
Stone, Mrs. Martha Evelyn	62/S/1	Cincinnati, OH	May 12, 1924
Bonnell, Miss Elizabeth	58/S/1	Cleveland, OH	?
Crease, Mr. Ernest James	19/S/3	Cleveland, OH	April 15, 1912
Rouse, Mr. Richard Henry	50/S/3	Cleveland, OH	April 15, 1912
Stanley, Mr. Ernest Roland	21/S/3	Cleveland, OH	April 15, 1912
Sunderland, Mr. Victor Francis	19/S/3	Cleveland, OH	Aug. 21, 1973
Ayoub, Miss Banoura	12/C/3	Columbus, OH	?
Daher, Mr. Tannous (Thomas)	/C/3	Columbus, OH	April 15, 1912
Thomas, Mr. John	37/C/3	Columbus, OH	April 15, 1912
Thomas, Mr. Tannous J.	15/C/3	Columbus, OH	April 15, 1912
Trout, Mrs. Jessie Bruce	28/S/2	Columbus, OH	?
Yousseff (Joseph), Mr. Gerios	26/C/3	Columbus, OH	April 15, 1912
Leeni (Philip Zenni), Mr. Fahim	25/C/3	Dayton, OH	Dec. 2, 1927
Vanderplancke, Miss Augusta M.	18/S/3	Fremont, OH	April 15, 1912
Vanderplancke, Mr. Jules	31/S/3	Fremont, OH	April 15, 1912
Vanderplancke, Mr. Leo Edmond	15/S/3	Fremont, OH	April 15, 1912
Vanderplancke, Mrs. Emily	31/S/3	Fremont, OH	April 15, 1912
Stewart, Mr. Albert A.	/C/1	Gallipolis, OH	April 15, 1912
Otter, Mr. Richard	39/S/2	Middleburg Hts, OH	April 15, 1912
Waelens, Mr. Achille	22/S/3	Stanton, OH	April 15, 1912

Osmon, Miss Maria	31/S/3	Steubenville, OH	?
Harbeck, Mr. William H.	44/S/2	Toledo, OH	April 15, 1912
Bonnell, Miss Caroline	30/S/1	Youngstown, OH	March 13, 1950
George, Mrs. Shanini Whabee	40/C/3	Youngstown, OH	April 21, 1947
Karajic, Mr. Milan	30/S/3	Youngstown, OH	April 15, 1912
Turcin, Mr. Stefan	36/S/3	Youngstown, OH	April 15, 1912
Wick, Col. George Dennick	57/S/1	Youngstown, OH	April 15, 1912
Wick, Mrs. Mary Hitchcock	45/S/1	Youngstown, OH	Jan. 29, 1920
Wick, Miss Mary Natalie	31/S/1	Youngstown, OH	Oct. 13, 1944
Garfirth, Mr. John	22/S/3	Berlin, ON	April 15, 1912
Patchett, Mr. George	19/S/3	Berlin, ON	April 15, 1912
Krekorian, Mr. Neshan	25/C/3	Brantford, ON	May 21, 1978
Sirayanian, Mr. Arsun	22/C/3	Brantford, ON	April 15, 1912
Vartanian, Mr. David	22/C/3	Brantford, ON	Aug. 3, 1966
Zakarian, Mr. Artun	27/C/3	Brantford, ON	April 15, 1912
Zakarian, Mr. Maprieder	26/C/3	Brantford, ON	April 15, 1912
Boulos, Mrs. Joseph (Sultana)	40/C/3	Chatham, ON	April 15, 1912
Boulos, Miss Laura (Nourelian)	9/C/3	Chatham, ON	April 15, 1912
Boulos, Master Akar (Farrand)	6/C/3	Chatham, ON	April 15, 1912
Allison, Mr. Hudson Joshua	30/S/1	Chesterville, ON	April 15, 1912
Allison, Mrs. Bessie Waldo	25/S/1	Chesterville, ON	April 15, 1912
Allison, Master Hudson Trevor	1/S/1	Chesterville, ON	Aug. 7, 1929
Allison, Miss Helen Lorraine	2/S/1	Chesterville, ON	April 15, 1912
Brown, Mildred (Allison cook)	/S/2	Chesterville, ON	?
Cleaver, Alice (Allison nursemd)	22/S/1	Chesterville, ON	Nov. 1, 1984
Daniels, Sarah (Allison maid)	33/S/1	Chesterville, ON	?
Swain,George(Allison chauffeur)	18/S/2	Chesterville, ON	April 15, 1912
Pain, Dr. Alfred	24/S/2	Hamilton, ON	April 15, 1912
Assaf, Mr. Gerios	21/C/3	Ottawa, ON	April 15, 1912
Assaf, Mrs. Mariana	45/C/3	Ottawa, ON	?
Barbara, Mrs. Catherine	45/C/3	Ottawa, ON	April 15, 1912
Barbara, Miss Saude	18/C/3	Ottawa, ON	April 15, 1912
Boulos, Mr. Hanna	18/C/3	Ottawa, ON	April 15, 1912
Caram, Mr. Joseph	28/C/3	Ottawa, ON	April 15, 1912
Caram, Mrs. Marid Elias	18/C/3	Ottawa, ON	April 15, 1912
Elias, Mr. Joseph	39/C/3	Ottawa, ON	April 15, 1912
Elias, Mr. Joseph, Jr.	17/C/3	Ottawa, ON	April 15, 1912
Elias, Mr. Tannous	15/C/3	Ottawa, ON	April 15, 1912
Khalil, Mr. Betros	25/C/3	Ottawa, ON	April 15, 1912
Khalil, Mrs. Zahie	20/C/3	Ottawa, ON	April 15, 1912
Khalil, Mr. Solomon	27/C/3	Ottawa, ON	April 15, 1912
McCrie, Mr. James Matthew	30/S/2	Sarnia, ON	April 15, 1912
Sjostedt, Mr. Ernest Adolf	59/S/2	Sault Ste. Marie, ON	April 15, 1912
Aijo-Nirva, Mr. Isak	41/S/3	Sudbury, ON	April 15, 1912
Kallio, Mr. Nikolai Erland	17/S/3	Sudbury, ON	April 15, 1912

Maenpaa, Mr. Matti Alexander	22/S/3	Sudbury, ON	April 15, 1912
Rintamaki, Mr. Matti	35/S/3	Sudbury, ON	April 15, 1912
Borebank, John James	41/S/1	Toronto, ON	April 15, 1912
Peuchen, Maj. Arthur Godfrey	52/S/1	Toronto, ON	Dec. 7, 1929
Reynolds, Mr. Harold J.	12/S/3	Toronto, ON	April 15, 1912
Panula, Mrs. Maria Ojala	41/S/3	Coal Center, PA	April 15, 1912
Panula, Mr. Ernesti Arvid	16/S/3	Coal Center, PA	April 15, 1912
Panula, Mr. Jaako Arnold	14/S/3	Coal Center, PA	April 15, 1912
Panula, Master Juha Niilo	7/S/3	Coal Center, PA	April 15, 1912
Panula, Master Urho Abraham	2/S/3	Coal Center, PA	April 15, 1912
Panula, Master Eino (William)	1/S/3	Coal Center, PA	April 15, 1912
Riihiivuori, Miss Sanni	22/S/3	Coal Center, PA	April 15, 1912
Makinen, Mr. Kalle Edvard	29/S/3	Glassport, PA	April 15, 1912
Hakkarainen, Mr. Pekka Pietari	28/S/3	Monessen, PA	April 15, 1912
Hakkarainen, Mrs. Elin Dolck	24/S/3	Monessen, PA	1957
Hirvonen, Mrs. Helga Lindqvist	22/S/3	Monessen, PA	1961
Hirvonen, Miss Hildur E.	2/S/3	Monessen, PA	1959?
Jussila, Mr. Erik	32/S/3	Monessen, PA	?
Lindqvist, Mr. Eino William	20/S/3	Monessen, PA	?
Corey, Mrs. Mary Phyllis	/S/2	Pittsburgh, PA	April 15, 1912
Karnes, Mrs. Claire Bennett	22/S/2	Pittsburgh, PA	April 15, 1912
Kenyon, Mr. Frederick R.	41/S/1	Pittsburgh, PA	April 15, 1912
Kenyon, Mrs. Marion Stauffer	31/S/1	Pittsburgh, PA	Oct. 3, 1958
Wirz, Mr. Albert	27/S/3	Beloit, WI	April 15, 1912
Olsvigen, Mr. Thor Anderson	20/S/3	Cameron, WI	April 15, 1912
Minahan, Dr. William Edward	44/Q/1	Fond du Lac, WI	April 15, 1912
Minahan, Mrs. Lillian Thorpe	37/Q/1	Fond du Lac, WI	Jan. 13, 1962
Minahan, Mrs. Daisy E.	33/Q/1	Green Bay, WI	April 30, 1919
Johansson, Oscar Olsson	32/S/3	Manitowoc, WI	April 5, 1967
Coxon, Mr. Daniel	39/S/3	Merrill, WI	April 15, 1912
Katavelas, Mr. Vassilios	18/C/3	Milwaukee, WI	April 15, 1912
Crosby, Capt. Edward Gifford	70/S/1	Milwaukee, WI	April 15, 1912
Crosby, Mrs. Catherine Halstead	69/S/1	Milwaukee, WI	July 29, 1920
Crosby, Miss Harriette R.	36/S/1	Milwaukee, WI	Feb. 11, 1941
Kink, Mr. Anton	29/S/3	Milwaukee, WI	1959
Kink, Mrs. Louise Heilmann	26/S/3	Milwaukee, WI	Oct. 9, 1979
Kink, Miss Louise Gretchen	4/S/3	Milwaukee, WI	Aug. 25, 1992
Kink, Miss Maria	22/S/3	Milwaukee, WI	April 15, 1912
Kink, Mr. Vincenz	26/S/3	Milwaukee, WI	April 15, 1912
Ridsdale, Miss Lucy	50/S/2	Milwaukee, WI	?
Hansen, Mr. Henrik Juul	26/S/3	Racine, WI	April 15, 1912
Hansen, Mr. Peter Claus	41/S/3	Racine, WI	April 15, 1912
Hansen, Mrs. Jennie Howard	45/S/3	Racine, WI	Dec. 15, 1952

Bibliography

Books

APPELBAUM, STANLEY. *The Chicago World's Fair of 1893, A Photographic Record.* New York: Dover Publications, Inc., 1980.

BIEL, STEVEN. *Down with the Old Canoe, A Cultural History of the Titanic Disaster.* New York: W. W. Norton & Company, 1997.

_____ed. *Titanica, The Disaster of the Century in Poetry, Song and Prose.* New York: W. W. Norton & Company, 1998.

BUTLER DANIEL ALLEN. *"Unsinkable," The Full Story of RMS Titanic.* Mechanicsburg, Pennsylvania: Stackpole Books, 1998.

CLARY, JIM. *Ladies of the Lakes.* Lansing, Michigan: Michigan Department of Natural Resources, 1981.

_____*The Last True Story of Titanic.* Brooklyn, New York: Domhan Books, 1998.

CUSSLER, CLIVE. *Raise the Titanic!* New York: The Viking Press, 1976.

DUNLAP, ORRIN E. *Marconi, The Man and His Wireless.* New York: The MacMillan Company, 1937.

EATON, JOHN P., AND CHARLES A. HAAS. *Titanic, A Journey Through Time.* New York: W. W. Norton & Company, 1999.

_____*Titanic, Triumph and Tragedy.* New York: W. W. Norton & Company, 1994.

EVERETT, MARSHALL, ed. *Wreck and Sinking of the Titanic, The Ocean's Greatest Disaster.* L. H. Walter, 1912.

GARDNER, MARTIN. *The Wreck of the Titanic Foretold?* Amherst, New York: Prometheus Books, 1998.

GELLER, JUDITH B. *Titanic, Women and Children First.* New York: W. W. Norton & Company, 1998.

GOLDSMITH, FRANK J. W. *Echoes in the Night.* Indian Orchard, MA: The *Titanic* Historical Society, 1991.

HAMPER, STAN. *Dowagiac Stories, Windows to the Past.* Dowagiac, Michigan: Stan Hamper, 1996.

_____*Dowagiac Stories, Windows to the Past, Vol. II.* Dowagiac, Michigan: Stan Hamper, 1998.

HILTON, GEORGE W. *Eastland, Legacy of the Titanic.* Stanford, California: Stanford University Press, 1995.

HUSTAK, ALAN. *Titanic, The Canadian Story.* Montreal: Véhicule Press, 1998.

HYSLOP, DONALD, AND ALASTAIR FORSYTH AND SHEILA JEMIMA, *Titanic Voices, Memories from the Fateful Voyage.* New York: St. Martin's Press, 1997.

KOHL, CRIS. *The 100 Best Great Lakes Shipwrecks, Volume II.* West Chicago, IL: Seawolf Communications, Inc., 1998.

_____*Dive Ontario! The Guide to Shipwrecks and Scuba Diving.* Chatham, Ontario: Cris Kohl, 1990; revised edition, 1995.

_____*Treacherous Waters: Kingston's Shipwrecks.* Chatham, Ontario: Cris Kohl, 1997.

KUNTZ, TOM, (ed.) *The Titanic Disaster Hearings: The Official Transcript of the 1912 Senate Investigation.* New York: Pocket Books, 1998.

LORD, WALTER. *A Night to Remember.* New York: Henry Holt and Company, 1955.

_____*A Night to Remember, Illustrated Edition.* New York: Holt, Rinehart and Winston, 1976.

_____*The Night Lives On.* New York: William Morrow and Company, Inc., 1986.

LYNCH, DON, and illustrations by KEN MARSCHALL. *Titanic, An Illlustrated History.* New York: Hyperion, 1992.

MARSHALL, LOGAN, ed. *The Sinking of the Titanic and Great Sea Disasters.* Philadelphia: John C. Winston Company, 1912.

MAXTONE-GRAHAM, JOHN. *The Only Way To Cross.* New York: Macmillan, 1972.

MCMILLAN, BEVERLY, AND STANLEY LEHRER, and The Mariners' Museum, Newport News, Virginia. *Titanic, Fortune & Fate.* New York: Simon & Schuster, 1998.

MERIDETH, LEE W. *1912 Facts About Titanic.* Mason City, Iowa: Savas Publishing Company, 1999.

O'DONNELL, E. E. *The Last Days of the Titanic.* Niwot, Colorado: Roberts Rinehart Publishers, 1997.

PEARSON, MICHAEL. *The £5 Virgins.* New York: Saturday Review Press, 1972.

PELLEGRINO, CHARLES. *Her Name, Titanic.* New York: McGraw-Hill Publishing Company, 1988.

_____*Ghosts of the Titanic.* New York: HarperCollins Publishers, Inc., 2000.

QUINN, PAUL J. *Titanic at Two A. M.* Saco, Maine: Fantail, 1997.

_____*Dusk to Dawn.* Saco, Maine: Fantail, 1999.

ROBERTSON, MORGAN. *The Wreck of the Titan or, Futility,* Salem, New Hampshire:, Massachusetts: Ayer Company, 1970 reprint.

_____*The Wreck of the Titan or, Futility,* and *Morgan Robertson, The Man.* Ludlow, Massachusetts: 7 C's Press, 1995.

RUFFMAN, ALAN. *Titanic Remembered, The Unsinkable Ship and Halifax.* Halifax: Formac Publishing Company, 1999.

SEBAK, PER KRISTIAN. *Titanic, 31 Norwegian Destinies.* Oslo, Norway: Genesis Forlag, 1998.

SPIGNESI, STEPHEN J. *The Complete Titanic.* Secaucus, New Jersey: Birch Lane Press, 1998.

USHER, ELLIS BAKER. *History of Wisconsin,* Volume 7, 1914.

VAN DER LINDEN, REV. PETER, ed., AND THE MARINE HISTORICAL SOCIETY OF DETROIT. *Great Lakes Ships We Remember.* Cleveland: Freshwater Press, 1979, revised 1984.

_____*Great Lakes Ships We Remember II.* Cleveland: Freshwater Press, 1984.

_____*Great Lakes Ships We Remember III.* Cleveland: Freshwater Press, 1994.

VESS, JOHN W. *The Titan and the Titanic: The Life, Works, and Incredible Foresight of Morgan Robertson.* Chapmansboro, Tennessee: John Vess, 1990.

WADE, WYN CRAIG. *The Titanic: End of a Dream.* New York: Rawson, Wade Publishers, Inc., 1979.

WELS, SUSAN. *Titanic, Legacy of the World's Greatest Ocean Liner.* Del Mar, California: Tehabi Books/Time-Life Books, 1997.

WINOCUR, JACK, ed. *The Story of the Titanic as Told by its Survivors.* New York: Dover Publications, 1960.

Periodicals

"Alden Gates Caldwell: *Titanic* Survivor." *The Titanic Commutator* (Journal of the *Titanic* Historical Society). Vol. 17, No. 2 (1993): 29.

BEHE, GEORGE. "The Night God Chose between the Quicks and the Dead." *The Titanic Commutator* (Journal of the *Titanic* Historical Society). Vol. 17, No. 2 (1993): 50-58.

DATTILE, PHILIP T. "A Daughter Remembers...*Titanic* David." *The Titanic Commutator* (Journal of the *Titanic* Historical Society). Vol. 23, No. 145 (1999): 28-35.

DRAEGER, CAREY L. "They Never Forgot: Michigan Survivors of the *Titanic.*" *Michigan History Magazine.* Vol. 81, No. 2 (March/April, 1997): 28-43.

FINDLAY, MICHAEL. "Sinking the Unsinkable." *Minnesota Monthly,* Vol 33, No. 1 (January, 1999): 46-49, 156-157.

HARPER, JAMES T. "Carpathia Passenger Frank Blackmarr's Collection of Letters, Documents and Photographs." *The Titanic Commutator* (Journal of the Titanic Historical Society). Vol. 23, No. 147 (1999): 164-175.

Marine Review (Cleveland, Ohio). *"City of Detroit III."* Vol. 42, No. 2 (February, 1912): 57-58.

_____"Loss of the Steamship *Titanic.*" Vol. 42, No. 5 (May, 1912): 156-160.

_____"Side Wheel Steamer *City of Detroit III.*" Vol. 42, No. 7 (July, 1912): 215-222.

MILLET, FRANCIS D. "The Decoration of the Exposition." *Scribner's Magazine,* Vol. XII, No. 12 (December, 1892): 692-709.

Scientific American. Vol. CVI, No. 17 (April 27, 1912): 377-381.

Scientific American. Vol. CVI, No. 19 (May 11, 1912): 417-418.

Newsletters, Journals, Reports, Brochures & Directories

Beeson's Marine Directory of the Northwestern Lakes. Chicago: Harvey C. Beeson. For the years 1903, 1909, 1911, 1912, 1913, 1915, 1916.

BUGBEE, GORDON P. "A Prehistory of the White Star Line: St. Clair River Steam Navigation in the Late Nineteenth Century." *Telescope* (Journal of the Great Lakes Maritime Institute), Vol. 15, No. 11 (November, 1966): 250-265.

_____"The *City of Detroit III:* Grandest Ship of the Lakes." *Telescope* (Journal of the Great Lakes Maritime Institute), Vol. 14, No. 2 (February, 1965): 27-47.

Directory of Milwaukee, Wisconsin, for the years 1911, 1912, 1930, 1933, 1934 and 1935.

DOWLING, REV. EDWARD J. "The Crosby Fleets." Published in four parts plus an update. *Detroit Marine Historian* (Journal of the Marine Historical Society of Detroit), Vol. 40, Nos. 4-7 (December, 1986-March, 1987) and Vol. 41, No. 10 (June, 1988).

FOLKMAN, RALPH C. "'Sparks' on the Great Lakes." *Inland Seas* (Journal of the Great Lakes Historical Society), Vol. 31, No. 3 (Fall, 1975): 201-206.

_____"The 'Erie' Episode." *Inland Seas* (Journal of the Great Lakes Historical Society), Vol. 32, No. 4 (Winter, 1976): 294-297.

FOX, WILLIAM A. "Samuel Ward Stanton, 1870-1912." *Steamboat Bill* (Journal of the Steamship Historical Society of America), Number 196 (Winter, 1990): 260-274.

HENRY, JOHN. "Lost Pleasures, Memories of the D&C Night Boats." *Steamboat Bill* (Journal of the Steamship Historical Society of America), Number 192 (Winter, 1989): 285-294.

MEAKIN, ALEXANDER C. "Four Long and One Short, A History of the Great Lakes Towing Company." *Inland Seas* (Journal of the Great Lakes Historical Society), Vol. 32, No. 1 (Winter, 1976): 12-25.

PENFIELD, DR. LIDA S. "Morgan Robertson and His Sea Stories." Paper given before the Oswego County Historical Society on March 10, 1942. Oswego Historical Society. Sixth Publication (1942): 21-26.

Summer Days on the Route of the White Star Line Steamers, 1900. Detroit: White Star Line, 1900.

Government Documents

U.S. CONGRESS, HOUSE, *Inspection of Steam Vessels*, 62nd Congress, 2nd Session, May 4, 1912, H. Rept. 657 (#6131).

U.S. CONGRESS, HOUSE, *Regulation of Radio Communication*, 62nd Congress, 2nd Session, April 20, 1912, H. Rept. 582 (#6131).

U.S. CONGRESS, SENATE, *Hearings of a Subcommittee of the Senate Commerce Committee pursuant to S. Res. 283, to Investigate the Causes leading to the Wreck of the White Star liner "Titanic."* 62nd Congress, 2nd Session, 1912, S. Doc. 726 (#6167).

U.S. CONGRESS, SENATE, *Report of the Senate Committee of Commerce pursuant to S. Res. 283, Directing the Committee to Investigate the Causes of the Sinking of the "Titanic," with speeches by William Alden Smith and Isidor Rayner*, 62nd Congress, 2nd Session, May 28, 1912, S. Rept. 806 (#6127).

U.S. CONGRESS, SENATE, *International Conference on Safety of Life at Sea*, 63rd Congress, 2nd Session, 1914, S. Doc. 463 (#6594).

U.S. CONGRESS, SENATE, *Safety of Life at Sea: Analysis and Explanatory Notes of the London Convention on Safety of Life at Sea in relation to the American Merchant Marine*, Prepared by Andrew Furuseth, 63rd. Congress, 2nd Session, May 1, 1914, S. Doc. 476 (#6594).

Newspapers

Akron (OH) *Beacon Journal*
Albion (NY) *Advertiser*
Ashtabula (OH) *Beacon*
Ashtabula (OH) *Star Beacon*
Auburn (NY) *Daily Advertiser*
Aurora (IL) *Daily Beacon-News*
Beloit (WI) *Daily Free Press*
(Benton Harbor, MI) *News-Palladium*
Bloomington (IL) *Daily Pantagraph*
Bradenton (FL) *Herald*
Brantford (ON) *Courier*
Brown County (WI) *Democrat*
Buffalo (NY) *Courier*
Calumet (MI) *News*
Chatham (ON) *Daily News*
Chelsea (MI) *Standard*
Chicago Daily Journal
Chicago Inter-Ocean
Chicago Record-Herald
Chicago Tribune
Cleveland Leader
Cleveland Plain Dealer
Columbus (OH) *Evening Dispatch*
(Cooperstown, NY) *Freeman's Journal*
(Dupage County, IL) *Daily Herald*
Dayton (OH) *Journal*
Detroit Free Press
Detroit News
Detroit News-Tribune
(Dowagiac, MI) *Cass County Weekly*
Dowagiac (MI) *Daily News*
(Dowagiac, MI) *Herald Republican*
(Dowagiac, MI) *Moon's Weekly*
Duluth (MN) *Herald*
(Duluth, MN) *Labor World*
Duluth (MN) *News Tribune*
(Elgin, IL) *Courier-News*
Flint (MI) *Journal*
(Fond du Lac, WI) *Daily Commonwealth*
(Galesburg, IL) *Republican Register*
Geneva (IL) *Republican*
Grand Rapids (MI) *Evening Press*
Grand Rapids (MI) *Herald*
Grand Rapids (MI) *News*
Green Bay (WI) *Gazette*
Green Bay (WI) *News-Chronicle*
Green Bay (WI) *Press-Gazette*
Hamilton (ON) *Spectator*
Hancock (MI) *Daily*
Holley (NY) *Standard*
Houghton (MI) *Daily Mining Gazette*
Indianapolis News
Indianapolis Star
Ithaca (NY) *Daily News*
Joliet (IL) *News*
Kalamazoo (MI) *Gazette*
Kane County (IL) *Chronicle*

Lindsay (ON) *Post*
London (ON) *Advertiser*
Lorain (OH) *Journal*
Manistee (MI) *Daily Advocate*
Manistee (MI) *Daily News*
Manitoulin Expositor (Little Current, ON)
Manitowoc (WI) *Daily Herald*
Marquette (MI) *Daily Mining Journal*
Milwaukee Free Press
Milwaukee Herold und Seebote (German)
Milwaukee Journal
Milwaukee News
Milwaukee Sentinel
Minneapolis Journal
Minneapolis Tribune
(Monessen, PA) *Daily Independent*
(Monmouth, IL) *Daily Review*
New York Times
New York Tribune
Niagara Falls (NY) *Gazette*
(Niagara Falls, ON) *Daily Record*
Orleans American (Albion, NY)
Oswego (NY) *Palladium*
Ottawa (IL) *Republican-Times*
Ottawa (ON) *Evening Journal*
Peoria (IL) *Herald-Transcript*
Pittsburgh Dispatch
Pittsburgh Leader
Pittsburgh Post
Pittsburgh Press
Pontiac (MI) *Press Gazette*
Port Huron (MI) *Times-Herald*
Racine (WI) *Journal-News*
Red Wing (MN) *Daily Republican*
(Rochester, NY) *Democrat and Chronicle*
Rockford (IL) *Republic*
Sarasota (FL) *Herald-Tribune*
Sarnia (ON) *Daily Observer*
(Sault Ste. Marie, MI) *Evening News*
Sault Daily Star (Sault Ste. Marie, ON)
Sheboygan (WI) *Press*
St. Charles (IL) *Republican*
St. Paul (MN) *Pioneer Press*
South Bend (IN) *Tribune*
Toledo (OH) *Blade*
Toledo (OH) *News-Bee*
Toledo (OH) *Record*
Toronto Evening Telegram
Toronto Globe
Toronto World
Washington (PA) *Observer*
Washington (PA) *Reporter*
Watchman-Warder (Lindsay, ON)
Wiarton (ON) *Echo*
Windsor (ON) *Evening Record*
Windsor (ON) *Star*
Youngstown (OH) *Telegram*
Youngstown (OH) *Vindicator*

Archives and Libraries

Canada

Archives of Ontario, Toronto, Ontario.

Maritime Museum of the Atlantic, Halifax, Nova Scotia.

Public Archives of Nova Scotia, Halifax, Nova Scotia. Records of the Coroner's Office, April 22-May 15, 1912.

St. Marys (Ontario) Museum.

University of Toronto Archives.

United States

Grand Rapids Public Library, Grand Rapids, Michigan.

Great Lakes Historical Society, Vermilion, Ohio.

Great Lakes Marine Collection of the Milwaukee Public Library/Wisconsin Marine Historical Collection. The Herman G. Runge Collection.

Great Lakes Maritime Institute, Detroit, Michigan.

Historical Collections of the Great Lakes, Bowling Green State University, Bowling Green, Ohio. The Dr. Richard Wright Collection.

Illinois State Historical Library, Springfield, Illinois.

Indiana State Historical Library, Indianapolis, Indiana.

Mariner's Museum, Newport News, Virginia.

Michigan State Historical Library, Lansing, Michigan.

Minnesota Historical Society Library, St. Paul, Minnesota.

New York State Historical Library, Albany, New York.

Ohio Historical Society Library, Columbus, Ohio.

Oswego County Historical Society, Oswego, New York.

State Library of Pennsylvania, Harrisburg, Pennsylvania.

Steamboat Historical Society of America, Providence, Rhode Island.

Titanic Historical Society, museum and archives at Indian Orchard, Massachusetts and at Falls River, Massachusetts.

Wisconsin State Historical Society Library, Madison, Wisconsin.

United Kingdom

Harland and Wolff Shipyards, Belfast, Northern Ireland. Historical Section.

Ulster Folk and Transport Museum, Belfast, Northern Ireland. Department of Archival Collections, R.C.W. Courtney Collection.

Unpublished Material

CAIN, J. D., President, Lorain Electronics Corporation, Lorain, Ohio. "Forty Years of Safety Communications on the Great Lakes by Means of Radio." An essay presented at the meeting of the National Safety Council, Marine Section, at Palmer House, Chicago, Illinois, on Tuesday, October 18, 1977.

Communications: Alan Hustak, Walter Lord, Ethel Rudolph (Anna Turja's daughter), Alice Solomonian (Neshan Krekorian's daughter), Joan Stickley (Samuel Ward Stanton's granddaughter).

Interviews: Jim Clary, Dennis Hale, and Bob McGreevy.

Index

Words in *italics* denote a ship's name

An asterisk (*) denotes a photograph or drawing